Windows® 8
For Tablets

FOR

DUMMIES®

A Wiley Brand

by Andy Rathbone

FOR

DUMMIES®

A Wiley Brand

Windows® 8 For Tablets For Dummies®

Published by
John Wiley & Sons, Inc.
111 River Street
Hoboken, NJ 07030-5774

www.wiley.com

Copyright © 2013 by John Wiley & Sons, Inc., Hoboken, New Jersey

Published by John Wiley & Sons, Inc., Hoboken, New Jersey

Published simultaneously in Canada

No part of this publication may be reproduced, stored in a retrieval system or transmitted in any form or by any means, electronic, mechanical, photocopying, recording, scanning or otherwise, except as permitted under Sections 107 or 108 of the 1976 United States Copyright Act, without either the prior written permission of the Publisher, or authorization through payment of the appropriate per-copy fee to the Copyright Clearance Center, 222 Rosewood Drive, Danvers, MA 01923, (978) 750-8400, fax (978) 646-8600. Requests to the Publisher for permission should be addressed to the Permissions Department, John Wiley & Sons, Inc., 111 River Street, Hoboken, NJ 07030, (201) 748-6011, fax (201) 748-6008, or online at http://www.wiley.com/go/permissions.

Trademarks: Wiley, the Wiley logo, For Dummies, the Dummies Man logo, A Reference for the Rest of Us!, The Dummies Way, Dummies Daily, The Fun and Easy Way, Dummies.com, Making Everything Easier, and related trade dress are trademarks or registered trademarks of John Wiley & Sons, Inc. and/or its affiliates in the United States and other countries, and may not be used without written permission. Microsoft and Windows are registered trademarks of Microsoft Corporation. All other trademarks are the property of their respective owners. John Wiley & Sons, Inc. is not associated with any product or vendor mentioned in this book.

For general information on our other products and services, please contact our Customer Care Department within the U.S. at 877-762-2974, outside the U.S. at 317-572-3993, or fax 317-572-4002.

For technical support, please visit www.wiley.com/techsupport.

Wiley publishes in a variety of print and electronic formats and by print-on-demand. Some material included with standard print versions of this book may not be included in e-books or in print-on-demand. If this book refers to media such as a CD or DVD that is not included in the version you purchased, you may download this material at http://booksupport.wiley.com. For more information about Wiley products, visit www.wiley.com.

Library of Congress Control Number: 2013932121

ISBN 978-1-118-32958-0 (pbk); ISBN 978-1-118-40180-4 (ebk); ISBN 978-1-118-40181-1 (ebk); ISBN 978-1-118-40179-8 (ebk)

Manufactured in the United States of America

10 9 8 7 6 5 4 3 2 1

About the Author

Andy Rathbone started geeking around with computers in 1985 when he bought a 26-pound portable CP/M Kaypro 2X. Like other nerds of the day, he soon began playing with null-modem adapters, dialing computer bulletin boards, and working at Radio Shack.

He wrote for various techie publications before moving to computer books in 1992. He's written the *Windows For Dummies* series, *Surface For Dummies, Motorola Xoom For Dummies, Upgrading and Fixing PCs For Dummies,* and many other computer books.

Today, he has more than 15 million copies of his books in print, and they've been translated into more than 30 languages. You can reach Andy at his website, www.andyrathbone.com, where he answers a reader's question online each week.

Author's Acknowledgments

Special thanks to Dan Gookin, Matt Wagner, Tina Rathbone, Steve Hayes, Linda Morris, Russ Mullen, Melba Hopper, and Cynthia Fields.

Thanks also to all the folks I never meet in editorial, sales, marketing, layout, and graphics who work hard to bring you this book.

Publisher's Acknowledgments

We're proud of this book; please send us your comments at http://dummies.custhelp.com. For other comments, please contact our Customer Care Department within the U.S. at 877-762-2974, outside the U.S. at 317-572-3993, or fax 317-572-4002.

Some of the people who helped bring this book to market include the following:

Acquisitions and Editorial

Project Editor: Linda Morris

Executive Editor: Steve Hayes

Technical Editor: Russ Mullen

Editorial Manager: Jodi Jensen

Editorial Assistant: Annie Sullivan

Sr. Editorial Assistant: Cherie Case

Cover Photo: Background © Michał Krakowiak; Tablet computer photographed by Wiley Creative Services

Composition Services

Project Coordinator: Sheree Montgomery

Layout and Graphics: Jason Guy, Joyce Haughey, Christin Swinford

Proofreaders: Cynthia Fields, John Greenough

Indexer: Ty Koontz

Special Help Melba Hopper

Wiley Publishing Technology Publishing Group

Richard Swadley, Vice President and Executive Group Publisher

Andy Cummings, Vice President and Publisher

Mary Bednarek, Executive Acquisitions Director

Mary C. Corder, Editorial Director

Publishing for Consumer Dummies

Kathleen Nebenhaus, Vice President and Executive Publisher

Composition Services

Debbie Stailey, Director of Composition Services

Contents at a Glance

Table of Contents

Introduction

● ●

*W*elcome to *Windows 8 For Tablets For Dummies!*

If you've been frustrated when running Windows 8 on a desktop PC, there's a reason: Microsoft designed Windows 8 to run on *tablets*. So, rest assured that with your tablet, you're now running Windows 8 the way it was supposed to be run.

You'll enjoy running Windows 8 on a tablet much more than on a desktop. Desktop PCs sit on boring desktops, which usually mean work. Tablets, by contrast, represent travel and leisure, and that's where they excel.

About This Book

Today, most people think of a desktop PC as a workhorse for creating: They create documents, spreadsheets, and whatever other boring files their boss requires. And they usually require a mouse and keyboard.

Tablets, by contrast, work best at letting you consume: videos, music, the Internet, and e-mail. And it's often done on the couch, with your fingertips.

But what if one tablet straddled both worlds, letting you both consume and create?

That's the promise of a Windows 8 tablet. Its finger-friendly Start screen lets you watch videos, listen to music, read e-books and e-mail, and browse the web. And, come Monday morning, you can switch to the Windows desktop, plug in a mouse and keyboard, and put on your working cap.

And how well does it hold up on that promise? That's where this book comes into play. I describe how it works in both work and play mode, and how to give it a few little tweaks to make it fit into your life a little more easily.

This book also explains how to run *Windows RT*, the slim-and-trim version of Windows 8. Both versions of Windows are almost identical. But when something in the book applies only to Windows RT, I mark that paragraph with the Windows RT icon, like the one shown in the margin.

How to Use This Book

This book works best as a reference that dishes up answers to your questions about running Windows 8 on a tablet. Instead of trying to read it all the way through, treat it like a specialized dictionary. When Windows 8 does something unexpected — or when you try to do something but Windows 8 seems to be ignoring you — pick up the book.

Using the book's index, table of contents, or even chapter titles atop each page, find the section you need, read the answer, and put the book away until you need it again.

Everything presented here works with a tap of your Surface's touchscreen. On those rare occasions where you need to type information on a keyboard, you see easy-to- follow bold text like this: Type **Crispy French Fries** into the Orders box.

And What About You?

This books assumes you're fairly familiar with a desktop PC. You've probably used Windows on a desktop PC, so you know the basics. You know how to point and click with a mouse, for example. You know how to double-click, right-click, and even drag windows around on the screen.

But you're not sure how that knowledge translates to a touchscreen tablet, where everything relies on your fingertips.

To bring you up to speed, this book explains how to control your tablet with your fingers, including the Windows desktop. However, it also points out those times when you should simply give up, plug a mouse and keyboard into your tablet, and turn it into a familiar desktop PC. (And yes, most Windows 8 tablets can also turn into plain ol' desktop PCs when duty calls.)

I cover the desktop when needed in this book, and I explain all the adjustments you can make so it's as touch-friendly as possible. But if you plan on using your tablet's desktop *exclusively*, you might be better served with my other book, *Windows 8 For Dummies*, also published by John Wiley & Sons, Inc. (That book also covers tablets, but without as much detail as you find in this book.)

How Did Microsoft Change Windows 8?

In the past, Microsoft released an operating system and never changed it: Windows XP, for example, still works basically the same as it originally did, a decade later.

With Windows 8, Microsoft takes a different approach: Windows 8 and its apps change *constantly*. What I describe as a shortcoming in this book may be fixed automatically on your tablet in the days, or months ahead. If I complain about something that you find to be fixed in your tablet, treat it as a stroke of good luck.

How This Book Is Organized

This book is broken down into five parts, which are in turn broken down into chapters. Here's what you find in each part of the book:

Part 1: Getting Started with Windows 8 Tablets

This part of the book helps you choose the Windows tablet that meets your needs: Windows 8 or Windows RT. Then it walks you through setting it up for the first time.

It describes the tablet's touch controls, as well as the intricacies of typing on a glass keyboard. I explain how to finger your way through both Windows 8's new Start screen as well as the traditional Windows desktop.

Part II: Connecting, Playing, and Working

The meat of the book, this part explains how to connect your tablet with everything you're likely to come across: the Internet, wired and wireless networks, monitors, digital projectors, mice, keyboards, flash drives, and online storage spaces, including Windows SkyDrive.

The rest of this part explains how to browse the Internet, as well as how to manage your e-mail and contacts with Windows 8's built-in apps.

Tablets running Windows RT include a built-in copy of Microsoft Home and Office, Student edition, so I explain the basics of opening, creating, and printing Word, Excel, PowerPoint, and OneNote documents.

Part III: Media

Most people rely on their tablets for leisure time just as much as work. This part of the book explains how to listen to music, take and browse photos, and watch movies on your tablet.

Part IV: Tweaks

Because they are built for a wide variety of scenarios, tablets come with a *lot* of settings. This part of the book explains Windows 8's two panels of switches that change how your tablet behaves.

And if flipping switches doesn't do the job, the troubleshooting chapter explains how to isolate the problem and return your tablet to normal.

Part V: The Part of Tens

Every *For Dummies* book comes with a Part of Tens, and this book's no exception. Here, you'll find lists: Ten things to do now to your tablet, ten essential apps, ten essential tips and tricks, ten handy accessories, and ten essential shortcut keys.

Icons Used in This Book

To keep things as easy to find as possible, this book puts little icons in the margin or in certain paragraphs. Some represent the icon you're supposed to be tapping during a step. The others call out these things:

Don't bother reading items marked with this icon unless you secretly yearn for an engineering degree.

This stuff is important enough to remember. (Or at least slap a sticky note next to the margin.)

Keep an eye out for this icon. It marks handy shortcuts, secret ways of doing things, and other stuff that saves you time.

Today's computers don't offer as many shock hazards as their ancestors. Still, this icon marks where you should tread carefully to avoid damaging your tablet, your data, or yourself.

Tablets running Windows RT differ subtly from tablets running Windows 8. This icon calls out information that explains those differences.

Where to Go from Here

New tablet owners should definitely start with a read-through of the first four chapters, with an emphasis on Chapter 3. Your tablet's keyboard changes slightly depending on what you're doing, and that chapter explains the changes.

After that, just start browsing, jumping to sections that explain things you initially found confusing about your tablet.

If you're reading this as an e-book, use your reader's Bookmark and Search features to find what you want.

Occasionally, our technology books have updates. If this book does have technical updates, they will be posted at `www.dummies.com/go/windows 8tabletsfdupdates`.

And with that, enjoy your tablet! It's a bold move by Microsoft that signals Windows' future, and you're at the forefront.

Part I

getting started with

Windows 8 For Tablets

Visit www.dummies.com for great Dummies content online.

In this part . . .

- ✔ Choose the Windows 8 tablet that meets your needs. Also, understand the difference between Windows 8 and Windows RT tablets.

- ✔ Set up your tablet for the first time.

- ✔ Know how to type on your tablet's built-in keyboard, as well as how to take notes on the tablet's screen.

- ✔ Find out how to navigate Windows 8's Start screen and desktop.

Chapter 1

Understanding Windows 8 Tablets

*N*ew on the scene and quite different from other tablets, Windows 8 tablets serve as quick conversation starters. If you mention one to your friends, or perhaps pull one out in a coffee shop, you'll soon hear these questions:

"Why buy a tablet instead of a laptop?"

"Why did you buy *that* Windows tablet?"

And, the clincher, "Why didn't you just buy an iPad?"

This chapter arms you with the answers to those questions. I explain how a tablet can be more versatile than a laptop or a desktop PC. I describe both types of Windows 8 tablets on the market, how to tell them apart, and which one best meets your needs.

Finally, I answer that nagging question you'll grow tired of hearing: "Why not just buy an iPad?"

Choosing a Tablet over a Laptop

Desktop PCs, laptops, and tablets each serve very different needs. Deskbound cubicle-dwellers, for example, need a bulky, powerful desktop PC with a spacious keyboard, large hard drive, and a large monitor. Unless you need to clean your desk, you'll never lift a desktop PC.

Travelers, by contrast, used to habitually reach for a laptop when heading out the door. Today, however, many travelers opt for a tablet, instead. That's because today's tablets outperform laptops in the following situations:

- ✔ While walking, either at a job site or when browsing a tradeshow or convention

- ✔ On an airplane, when the person in front of you has tilted their seat so far back that your laptop no longer opens wide enough

- ✔ In the back seat of a taxi

- ✔ In conference rooms, where you can easily pass your tablet to others

- ✔ At gatherings of friends or family, where you can quickly show off photos

- ✔ On the living room couch, where you can interact with TV shows

- ✔ In classrooms or client meetings, when you need to draw diagrams or quick notes for reference later

When you need a laptop or desktop PC, you can turn your tablet into one: Plug a mouse and a keyboard into your Windows 8 tablet and load the familiar Windows desktop. There, you can run the mainstays of Microsoft Office: Word, PowerPoint, Excel, Access, and OneNote.

When you're ready to hit the road again, unplug the accessories and run, taking all of your files with you:

- ✔ Tablets strip computing down to its essentials. Dropping the keyboard makes them lighter and thinner than laptops. Many people already have a spare keyboard and/or mouse at home or the office, and all Windows 8 tablets include a USB port for plugging in accessories.

- ✔ When you plug a monitor into your tablet's video port, you've created a two-monitor workstation. You can view your notes on your tablet, but compose your document using the second, larger monitor. (I explain how to manage two monitors in Chapter 6.) Or, you can extend your Windows desktop across both monitors, doubling or tripling its size.

- ✔ Touchscreens make many tasks much easier, faster, or both. It's easier to scroll through large documents with a flick of your finger, for example. Plus, touchscreens often seem more natural, especially when paging through digital books, maneuvering through maps, or resizing digital photos.

Deciding on a Windows 8 Tablet Instead of an iPad

Apple's iPad is the most popular tablet in the world. It's an extraordinarily well-built tablet that lets you do many things very well. The iPad's extensive app library fills nearly every niche, whether you need a bird-watching journal or a ukulele chord finder.

However, part of an iPad's success comes from its limitations. First, Apple kept things simple by designing an iPad for a single owner. That simplicity turns into awkwardness when you hand your iPad to a friend or coworker: They have access to your private e-mail, appointments, and photos.

Windows 8 tablets let you set up separate accounts for friends, family, or coworkers, keeping everyone's work separate. Even simpler, you can just turn on your tablet's Guest account. Your friend or coworker can use that to check e-mail or to browse the web.

The iPad also falls short when you need standard software like Word, Excel, PowerPoint, or OneNote. In fact, many iPad owners carry both their iPad *and* their laptop, so they'll be ready when work calls.

A Windows 8 tablet, by contrast, does it all:

✔ Just like the iPad, every Windows 8 tablet lets you read e-mail and browse the web, as well as download apps, movies, and songs. But when work calls, you needn't reach for a laptop. Every Windows 8 tablet can run Microsoft Word, Excel, PowerPoint, and OneNote.

✔ Unlike the iPad, your Windows 8 tablet has a USB port. With an iPad, until you buy an adapter, you can't add storage, download your camera's photos, or even access files on a flash drive. With a Windows 8 tablet, you can plug in a mouse, keyboard, portable hard drive, flash drive, or camera.

✔ iPads can't print, except to wireless printers. Although wireless printers are becoming more common, a Windows 8 tablet can print to nearly any printer: Just plug the printer into the USB port. (Windows 8 tablets can print to wireless printers, as well.)

✔ iPads lack a file browser. Unless you download third-party software, you can't browse your *own* files, much less share files on other networked computers. (The Windows 8 desktop lets you browse your own files, as well as those on connected networks.)

✔ Many Windows 8 tablets cost less than an iPad. And Windows 8 tablets work with nearly any accessories you use with your laptop or desktop PC. You're not locked into buying special adapters for your particular model.

Choosing the Right Windows 8 Tablet

Windows 8 tablets come in two basic models: *Windows RT* tablets, and Windows 8 tablets. Both run Microsoft's new Windows 8 operating system, but with slight differences. They're each designed to serve slightly different needs.

The next two sections help you decide whether you need a Windows RT or a Windows 8 tablet. After you've chosen your type of tablet, the following section explains what features to look for when shopping.

Windows RT tablets

The designers of Windows RT assume you'll spend most of your time on Windows 8's new Start screen, shown in Figure 1-1.

Figure 1-1: Tablets running Windows RT are designed to compete with the iPad.

Covered in Chapter 4, Windows 8's Start screen contains small programs known as *apps*. Just like the apps on a smartphone or an iPad, they let you browse the web, check e-mail, play movies and music, and keep in touch with friends on Facebook.

Windows RT is aimed at people who prefer a long battery life rather than speed and power. To preserve battery life, Windows RT differs from Windows 8 tablets in one key way: It won't let you install programs on the Windows desktop.

The desktop hasn't disappeared, however. When you open Windows RT's Desktop app, the same ol' Windows desktop appears. You can still manage files with File Explorer, call up the desktop's Control Panel, open windows, and perform the usual desktop mechanics.

But you're stuck with what comes built in to Windows RT's desktop. To make the anemic desktop more attractive, Microsoft tosses in free desktop versions of Microsoft Word, Excel, PowerPoint, and OneNote.

Combine those popular office programs, a long battery life, and a lower price tag, and a Windows RT tablet may be all you need. Instead of installing desktop programs, you can install apps onto the Start screen. (Some former desktop programs appear as Start screen apps.)

- ✔ Windows RT comes pre-installed on tablets or laptops. You can't buy the operating system separately, nor can you install it onto a different computer yourself.

- ✔ The Windows 8 Start screen works best with touchscreens, so you'll find it mostly on touchscreen tablets and touchscreen laptops. You won't find Windows RT sold on desktop PCs.

Windows 8 Tablets

Windows 8 tablets come in two types: *Windows 8* tablets, which are aimed at consumers, and *Windows 8 Pro* tablets, which are aimed at businesses. Because they're identical except for a few extra business tools in Windows 8 Pro, I refer to them both as Windows 8 tablets in this book.

Windows 8 tablets include the Start screen and its apps, just like Windows RT. However, these powerful tablets also include a *fully-functional* Windows desktop.

Microsoft refers to the Windows 8 tablet as "no compromises." It lets you run the finger-friendly Start screen apps while traveling. Then, when it's time to work, you can load the Windows desktop and fire up your favorite Windows programs.

Intel's Atom-ic tablets

Some Windows 8 tablets use the latest version of Intel's *Atom* processors, the ones found in the under-powered but inexpensive netbooks sold a few years back. The newer Atom chips are more powerful than the older versions, yet they still extend the battery life.

If you need long battery life as well as a fully functioning Windows desktop, look for a Windows 8 tablet with an Atom processor. Your desktop programs will run more slowly than they would on your desktop PC or a traditional Windows 8 tablet, but you'll still be able to run Windows programs on the desktop.

Of course, there's at least one compromise: These powerhouses weigh a little more, cost more, and don't include Microsoft Word or other Office programs. (Those can be purchased and installed separately.)

Perhaps most important, Windows 8 tablets lack the battery life to run all day. If you plan on using your tablet mainly between power outlets, however, you'll do fine.

Windows 8 Pro includes support for Windows Server domains, encryption, virtual hard drives, BitLocker, and other technical programs required in some businesses. Think of Windows 8 tablets as "real" computers that happen to be tablets, as well.

Understanding hybrid tablets

If you're looking mainly to *consume* content — watch movies, listen to music, read e-mail, or catch up with friends — a simple tablet works fine, and the Start screen apps easily handle all of those tasks.

But if you need to *create* content — write reports, crunch numbers in a spreadsheet, or whip up a PowerPoint presentation — you'll need the desktop. And although you can use your fingers on a tablet's touchscreen desktop, you'll work more quickly after attaching a mouse and keyboard.

To handle the need for an occasional mouse and keyboard, many tablets today come in the form of *hybrids* — a fancy term simply meaning they include keyboards and mice/trackpads that detach or fold back when not in use. Hybrid tablets give you the versatility of a tablet, but let you turn them back into a laptop for desktop work.

Windows 8 has stirred a flurry of excitement among computer manufacturers, and you find a wide variety of hybrid Windows 8 tablets. Some include detachable trackpads and keyboards, held in place by hinges, hoops, or magnets.

When choosing a hybrid, look at the weak link: the add-on mouse and keyboard:

- Are they easy to remove, yet still easy to carry around?
- Are they sturdy enough to stand up to road wear?
- Do the detachable parts serve another purpose when detached? Or are they deadweight you'll still have to carry around when not in use?
- How much do they add to the price?
- Are they a better solution than simply carrying around a small mouse and keyboard in your gadget bag?

After deciding on a tablet that's right for you, you'll find two things left to compare:

- **Hard-disk space:** Tablets lack the large hard drives found in desktop PCs. As I write this, most come with 32GB to 256GB of hard-disk space. If that's still not enough storage space, slip a thin portable hard drive into your bag to carry your files. (Both Windows RT and Windows 8 tablets accept most portable hard drives.)
- **Price:** The bottom line comes down to price, and that's a decision only you can make. As of this writing, Windows RT tablets cost between $500 and $800, and Windows 8 tablets will set you back between $600 and $1,200.

Chapter 2

Setting Up Your Tablet

*Y*ou can add accessories to a tablet, just as you can with any computer. But before filling up your gadget bag with accessories, spend a few minutes in this chapter.

Here, I describe every port, switch, and sensor already built in to your Windows 8 tablet. I explain how to find them all, as well as how to put them to work.

If your tablet isn't well-stocked enough out of the box, I list some lightweight, handy accessories in Chapter 18. But after reading this chapter, you may discover that your tablet already includes everything you need.

After you've identified your tablet's parts and flipped its On switch, you'll be ready for the next step: signing into Windows 8 with your own user account.

Identifying Your Tablet's Parts

Microsoft dictated a lengthy list of requirements for Windows 8 tablets, so you'll find yours stuffed with buttons, ports, and sensors. However, many of them are not labeled, leaving them unidentified unless you pore over your tablet's boring manual.

This section runs you through a quick ID check, and explains when or if you'd ever need to use it.

Perhaps the hardest part is finding each part again on-the-fly: Your tablet always rotates its screen to be right-side up, so you may relocate the buttons on the *opposite* side of where you first found them.

To tell which way is "right-side up" on your tablet, look for its Windows key button. The Windows key button always appears on the tablet's bottom front edge, centered below the screen.

Buttons

Different tablets from different manufacturers include a variety of buttons and switches. But every Windows 8 tablet includes these four mainstays.

Power button

The power button, a push-button switch, usually lives on the tablet's right edge, where it's easy to reach unless you're left-handed. Press the button (try using a fingernail on really thin buttons), and your tablet either comes to life or turns itself off.

Technically, it's *not* an on/off switch. Instead, it puts your tablet to *sleep* — a lower power state that saves your work, but allows for quick start-up times.

If you want the power switch to *really* turn off your tablet, I describe how to configure your power switch to do that in Chapter 13.

Keeping tabs on battery strength

After you find your tablet's power switch, the second most important part of your tablet could be its battery: Your tablet won't wake up without it.

To see your current battery strength, bring up the Charms bar by swiping inward from the screen's right edge. Windows 8's new Charms bar appears, as I describe in Chapter 4. But also notice the tile to the left that displays the current date and time. Beneath the date lives an icon for your current battery strength, as well as for your Internet strength.

That same tile also appears on the Windows Lock screen. Make a habit of glancing at the battery strength icon: It's a quick way to see whether you should start prowling for a nearby power outlet.

Windows Key button

All Windows 8 tablets include a dedicated Windows Key button on their front panel, centered below the Start screen. (The button wears Microsoft's new Windows logo.) Pressing or touching that button does one of two things:

✔ It returns you to the Start screen, Windows's center of operations.

✔ If you're already on the Start screen, it returns you to your last-used application.

So, don't consider the Start button as simply another way to summon the Start screen. It's also a handy way to return to your work.

When your tablet's turned off or sleeping, touching the Windows key does nothing. That's exactly what you want from a tablet stuffed into a bag, where the Windows key can be inadvertently touched.

Screen Rotation Lock button

Tablets automatically rotate their screen to match how you're holding the tablet. That ensures you're always viewing them "right-side up." But sometimes you don't want the screen to rotate. When you unconsciously tilt the tablet while reading a digital book, for example, it's annoying when the pages rotate.

To prevent the screen from rotating automatically, press the Screen Rotation Lock button. (Found on the tablet's side, the button usually bears a padlock icon with two arrows.) When locked, the Screen icon on the Charm bar's Settings pane wears a lock, as shown in the margin. Press the Screen Rotation Lock button again to unlock it, returning screen rotation to normal.

You can also toggle the rotation lock directly from the Charms bar's Settings pane by following these steps:

1. **Slide your finger inward from the screen's right edge to summon the Charms bar.**

   I explain the Charms bar in Chapter 4.

2. **Tap the Settings icon, and then tap the Screen icon.**

   The Brightness sliding control appears.

3. **Tap the monitor icon at the top of the sliding brightness control.**

Oddly enough, that toggles the Rotation Lock; the top of the brightness control sports a padlock when the Rotation Lock is on.

Note: Tablets always turn off screen rotation when you plug in a second monitor, described in Chapter 6.

Volume switch

Most tablets include a toggle switch on their side for volume. Press the switch's top end to increase the volume; press the bottom end to cool down the party.

You can also change the volume from the Charms bar's Settings pane by following these steps:

1. **Slide your finger inward from the screen's right edge to summon the Charms bar.**

2. **Tap the Settings icon, and then tap the Volume icon.**

   The Volume sliding control appears.

3. **Slide the control up or down to raise or lower the volume.**

Tapping the Speaker icon atop the sliding control works as a toggle to mute the speakers.

Ports

Tablets usually include at least four holes along their edges, technically called *ports*: USB, a display port, a docking port, and a headphone/microphone jack.

They each come in handy when plugging in accessories to let your tablet do more tricks.

USB

This simple port, lacking on the iPad and not fully supported by Android tablets, lets you plug in nearly any item that works on a desktop computer: flash drives, portable hard drives, a mouse, a keyboard, a TV tuner, a digital camera, and other common gadgets. Windows 8 recognizes most items as soon as you plug them in.

If you're connected with the Internet, Windows installs drivers for them automatically, so they work without your intervention.

Tablets running Windows RT don't accept nearly as many USB devices as tablets running Windows 8. They accept most mice, keyboards, and storage devices, including most digital cameras. Forget about installing TV tuners, dial-up modems, or anything else that comes bundled with software.

Video

All Windows 8 tablets include a tiny video port that lets you plug in an external monitor or HDTV — if you have the correct type of cable, that is. Unfortunately, very few tablets include that cable in the box.

Most tablets send their video through either a Micro HDMI port or the newer miniDisplayPort. The two ports look almost identical, but the Micro HDMI port nearly always has the word "HDMI" stamped next to it.

I describe the nuances of connecting a cable between your Windows 8 tablet and a monitor and HDTV in Chapter 6.

Docking

Many tablets offer optional *docking stations* — little props that serve as stands. When you slide your tablet into its docking station, your tablet sits facing you, much like a traditional monitor.

Most docking stations include a set of ports for attaching a full-sized keyboard and mouse. That lets you use your tablet like a regular PC by nestling it into its dock.

When shopping for a dock, make sure you buy one made specifically for your particular Windows 8 tablet. Different manufacturers' docks use slightly different connectors, and they're rarely interchangeable between models.

Microphone and speakers

All tablets include a built-in microphone, usually visible as a pinhole (or two, for stereo) along one of the tablet's edges. The built-in microphone works fine for recording meetings, classes, dictation, or even soundtracks to home movies shot with your tablet's built-in camera.

But if that's not enough quality, move to the headphone jack: Those jacks also work with special microphones created for iPods, iPads, and iPhones. (The headphone jack has extra depth, and senses when you insert a specially designed microphone.) Most iPod microphones cost under $20.

For a professional-quality recording, however, buy a microphone that plugs into the USB port. These range from around $50 to several hundred dollars.

As for speakers, all tablets include stereo speakers that work fine for casual listening. You can plug a set of headphones into the headphone jack, of course, for private listening. To fill the room with sound, plug in a pair of standard desktop computer speakers.

For the best sound, head to Chapter 6, where I describe how to connect your tablet to your home stereo or home theater.

Memory card slot

Most Windows 8 tablets come with small hard drives of 32, 64, or 128 GB. Most desktop PCs, by contrast, include at least 300GB of space — more than twice as much.

If your tablet begins running out of room for your files, turn to the memory card slot. Most tablets come with slots that accept micro-sized memory cards — the ones about the size of your little fingernail.

How big of a memory card do you need? In short, as large as you can afford. They come in sizes of 32, 64, or 128GB.

Table 2-1 shows the approximate amount of information you can pack onto different-sized memory cards. Each cell in the table shows how many albums, photos, high-definition video hours, or apps it would take to fill the card.

Table 2-1	Approximate Memory Card Storage Capacities			
Size	*Albums*	*Photos*	*HD Video*	*Apps*
16GB	80	400	2 hours	16
32GB	160	800	4 hours	32
64GB	320	1,600	8 hours	64
128GB	640	3,200	16 hours	128

Most tablets include a microSDXC card slot, the type of slot commonly found in smartphones. MicroSDXC slots accept three types of cards, ranked according to how much information they can store. (The slots are backward-compatible, so the newer card slots can still read the older types of cards.)

The slots on most tablets accept all of these cards:

- **Micro Secure Digital (microSD):** The oldest version, these cards rarely held more than 2GB in capacity.

- **Micro Secure Digital High Capacity (microSDHC):** These cards hold up to 32GB in capacity.

- **Micro Secure Digital eXtended Capacity (microSDXC):** These newer cards currently come in 64GB sizes, but expect to see 128GB cards out soon. (Theoretically, they can hold up to 2TB in capacity.)

Your tablet's speedy hard drive

Replacing the mechanical drives of yesteryear, drives called Solid State Drives (SSDs) work much like gigantic flash drives. Lacking the spinning wheels inside older drives, SSDs work with a different set of rules.

First, they're smaller, with enough room for Windows, a few of your favorite programs, and your personal information. If you need more room, insert a large memory card or plug a portable hard drive into a USB port.

Second, SSD drives don't need defragmenting. Windows 8 knows this, so it automatically turns off its built-in defragmentation tool.

Most tablets come with 32, 64, or 128GB of storage space. Remember, when the drive is formatted or prepared to accept information, that number drops by about ten percent. Windows and its recovery tools eat up to 13GB of space, and any bundled programs eat even more.

The moral? When you buy that 128GB tablet with Windows installed, don't expect to find 128GB of storage space waiting for you when you turn it on.

Display

Most Windows 8 tablets come with a resolution of 1366×768. Nerds gave that particular resolution the official moniker of *XVGA*, in case you find that listed on some of the thin sheets of paper tossed in with your tablet in lieu of a manual.

Windows 8 requires that resolution in order to "dock" an app along the side of your screen, described in Chapter 5.

I describe how to change your resolution in Chapter 13.

Sensors

Your tablet's built-in *sensors* constantly measure the world around them, translating those measurements into numbers, and feeding them to Windows 8's various programs. Fortunately, many sensors can be safely ignored.

But if you're holding your thumb over the light sensor, for example, the tablet thinks it's in a dark room and quickly brightens the screen.

This section points out how to locate the sensors built into most tablets, and what they do.

Ambient light

This sensor, located as a faint dot along the front panel, constantly checks the available light around you. As the ambient light fades or brightens, Windows subsequently dims or brightens the screen. When you're in a dark room, for example, the screen dims to save your eyes, as well as the tablet's battery.

Step into the sunshine, and the screen brightens to stay visible.

Unfortunately, some light sensors are overly sensitive, and your tablet's constant screen changes can become a distraction. If you notice the screen constantly dimming and brightening, I explain how to turn off Windows' Adaptive Brightness in Chapter 13.

Rotation/accelerometer

These sensors live deep inside your tablet's case. The rotation sensor lets the tablet know how it's being held — portrait or landscape mode, for example — so it can rotate the screen accordingly.

The accelerometer, by contrast, detects changes in physical speed. Some apps tap into the accelerometer to detect when two devices bump together. When each device detects a quick simultaneous stop, they know you've bumped them together, and your app is ready to exchange business cards, for example.

GPS

Found mostly on tablets that offer cellular Internet access, a Global Positioning System (GPS) sensor lets the tablet know your exact location to within about 30 feet. With your permission, your tablet gives this information to apps, which can then find your location on a map or locate the closest coffee shop.

If your tablet doesn't include cellular access, you can plug a GPS into your tablet's USB port. Before buying one, though, make sure it's listed as compatible with the app that needs to use it.

Note: Even if your tablet lacks a GPS, it can usually narrow down your location to within several hundred feet by using your wireless Internet connection.

Cameras

Most tablets come with two separate cameras: one on the front, the other on the back. You'll notice them as small round holes beneath the glass, usually about 1/8-inch in diameter.

The front-facing camera works best for taking photos of yourself, mainly to create profile photos: your user account photo, for example, or photos to represent you on websites. It works best when shooting fairly close-up — about two or three feet away.

Treat the rear-facing camera like a "real" camera. Use it for shooting panoramic landscapes, for example, groups of friends, or party pictures.

Most tablets place their highest-quality camera facing rear; the lousy camera, unfortunately, faces you. But since you're usually shooting close-up portraits that end up as tiny Facebook profiles, you probably don't need much resolution, anyway.

I explain more about cameras in Chapter 11.

Wi-Fi (Wireless Internet access)

Standard on most tablets, Wi-Fi lets you connect with wireless networks, either your own or those you find in public at coffee shops, airports, and hotels. When you're within range, which is usually within 200 feet of a transmitter, you can access the Internet.

When you're out of range, however, you're also out of luck.

3G/4G cellular access

Some tablets include a data plan from a cellphone provider — at an extra cost, of course, usually through a monthly fee. You're usually locked into the contract for about two years. After that, you can cancel and stick with Wi-Fi. When traveling, however, you may miss your "always on" Internet access.

Connections using 3G aren't as fast, but also don't drain the battery as rapidly. The 4G connections, by contrast, are speedy when within range, but suck the power from your battery more quickly.

Turning On Your Tablet

To turn on your tablet, press its power button, described earlier in this chapter. (The button's usually marked with the symbol shown in the margin.) Windows 8 tablets usually load within a few seconds — much faster than your desktop computer.

Another press of your tablet's power button puts it to *sleep,* a low-power slumbering mode that saves power, but allows for quick startup times when you need to jot something down. Sleep mode still consumes battery life, but at barely a trickle.

Turning on your tablet for the first time

When you first turn on your tablet, Windows 8 runs you through a series of fairly simple steps, all described here:

1. **Choose your favorite color scheme.**

   These colors then appear on your screen's background. If you change your mind later or grow tired of your first choice, I describe how to switch these colors to something else in Chapter 13.

2. **Choose a wireless network and password, if asked.**

   You can skip this and connect later, if you wish. I explain how to connect with wireless networks in Chapter 6.

3. **Choose Express Setup.**

   This tells your tablet to connect with your wireless network, if you have one, as well as to turn on automatic updates to download security patches and new drivers.

4. **Sign in with a Microsoft account.**

   I describe this step in this chapter's "Creating a Microsoft Account and Signing In" section.

   Welcome to Windows 8!

To turn off your tablet *completely,* press and hold the On/Off button. When all the tablet's lights turn off, the tablet's turned off. It takes a few seconds longer to turn back on, but you conserve a little bit of extra battery life, a handy trick when your next power outlet is two villages down the road.

When you first turn on your tablet, note the location of the switch's glowing power light. As you hold your tablet in different positions, the screen constantly rotates to be right-side up. But by remembering the location of the power light, you'll always find your glowing power button, even in a dark room.

Unlocking the Lock Screen

Whenever you turn on your computer, you always encounter Windows 8's Lock screen. Shown in Figure 2-1, it's simply a screen showing the current time and date, as well as a few notifications, including the strength of your battery and network connection. Depending on your tablet's settings, you may also see your latest appointment, the current weather conditions, your amount of unread e-mails, and any waiting instant messages.

To unlock the Lock screen, swipe your finger up the screen. Windows 8 quickly unlocks your tablet, leaving you at the sign-in screen.

Current time   Next appointment   Current day and date

Figure 2-1:
Your Lock
screen
displays the
current time
and date, as
well as your
network
strength and
battery life
indicator.

11:21

Deborah Rathbone's birthday
All day

Sunday, September 9

Number of unread e-mails

Battery strength (Full)

Network indicator (Wired access)

The Lock screen shows notifications only if you're currently signed in. If nobody is signed in on the tablet, a generic Lock screen appears, showing only the date, time, and the strength of the battery and network signal.

Creating a Microsoft Account and Signing In

Microsoft designed Windows 8 around a *Microsoft account,* which is simply an e-mail address and password. Without a Microsoft account, you can't install apps, which defeats the purpose of owning a tablet. Although you can log in without a Microsoft account, you'll definitely want one to make full use of your tablet.

In fact, you may already have a Microsoft account and don't know it, as all of these addresses qualify:

- ✔ Xbox Live account
- ✔ An e-mail address from Hotmail.com, Outlook.com, or Live.com
- ✔ Microsoft Passport

If you don't already have one of these e-mail addresses, Microsoft asks you to create a Microsoft account at the screen similar to the one shown in Figure 2-2. (Every account holder on your tablet eventually encounters this screen or some variation of it.)

Figure 2-2: Create a Microsoft account, if necessary, and then sign in.

After you've jumped through a few more hoops, you're left at the Windows 8 Start screen, which I cover in Chapter 3.

- ✔ Don't have a Microsoft account? Then choose Sign Up for a New E-Mail address to create one.

- ✔ Don't *want* a Microsoft account? Then choose Sign in Without a Microsoft Account. That lets you create a local account. It lets you use your tablet, but without many of Windows 8's benefits. You can't download apps, or use Windows 8's built-in Mail, People, Messaging, and Calendar apps.

- ✔ Not sure what to do? Create a local account and spend some time poking around your tablet. You can always convert it to a Microsoft account later.

- ✔ I explain how to add separate accounts for other people, as well as how to turn on a guest account in Chapter 13.

Chapter 3

Touching, Typing, and Drawing on Your Tablet

Chances are, you've grown used to using a laptop or desktop PC. You know how to click a mouse or manipulate a laptop's trackpad. A touchscreen tablet changes all that.

Now your *fingertips* tell your tablet how to behave. This chapter covers the touch control tricks stashed inside every tablet warrior's arsenal.

Here, you discover the seven main touch commands that Microsoft built into Windows 8. Although these may sound complicated when reading about them, envision your tablet's display as a piece of paper: Most of a tablet's finger commands are as intuitive as manipulating a sheet of paper as it lies flat on a table.

I also explain the mechanics of typing on a glass keyboard, as well as a few tricks to speed up your typing.

Finally, I explain a Windows tablet's hidden power: It lets you draw on the screen with a stylus, a special plastic-tipped pen. Windows 8 recognizes your handwriting, letting you treat your tablet like pen and paper — or even a brush and canvas.

Whether or not it unleashes your artistic soul, the stylus lets you sign that e-mailed invoice.

Controlling a Touchscreen with Your Fingers

Controlling a touchscreen sounds easy enough. You just touch it. Complicating matters, though, is the fact that you can touch tablets in *seven* different ways, and each type of touch does something very different.

This section describes the seven main ways to touch a tablet, as well as examples of when to use each one.

Tap

The equivalent of a mouse click, this is a quick tap and release of your finger. You can tap any item on the screen, be it a button, icon, or other bit of computer viscera. When in tight quarters, a fingertip often works better than the pad of your finger.

Example: Tap the Next button to move to the next step; tap the Charms bar's Start button to return to the Start screen. Tap an app on the Start screen to open it.

Double-tap

The equivalent of a mouse double-click, the double-tap involves two quick taps of your finger. Double-tap any item on the screen that you'd like to double-click on.

Example: Double-tap a desktop folder to open it. Double-tap a web page to make it larger.

On a tablet, many things can be opened by merely tapping. So, if a tap doesn't open an item, try the double-tap, instead.

Press and hold

The equivalent of a mouse right-click, touch the item and *hold down your finger.* A second or two later, a square will appear onscreen. Lift your finger, and the square becomes a menu, just as though you'd right-clicked the item with your mouse.

Example: Press and hold your finger on a blank portion of the Windows desktop. When the square appears, lift your finger; a menu appears, enabling you to choose between your desktop's options.

Pinch and/or stretch

As a handy way to zoom in or out of a photo, pinch the screen between two fingertips (usually your thumb and index finger). The photo, text, or window shrinks as your fingers move inward. (Lift your fingers when you've found the right size.)

To enlarge something, spread your two fingers across the screen. As your fingers spread, the object beneath them grows along with their movements.

Example: Stretch your fingers across hard-to-read items like web pages, photos, and documents until they reach a suitable size or level of detail. Pinch the items to reduce their size and to fit more of them on the screen.

Slide

Press your finger against the screen; then, without lifting your finger, slide your finger across the glass. When you lift your finger, the item stays in its new location.

Example: To reposition a window across the desktop, press your finger on the window's *title bar* — that colored strip along the top edge. Slide your finger to the window's desired position; then lift your finger to set the window in its new place.

Rotate

Press and hold the screen with two fingers; then rotate your fingers. The item turns as though it were paper on a table.

Example: When viewing maps or photos, rotating your two fingers repositions the items along with your fingers' movements.

Swipe

Slide your finger in a certain direction, usually inward from one of the screen's edges. Throughout Windows 8, you'll constantly find yourself swiping inward from your tablet's edges because doing so summons hidden menus.

Example: Swiping almost always seems natural. You swipe across a digital book to turn its pages, for example. You swipe across a web browser's screen to scroll up or down a web page. You swipe across the Start menu to see tiles hidden along the left or right edges.

Note: You can also swipe to *select* items. To do that, swipe in the opposite direction the item usually moves. For example, the Start screen scrolls to the left or right. So, to select a particular Start screen tile, swipe it *downward* and release. Windows highlights the tile and places a check mark in its upper-right corner, indicating that you've selected it for further action. (I describe the Start screen in Chapter 4.)

Typing on a Glass Keyboard

Tablets can display anything onscreen, from photos and movies to buttons and words. So, it's only natural that tablets can toss a convenient keyboard onto the screen when you need to type something.

Although a keyboard is the fastest way to enter text, your tablet's *glass* keyboard brings a few challenges. First, the keyboard consumes the lower half of the screen, removing half of your work from view.

Second, the keys don't physically move, so you never know if you've correctly aligned your fingers. You'll find yourself staring at the keyboard, rather than focusing on your work above it.

On the positive side, each key clicks and lights up when touched, helping you see which one you've pressed. And the keyboard autocorrects fairly well; when your fumbling fingers type *thw*, the keyboard automatically substitutes *the*. Chances are, you'll never notice the correction.

Also, your tablet's glass keyboard is often larger than the cramped layouts stuffed onto small laptops. Glass keyboards are always cleaner, too, as they lack the cracks that attract sandwich crumbs and cat hairs.

Finally, glass keyboards change characters on-the-fly, easily letting you type symbols and foreign characters once you know the tricks I describe in this section.

Glass keyboards will never outperform real keyboards for speed. But with practice, your typing speed will improve. The rest of this section helps you make the most out of the keyboard that's built into every Windows 8 tablet.

Every Windows 8 tablet includes a USB port. If the glass keyboard drives you crazy, plug in a real keyboard snatched from a neighboring computer, be it in the hotel's Guest Office, a nearby cubicle, or on a roommate's desk.

Summoning the main keyboard

To type something on the Windows 8 new Start screen or its apps, you simply tap the area where you'd like to type. As you tap, a keyboard fills the screen's bottom half, ready for you to begin typing.

The desktop isn't as friendly, unfortunately. When you need to type, you must *manually* summon the keyboard by tapping the Keyboard icon (shown in the margin) on the taskbar along the bottom of the screen.

Whether you're typing from the Start screen or the desktop, the Windows 8 keyboard appears, as shown in Figure 3-1.

The keyboard looks and behaves much like a real keyboard, with many of the same keys. Position your fingers over the keys the best you can, and start typing. As you type, the letters appear onscreen.

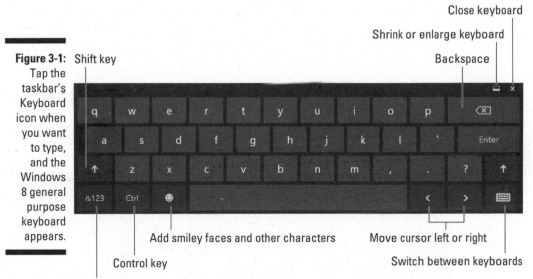

Figure 3-1:
Tap the taskbar's Keyboard icon when you want to type, and the Windows 8 general purpose keyboard appears.

Shift key

Close keyboard

Shrink or enlarge keyboard

Backspace

Add smiley faces and other characters

Control key

Move cursor left or right

Switch between keyboards

Add numbers and symbols from keyboard's top row, as well as numeric keypad

Typing on glass is completely foreign to many people, and it's an oddly unsettling experience. Try these tips during your first few days of typing:

✔ Because you can't feel the keys with your fingertips, you'll stare at your fingers rather than your work onscreen. Once you grow more comfortable with the keyboard, though, train yourself by shifting your gaze upward, toward your work.

✔ Tap the Shift key to type an uppercase letter. (The Shift key automatically turns off after you've typed that first letter.) To turn on Shift Lock, tap the Shift key twice. When you're through typing uppercase letters, tap the Shift key again to turn off Shift Lock.

✔ If you're accustomed to pressing keyboard commands such as Ctrl+V for Paste, press the Ctrl key, and some of the keyboard's keys will change. The word Paste will appear on the V key, for example. Other keys will sprout labels, as well, letting you know which key you need to press to Select All, Undo, Cut, Copy, or Paste.

✔ Need a numeric keypad? Press the &123 key in the lower-left corner, and the numeric keypad appears, along with a Tab key, and the brackets and symbols usually found on most keyboards' top row.

✔ Want a different keyboard? Press the Switch Keyboards button in the keyboard's lower-right corner to switch between each of the Windows 8 keyboards, as shown in Figure 3-2. (I describe the other keyboards in the following sections.)

Figure 3-2:
Tap the
Switch
Keyboards
button to
choose
between
the four
ways of
entering
text in
Windows 8.

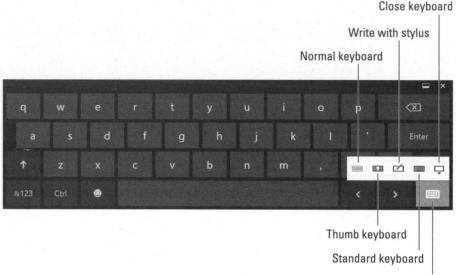

Close keyboard

Write with stylus

Normal keyboard

Thumb keyboard

Standard keyboard

Select a different keyboard

 When you're through typing, remove the keyboard from view by pressing the X in the keyboard's upper-right corner. (Or press the Switch Keyboards button and tap the keyboard icon with the downward-pointing black triangle.) The keyboard vanishes, leaving you with a full-screen view of your work in progress.

Typing with the Thumb keyboard

Built for a generation raised on smartphones, this peculiar keyboard lets you hold your tablet vertically like a giant phone. The keyboard appears in two halves, each clinging to a bottom edge (see Figure 3-3). Your left and right thumbs can then poke at the letters while typing. (You've probably seen texting teens do this under the table at family gatherings.)

 To switch to the Thumb keyboard, press the Switch Keyboards button in the keyboard's lower-right corner and choose the Thumb Keyboard option, shown in the margin.

Figure 3-3:
The Thumb keyboard lets you type with your thumbs.

 If the Thumb keyboard is too large for your hands, tap and hold the three dots (shown in the margin) next to the mini-spacebar on the keyboard's left side. Three options appear on a sliding bar: Small, Medium, and Large. The Thumb keyboard comes set to Large, so slide over to the Medium or Small option, and see if one of them fits better.

Handwriting

Windows 8 also recognizes your handwriting, translating it into text as you write on the screen. However, writing or drawing requires a *stylus* — a type of pen with a special plastic tip. Some tablets include a stylus; others make you buy one as an option.

 To switch to drawing mode, tap the Switch Keyboards button in the keyboard's lower-right corner and tap the Stylus option, shown in the margin.

I describe how to draw and write on a tablet in "Drawing and Writing with a Stylus" later in this chapter.

Standard keyboard

Windows normally sticks with the keyboard shown earlier in Figure 3-1. Because that keyboard shows only letters, the keys are as large as possible, making it a little easier to type on a glass surface.

But if you need a desktop PC-style keyboard, complete with numbers and function keys across the top, Windows can bring one up. Shown in Figure 3-4, it's the real deal, complete with the Windows key, the Alt key, and even four arrow keys for navigating menus.

Figure 3-4:
The
Standard
keyboard
adds every
key, but
makes for
cramped
typing.

The keyboard makes for some mighty cramped typing, though. But it's nice to have in a pinch, when you need certain keys that aren't available elsewhere.

I explain how to add the Standard keyboard as a keyboard option in the upcoming section, "Adjusting Your Keyboard Settings."

Adding the Standard Keyboard option doesn't force you into using that keyboard forever. It's merely added as an option when you touch the Switch Keyboards button that appears in every keyboard's lower-right corner.

Speeding Up Your Typing

Oddly enough, hunt-and-peck typists have an advantage with a glass keyboard. They'll transition to glass more quickly than touch typists. In fact, they'll probably enjoy the Standard keyboard described in the previous section, as it shows *all* its letters and numbers.

But if you're a touch typist with a fairly fast typing speed, you'll be as frustrated as a kid in his first day of a typing class. A glass keyboard simply doesn't work or feel right.

It just takes time. It took practice to master typing on a regular keyboard, and practice will also bring you up to speed on the glass keyboard. Many websites offer free typing speed tests. Spend ten or twenty minutes playing with them, working for accuracy over speed. When your accuracy improves, you can try to speed up your typing.

The next few sections explain other ways to speed up your typing, either by changing the keyboard's settings or by using the special shortcut keys that appear as you type.

Adjusting your keyboard's settings

Windows 8 offers numerous settings to tweak the keyboard's behavior. Most options come turned on by default, so if something about the keyboard bugs you, you can often fix the problem simply by turning off that particular setting.

But whether or not you're happy with your keyboard, drop by the keyboard's settings area to make sure the keyboard is customized to meet your own needs.

To view and change your keyboard settings, follow these steps:

1. **From any screen, swipe your finger inward from the right edge to fetch the Charms bar.**

2. **From the Charms bar, tap the Settings icon; then tap Change PC Settings from the Settings pane.**

3. **When the PC Settings window appears, tap the General section.**

4. **Scroll down to the Touch Keyboard section, and touch any of the toggles to turn their features on or off.**

There, in the Touch Keyboard section shown in Figure 3-5 and the adjacent Spelling section, you can change how the keyboard responds to your fingertips. Most of the settings are self-explanatory. Simply tap the toggle switch to the right of the setting, and it switches On or Off.

Figure 3-5:
The General area of the PC Settings window offers switches to change your keyboard's behavior.

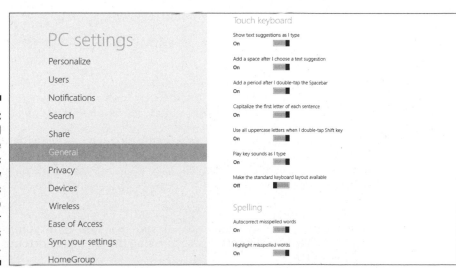

For example, the Capitalize the First Letter of Each Sentence option capitalizes the first letter you type after typing a period. This little timesaver saves you a trip to the Shift key, subtly speeding up your typing. Don't like it? Tap the On toggle to turn it to Off.

One gem here, which is normally turned off, is Make the Standard Keyboard Layout Available. When you turn on that option, your keyboard selection button includes an option to fetch a full keyboard, complete with a row of numbers along the top, function keys, a Windows key, and other keys you may find to be essential. (I show the Standard keyboard earlier in Figure 3-4.)

Down the road, should you stumble upon a program that insists upon your using those keys, Standard Keyboard will be listed as an option.

Typing special characters

Windows never made it particularly easy to enter foreign characters. To enter a foreign symbol into a word like sauté, for example, you'd need to consult a book or chart for the correct code and then enter a complex series of keystrokes to make the é appear.

The Windows 8 keyboard simplifies the process. To add the little hat on the letter é, for example, press and hold the **e** key. A little pop-up menu appears around the letter, shown in Figure 3-6, showing possible foreign characters based on the e key: è, ē, é, ê, ë. Slide your finger in the direction of the key you want, and let go: The desired key appears.

Figure 3-6: Press and hold a letter to see all possible variations. Slide your finger toward the character you want and lift your finger to type that character.

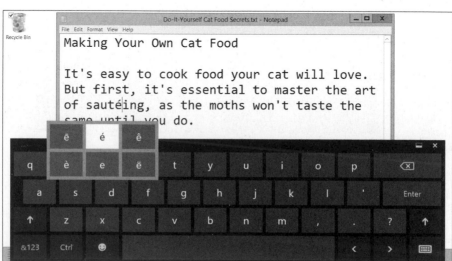

After you've done this a few times, you'll automatically know which way to slide your held-down finger to reach the key you want. To speed things up, just press the key and then slide your finger in the direction of the character you want to grab from the pop-up menu. Lift your finger, and that special character appears, just as though you'd waited for the pop-up menu to appear.

Holding down the question mark key lets you choose between eight other common symbols, including the semicolon, colon, brackets, hyphen, ampersand, and question mark.

Press the &123 key to bring up the numeric keypad. When the keypad appears, press either of the two arrow keys along its left edge to see even more characters, including symbols for copyright, mathematics, and popular currencies.

Typing smilies (emoticons)

Sometimes called *emoji* characters, these little characters grew from the simple smiley face created from a colon, a dash, and a right parenthesis: :-).

Windows 8 carries the text-based smiley into the future by supporting *dozens* of emoticons. To insert an emoticon, press the smiley key shown in the margin. The Emoticon keyboard appears, as shown in Figure 3-7.

Figure 3-7: Press the smiley key to the left of the spacebar to choose from among dozens of characters.

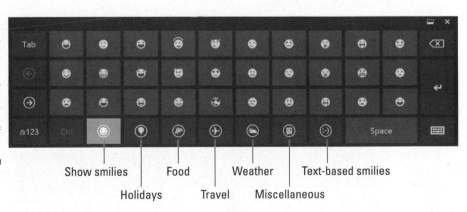

Show smilies   Food   Weather   Text-based smilies

Holidays   Travel   Miscellaneous

The keyboard first shows the smiley faces shown in Figure 3-7. However, pressing any of the keys along the bottom lets you choose among six other categories of symbols: holiday, food, travel, weather, miscellaneous, and text. The text category is a quick way to add text-based smiley faces when sending e-mail.

And that brings us to the problem with special characters: Few of these little symbols translate well between programs, computers, and e-mail systems. They'll work most reliably if you're sending them between two Windows 8 computers.

However, if you're sending them to somebody not using Windows 8, stick with the last emoticon button, which lets you insert the time-tested text-based smileys: :-(.

You can still use emoticons as clipart when creating flyers and posters. Insert them into your document; then enlarge their font size to make them as large as you want.

Predictive typing

Predictive typing is a computer term that describes Windows' psychic abilities. Whenever you type, Windows tries to guess what you're about to type. When Windows feels particularly prescient, it lists the word you're about to type. It simultaneously places an orange key named Insert on the keyboard, as shown in Figure 3-8.

Figure 3-8: If Windows guesses your intended word correctly, tap the Insert key, and Windows fills in the rest of your word.

If Windows has guessed correctly, tap the orange Insert key, and Windows fills in the rest of your word. If you notice that Windows has guessed incorrectly, simply ignore the Insert key, and breathe a sigh of relief, knowing that computers won't be smart enough to overthrow us within our lifetimes.

Windows' accuracy rate differs between individuals. Personally, I tap Insert whenever the key appears. It's never 100 percent correct, but it's correct often enough that even on the rare times that I've had to backspace over the correction, I've still saved typing time.

Test it for awhile to determine its accuracy rate for your own typing style.

Windows' keyboard includes prediction in other ways, tossing in extra keys that come in handy depending on the program that's accepting your text:

- ✔ If you're tying a web address in Internet Explorer, two new keys straddle the spacebar: On the right, you see a .COM key. Tap that to insert . **COM**, saving you from typing in those four characters. On the left, the backslash key appears, simplifying things when typing in long web addresses.

- ✔ Tap and hold the .COM key, and a pop-up menu appears, letting you choose to insert the .net, .org, .us, or .edu characters, as well.

- ✔ When you type an e-mail address into the Mail app, the keyboard sprouts the .COM key, as well as the @ key, speeding up your e-mail address entry.

- ✔ When typing into the Search field in Microsoft's Bing search engine, the Enter key transforms into a Search key. Tap that key, and Bing immediately starts its search.

- ✔ Typing in a logon password? If strangers are nearby, tap the keyboard's Hide Keypress key that appears in the keyboard's lower-right corner. That prevents the keys from lighting up when tapped, keeping your password safer from prying eyes.

Editing Text

Without the pinpoint precision of a mouse pointer, editing a few lines of text seems insurmountable. How do you place the cursor in the exact location necessary to excise the unwanted text?

Like nearly anything else on your tablet, it starts with a strategically placed tap.

Double-tap a word near where you want to edit. Windows highlights the word, surrounding it with a small marker on each side. To extend the selection, drag the first marker to the selection's beginning; drag the second marker to the section's end, as shown in Figure 3-9.

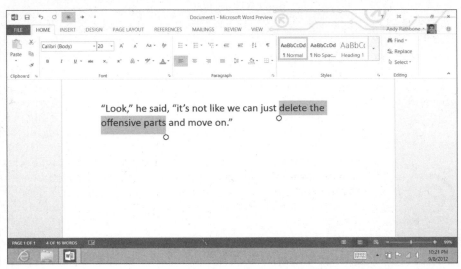

Figure 3-9:
Tap a word
to select it.
Drag the
markers
until you've
surrounded
the portion
you'd like to
delete; then
press Delete
to remove
the text.

Different programs vary a little bit from these steps:

✔ Sometimes double-tapping a word highlights it, but doesn't place the markers on each side. If this happens, hold down the Shift key: As you slide your finger, Windows highlights adjacent words. When you've highlighted the desired words, lift your finger and press Delete to delete them.

✔ Sometimes a tap will simply place a marker on the screen. Then you can drag the marker to the right or left until it's at the position where you'd like to begin typing.

✔ Having trouble putting the cursor where you want it? Try zooming in with your fingers: Straddle the words with your fingertips; then spread your fingers. In many programs, the text increases in size, making it much easier to touch *exactly* where you want to begin typing or editing.

✔ If your tablet came with a stylus, keep it handy. You can quickly and easily mark text for changes by drawing over it with your stylus, much like using a highlighter. (I cover drawing and using a stylus in the "Drawing and Writing with a Stylus" section, coming up shortly in this chapter.)

Typing on a Detachable Keyboard

Typing on glass works well for impromptu notes and quick e-mails. But if you're craving something more substantial, you can easily plug a real keyboard into your keyboard. Windows 8 tablets all include a USB port, which accepts almost all the keyboards available today.

Nearly all wireless keyboards sold for the iPad will also work with Windows 8 tablets.

If you're shopping for a tablet keyboard, look for one designed around Windows 8, complete with dedicated Charms bar keys, as well as a Windows key, and keys for adjusting the volume.

All Windows 8 tablets also accept *Bluetooth* keyboards — a popular wireless option. I explain how to add both USB and Bluetooth accessories in Chapter 6.

Drawing and Writing with a Stylus

When Microsoft first released tablets a decade ago, the company thought people would treat them as digital notepads: Doctors would carry them from room to room, scribbling notes, consulting charts, and viewing x-rays taken minutes before. That dream never quite caught on.

Instead, people today think of tablets as easy ways to watch movies, read books, or browse websites. Yet, all of Microsoft's pioneering "digital notepad" work isn't lost. Your Windows tablet still accepts your handwriting when you draw on it with a *stylus* — a specially designed, plastic-tipped pen.

As you write in either cursive or block letters, Windows recognizes your scrawls, converting your words into text. In some programs, Windows saves your handwritten journals, but it indexes their contents, making them easy to retrieve.

This section explains how you can treat your expensive new tablet like a plain ol' pencil and paper.

Calibrating your stylus

The Windows 8 handwriting recognition works quite well, because Microsoft's been perfecting it for many years. However, to make Windows recognize your writing style even more accurately, calibrate it: Let Windows watch as you tap a set of crosshairs on the screen.

Windows compares your onscreen touch with the actual location of the crosshairs, and behaves more accurately. To calibrate your tablet, follow these steps:

1. **From the Desktop, swipe in from your tablet's right edge to fetch the Charms bar; then tap the Settings icon.**

2. **From the Settings pane, choose Control Panel at the top.**

   The Control Panel appears.

3. **Tap the Hardware and Touch category; then tap the Tablet PC Settings section.**

   The Tablet PC Settings window appears.

4. **From the Tablet PC Settings window, tap the Calibrate button.**

   The Calibrate Pen or Touch Input Screens window appears.

5. **Tap Pen Input.**

6. **Follow the instructions, tapping on the screen on the crosshairs; then tap the Yes button to save the data.**

Windows saves your calibration data, tracking the touch of your stylus that much more accurately. Feel free to repeat these steps anytime you feel Windows doesn't correctly recognize your stylus.

The Tablet PC Settings includes some other gems to simplify tablet computing:

✔ To right-click on a tablet with a stylus, press the stylus against the screen; when a circle appears, lift it, and the right-click menu appears. But if your hand covers the right-click menu, tell Windows you're *left-handed*: In Step 4 above, tap the Tablet PC Settings window's Other tab. Tap the Left-Handed option, and tap OK.

✔ While you're in the Tablet PC Settings area, calibrate your tablet for your *touch,* as well. In Step 5, choose Touch Input, and tap the crosshairs where they appear.

Converting handwriting to text

You can write by hand anywhere that Windows accepts typing. You can handwrite a letter in Microsoft Word, for example, or write in the name of a newly created folder.

As you write, Windows converts your handwriting to words and drops them into the appropriate place.

To convert your handwriting to text on your tablet, follow these steps:

1. **Tap where you'd like to enter text.**

   Tap any place that accepts text — an e-mail, a Word document, an entry in a calendar — even the name of a new file you're saving.

2. **If the handwriting panel doesn't appear, tap the taskbar's Keyboard icon, shown in the margin.**

3. **If a keyboard appears instead of the handwriting panel, tap the Switch Keyboard icon and choose the Stylus option, shown in the margin.**

   The handwriting panel appears.

4. **Begin writing in the handwriting panel, either in cursive, block letters, or even a combination.**

   As you write, Windows quickly begins recognizing the separate words, listing them in order along the panel's left edge. After you've written a short phrase, tap the Insert button. Windows inserts the words as text, as shown in Figure 3-10.

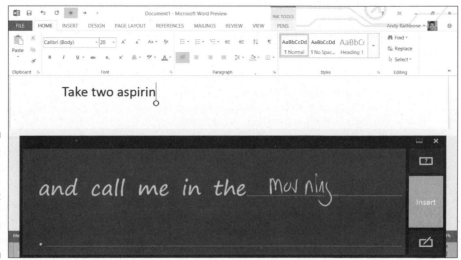

Figure 3-10:
Tap the Insert button to insert your recognized words as text.

If all goes according to plan, you'll write your words, insert them, and move on. If all doesn't go according to plan, you'll need to correct your mistakes, as described in the next section.

Correcting handwritten mistakes

Windows will inevitably make a mistake. It won't recognize one of your words correctly, for example, or it will turn an inadvertent keystroke into a period.

To correct mistakes in the handwriting panel before you've touched the Insert button, draw a line through the misspelled word or letters, as shown in Figure 3-11.

Figure 3-11:
Draw a line through mistakes, and Windows removes them from the panel, letting you write them correctly.

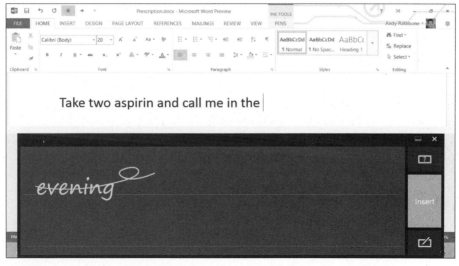

Spot a mistake in text that's already entered? Then run your stylus over the text that needs correcting, just as though you were highlighting it with a marker. As you highlight the text, it appears in the handwriting panel, as though you'd just written it by hand.

Once the text appears in the handwriting panel, draw a line through the words you'd like to remove, just as though you'd written them there. Then tap the Insert key to put the corrected version back in place.

You can correct mistakes several other ways inside the handwriting panel:

✔ To correct a single letter within a word in the handwriting panel, tap the word. Windows spaces the word out, letter by letter. Write the correct letter over the incorrect letter, and Windows replaces the wrong letter with the newly corrected letter.

✔ To add a symbol, tap In your document where the symbol should appear. When the handwriting panel appears, you'll see a symbol key (shown in the margin). Tap it to see the available symbols, and tap the one you'd like to place into the document.

✔ For more tips on how to correct items in the handwriting panel, tap the question mark icon (shown in the margin) in the handwriting panel's upper-right corner. Detailed animations show exactly how to correct, delete, split, and join letters and words.

Writing in Windows Journal

Windows' built-in handwriting-to-text translator works quite well in many situations. Sometimes, however, it's overkill. For example, nobody cares about grammar or even misspellings in a grocery list.

That's where the Windows Journal program comes in. It works just like paper: You write your notes, and the program saves them as handwritten notes — they aren't automatically converted into text.

There's a twist, however. Windows still recognizes your words enough to index them, making them searchable — a handy way to ensure that you can retrieve them down the road.

The Windows Journal program isn't available on tablets running Windows RT.

Shown in Figure 3-12, Windows Journal works well for taking notes in class or at a conference. It's handy whenever you want to jot down quick notes, but can't be bothered with finding a flat surface to set down your tablet and begin typing. (It even lets you write documents on an airplane; you can hold your tablet, leaving room for your snack of peanuts and a drink on the fold-down tray.)

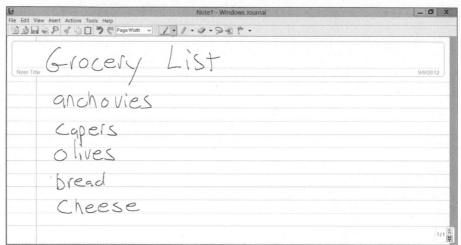

Figure 3-12:
Windows Journal saves your notes and drawings, just as you've written them, but it indexes the words so you can find them later.

Windows Journal simplifies note-taking in several different ways:

- ✔ Instead of facing a blank sheet of paper, begin with a template by tapping the File menu and choosing New Note from Template. There, you can choose from lined paper, graph paper, office memos, a monthly calendar, musical notation, or even a To Do list with check boxes.

- ✔ Describe your note's contents along the top in the Note Title box. Then, when you tap the Save button, Windows automatically saves your note using the words you've written as the Note Title.

- ✔ To find a note later, use the Charms bar's Search Files feature, and type a word from one of your notes. Because Windows indexes all of your journals, it will locate your note, where you can load it with a tap of its name. (I cover the Charms bar in Chapter 4.)

- ✔ To e-mail a note, tap the File menu, choose Send to Mail Recipient, and select the format to send it in. Unless the recipient also uses Windows Journal, choose Web Page as the format. Then the recipient can read your note — but not edit it — in the browser.

Drawing in Paint

A mainstay of Windows for nearly two decades, Paint lives on in Windows 8. Many people have tried Paint using a mouse; they grew frustrated, and moved on to more fruitful endeavors. But Paint takes on new life when used with a stylus

It's never going to be as capable as more expensive programs designed for graphic artists. But you'll still find Paint listed among the Start screen's apps. If you have a stylus, give Paint another try. You might be pleasantly surprised.

Chapter 4

Navigating the Windows Start Screen

In This Chapter

▶ Opening, closing, and switching between apps

▶ Understanding the Charms bar

▶ Finding the hot spots in Windows 8

▶ Organizing the Start screen

▶ Navigating the Start screen with an optional mouse and keyboard

*M*ost tablet owners will camp out quite comfortably on Windows 8's new Start screen. The Start screen, which Windows 8 transforms from a small menu into a full-fledged operating system, contains nearly all the tools a tablet owner needs.

Microsoft built the Start screen to be finger-friendly, yet information-packed. It excels at serving up quick, informational tidbits with the least amount of effort. Just turn on your tablet, for example, and you'll already see your next appointment, the number of your unread e-mails, and the strength of your Internet connection and battery.

If the Start screen lacks a tool you need for a particular task, visit the Microsoft Store and download an *app* to handle the job. Apps — small, touch-friendly programs — hail from the world of smartphones. In fact, a tablet works much like a smartphone with a larger screen.

This chapter explains how to get the most from Windows 8's Start screen and its bundled apps.

Windows 8's New Start Screen

If you've used Windows before, you're probably familiar with the Windows desktop. You've seen several open programs, each running inside its own resizable window.

That approach worked fine on desktop PCs with keyboards, mice, and large monitors. People could create spreadsheets and write reports all day, all the while looking forward to lunchtime.

Tablets, by contrast, serve different needs. Instead of creating documents inside an office cubicle, tablet owners manipulate bits of information in a variety of ways. They fill out forms at job sites, for example, read a book while on the couch, or glance at a map while walking along through a convention hall. Tablets let them do these tasks quickly, with a finger, and while on the go.

That's where Windows 8's new Start screen (shown in Figure 4-1) comes in.

Figure 4-1:
The Windows 8's Start screen includes some "live" tiles, which constantly update their information.

Designed specifically for tablets, the Windows 8 Start screen resembles a personalized billboard. Filled with colorful tiles, the Start screen spreads across your tablet's wide screen, extending off the right edge.

Each tile represents an *app* — a small program — and many tiles constantly percolate with new information. Your Mail app's tile, for example, constantly cycles through your latest unread e-mails. The Weather app displays the forecast for your location, and the Calendar app shows the time and location of your next appointment.

That's not to say you *can't* work on a Windows 8 tablet. Windows 8 still includes the traditional Windows desktop — it's an app waiting to be opened, like everything else in Windows 8. Open the Desktop app with a tap on its tile, and your tablet's Start screen quickly clears to reveal the desktop, complete with its movable windows.

- ✔ To see the portion of the Start screen that disappears off the screen's right edge, slide your finger along the screen from right to left, just as though you were sliding a piece of paper. As your finger moves, the Start screen travels along with it, bringing more tiles into view.

- ✔ Having trouble finding things on the Start screen? I explain how to organize your screen into neatly labeled groups in this chapter's "Organizing the Start screen" section.

- ✔ Need a new app to meet a particular need? I explain how to download and install new apps from the Windows Store app in Chapter 9.

- ✔ I cover the Desktop app in Chapter 5. Microsoft worked hard to make the desktop finger-friendly. But if you're looking for the same level of productivity you had on a desktop PC, plug a mouse and keyboard into your tablet.

- ✔ Although the desktop's certainly convenient to have around, you probably won't load it too often. The Start screen's apps serve most needs quite well.

Opening, Closing, and Switching Between Apps

The Start screen heralds a new way of working with Windows and its ecosystem of small, inexpensive apps rather than large, expensive desktop programs.

To help you figure out this new world, this section covers app basics: How to open and close them, switch between them, and find their menus when they need a few tweaks.

Opening an app

When first installed, Windows 8 doesn't bother to organize your Start screen, shown earlier in Figure 4-1. Your apps appear in a haphazard mess that sprawls out of view beyond the screen's right edge. As you slide your finger along the Start screen from right to left, the tiles move, bringing more into view.

If you spot the app you want to open, tap it with a finger: The app fills the screen, ready for action.

However, the bigger task may be simply *finding* the app you want to open. The sprawling Start screen doesn't alphabetize your apps or organize them into manageable groups. That leaves way too many hiding places.

When your sought-after app is lost in a sea of tiles, bring the app to the surface by following these steps:

1. **Swipe up from the screen's top or bottom. When the Start screen's menu appears along the bottom edge, tap the All Apps icon.**

   The Start screen lists of all your apps alphabetically, shown in Figure 4-2, followed by a list of your desktop programs, organized alphabetically by category. Still don't spot the app you're after? Move to Step 2.

Figure 4-2: Tapping the All Apps icon shows a list of all your installed apps, alphabetized by category.

2. **Pinch the All Apps screen.**

   The app icons disappear, and Windows lists the alphabet, from A to Z, shown in Figure 4-3. Touch the first letter of your app, and Windows redisplays all the apps. This time, the apps beginning with that letter begin at the screen's center, making them easier to pluck from the list.

   This trick works best for the Start screen's huge variety of apps. If you still can't find your app, move to Step 3.

Figure 4-3:
Pinch the
list of all the
apps, and
Windows
displays
the alpha-
bet and
program
categories,
letting you
jump to
an app or
program
beginning
with that
letter.

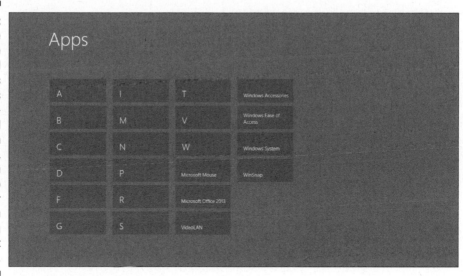

3. **Search for the app.**

   Swipe your finger in from the right edge to fetch the Charms bar,
   covered later in this chapter's "Understanding the Charms Bar" section.
   When the Charms bar appears, tap the Search icon. A keyboard appears
   ready for you to type the app's name (see Chapter 3 for more information
   on using the keyboard). As you type, Windows lists matching apps,
   narrowing down the list with each letter you type.

   Spot your app? Tap its icon to launch it.

If you've plugged a keyboard into your tablet, just begin typing the app's name
directly onto the Start screen. The screen quickly transforms into a list of
every app matching what you've typed so far. Once you spot your app's name
on the list, tap it, and it leaps onto the screen. (Or, if your typing has narrowed
down the list to one app, press Enter on the keyboard to launch the app.)

   ✔ Remember that the Start screen doesn't show *all* of your installed apps.
   It shows only the apps Microsoft chose to be listed.

   ✔ Want an unlisted app to appear on the Start screen? Put it there
   yourself. When looking at the app's tile from the All Apps layout shown
   earlier in Figure 4-2, select the app by sliding its icon up or down a bit.
   (A check mark appears to let you know it's selected, and the bottom
   menu appears.) Then tap the Pin to Start icon from along the bottom
   menu.

   ✔ Still don't see an app that meets your needs? It's time to download one
   from the Windows Store, a chore covered in Chapter 9.

Closing an app

Older Windows versions always wanted you to close a program after using it. You'd click the little box in the program's upper-right corner, and the program would disappear from the screen.

In Windows 8, though, you won't find any close buttons on apps: Apps aren't meant to be closed. When not being used, apps simply rest in the background, waiting in case you need them again. They consume very few resources, and they don't eat much, if any, battery power.

But if you *do* want to close an app, perhaps one that's making annoying noises in the background, doing so isn't difficult.

To close the app currently on the screen, slide your finger down from the screen's top edge all the way to its bottom edge. As you slide, the app follows your finger, shrinking and then disappearing completely when your finger reaches the screen's bottom edge.

It's oddly empowering to watch your finger slide that unwanted app off the screen. It's an easy trick to remember, and you'll find yourself doing it again and again.

Switching between apps

When not being used, apps slumber in the background, waiting to be summoned once again. These sleeping apps don't consume any resources, and your tablet devotes its attention to the app currently filling the screen.

If you want to return to a previously used app, you can summon it with this easy trick: To switch back to the app you've just used, swipe your finger inward from the tablet's left edge.

As your finger moves inward from the screen's edge, it drags your last-used app along with it. When you can see the app begin to appear onscreen, lift your finger. The app grows to fill the screen.

Keep repeating the same trick, sliding your finger in from the left, and you'll eventually cycle through *all* your currently open apps.

Can't remember whether an app's already open? To see a list of your last six open apps, follow these steps from any screen in Windows 8:

1. **Slowly slide your finger inward from screen's left edge.**

2. **When you see an app begin to slide into view, slide your screen back to the left edge.**

   All of your opened apps appear in a column clinging to the screen's left edge, as shown in Figure 4-4.

Figure 4-4: Swipe your finger in from the screen's left edge; then slide it back slightly until a column of recently used apps aligns itself against the screen's left edge.

Once you see the apps' thumbnails clinging to the screen's left edge, you can perform a few other circus tricks, as described here:

- ✔ **Return to an open app:** Tap an app's thumbnail from along the screen's left edge, and the app fills the screen. Simple.

- ✔ **Close an app:** With your finger, slide the app slightly to the right, and then down and off the screen. This one might take a little practice, because the app will try to muscle its way onto the screen. (If you've plugged a mouse into your tablet, close the app by right-clicking its thumbnail and choosing Close.)

- ✔ **Remove the app column:** Because that column of recently used apps consumes some real estate, it closes by itself after you open one of its apps. But if you want to close it manually, just tap the currently open app. That brings Windows attention back to your current app and closes the column of apps.

Installing and uninstalling an app

You install apps through the Windows Store app. I describe how to install and uninstall apps in Chapter 9.

Understanding the Charms Bar

Although it sounds like something dipped in milk chocolate, Windows 8's Charms bar is a menu. But more than that, it's a tool that unites every portion of Windows 8. The all-powerful Charms bar lives *everywhere*: on the Start menu, within every app, and even on the Windows desktop.

However, the Charms bar remains out of sight until you summon it with this trick: Slide your finger inward from any screen's right edge, and the Charms bar appears (see Figure 4-5). The Charms bar also fetches a notification in the screen's lower-left corner showing the current time and date, as well as the strength of your wireless signal and battery.

Figure 4-5: Swipe your finger in from the screen's right edge, and the Charms bar appears, complete with menus to control what you're currently viewing.

The Charms bar —

Search

Share

Start screen

Devices

Settings

Battery strength   Current date and time

Wireless strength

The Charms bar displays five handy icons, each described in the following sections.

Search

 When you need to find something in the sea of text you're currently viewing, fetch the Charms bar with a finger swipe inward from the screen's right edge. Then tap the Search icon, shown in the margin.

The Search pane appears along the screen's right edge, and a keyboard appears below, ready for you to type what you want to find. The Search icon provides a quick way to find a particular reference in your currently viewed website, a lost e-mail from within your Mail app, or even the forecast for a different city in the Weather app.

But Search isn't restricted to the app you're currently viewing. By tapping different items on the Search pane, you route your search to cover your entire tablet. The Search pane is shown in Figure 4-6.

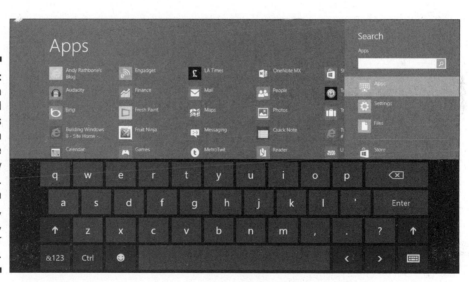

Figure 4-6:
The Search command searches through what you're currently viewing. To search other areas, tap Apps, Settings, or Files.

The Search pane offers these areas:

- ✔ **Search box:** This lets you search what you're currently viewing. Type what you're seeking inside this box; then tap Enter. Below the Search box, you often see names of items you've searched for previously, letting you retrieve them again with a quick tap.

- ✔ **Apps:** Choose this to find an app you can't locate on the Start screen. As you type, a list of matching apps appears onscreen. When you spot your app, launch it with a tap on its name.

When you tap Apps, a list of apps you've previously sought appears along the bottom of the Search pane, which saves you from having to retype the app's name. Tap an app's name, and it launches.

✔ **Settings:** A search in this box looks through every setting found in Windows' two control panels: the Start screen's PC Settings area and the more powerful desktop's Control Panel. Sometimes this search is the only way to find a helpful-but-rarely-used setting that's hidden deeply in the Control Panel's crevices.

✔ **Files:** Choose this to search through all the files on your computer, as well as files you've stored on SkyDrive, Microsoft's online storage space covered in Chapter 6. Searching for files turns up songs, videos, documents, and photos, bringing a list of matching names to the forefront. When you spot the one you want, launch it with a tap.

The Start screen's Search feature works well at finding information quickly and on the fly.

When you need to search other areas, though, or search for more specific items, try these tips:

✔ To search files on your *homegroup* — other computers on your home network — choose Files. Then tap the downward-pointing arrow next to the word *Files* in the screen's upper-left corner. When the drop-down menu appears, choose Homegroup instead of Files. That routes your search to computers on your home network's Homegroup.

✔ To route a search to the Internet, open Internet Explorer. Then summon the Charms bar, tap the Search icon, and type your search term.

✔ When you need more advanced searches — finding files created on a certain date, perhaps — open the Desktop app. Just as with Windows Vista and Windows 7, every desktop folder includes a Search box in its upper-right corner. To fine-tune your searches, tap the Ribbon menu's Search tab and tap the type of search you need.

Share

Computers excel at sharing information. There's little point in creating something unless you want somebody else to see it. That's where the Charms bar's Share icon comes in.

When you're viewing something you want to share, fetch the Charms bar with a swipe of your finger inward along the tablet's right edge.

When the Charms bar appears, tap the Share icon, shown in the margin. The Share pane appears, listing different ways you can share what you're seeing. You'll almost always see one universal sharing mechanism: the Mail app. Choose that to e-mail what you're seeing to a friend.

Choose the Share icon while viewing a website, for example, to e-mail its link to a friend, as shown in Figure 4-7.

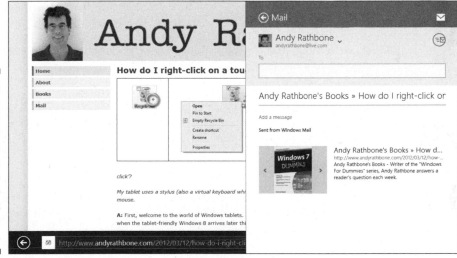

Figure 4-7: Tap the Share icon while viewing a website; then tap Mail to e-mail its link to a friend.

Not all apps support the Share command. If an app doesn't support it, there's no way to share that app's contents. Worst of all, the Windows desktop doesn't support the Charms bar's Share command.

Start

The Start icon is perhaps the most-often used portion of the Charms bar. When tapped, the Start icon always drops you off at the Start screen.

So, to return to the Start screen from anywhere within Windows 8, fetch the Charms bar by swiping your finger inward from the screen's right edge. Then tap the Start icon, shown in the margin. The Start screen returns to the forefront, ready for you to launch another app.

If you're already on the Start screen, tapping the Start icon returns you to your last-used app.

Pressing the Windows key just below your tablet's screen works just like the Charm bar's icon: It returns you to the Start screen or your last-used app.

Devices

This oddly named Charms bar icon doesn't say "Print," but that's probably what you'll use it for most often. Tapping the Charms bar's Devices icon lists all the devices attached to your computer that can interact with what's on the screen.

Most of the time, that device will be your printer. (Or your *printers,* if you're connected to more than one.)

To print something from an app on your tablet, summon the Charms bar by swiping inward from your tablet's right screen; then tap Devices. When the list of available devices appears in the Devices pane, tap your printer's name. Adjust any settings the printer offers, and tap the Print button.

I describe printers in more detail in Chapter 6.

You also tap the Charm bar's Devices icon to send your screen to a second monitor, also described in Chapter 6.

Settings

The Charms bar's Settings icon lets you tweak the settings of the app you're viewing. It also serves as a gateway for tweaking many of your tablet's most common settings.

To change your currently viewed app's settings, summon the Charms bar by sliding your finger in from the screen's right edge. When the Charms bar appears, tap the Settings icon. The Settings pane appears, as shown in Figure 4-8.

Along the top of the settings pane, you see the settings available for the app you're currently viewing onscreen, and along the bottom, you see settings for the things you're most likely to tweak on your tablet:

- ✔ **Networks:** Look here for your wireless signal strength, as well as the name of the wireless connection that's currently pouring the Internet into your tablet. (Tap it, and you can turn on Airplane Mode before flying.)

- ✔ **Volume:** Tap here to fetch a sliding volume control. Slide the bar up to increase the sound; slide it down to lower it.

✔ **Screen:** Tapping here brings a sliding control for screen brightness. (Tap the monitor icon atop the sliding control to lock your tablet's rotation control, keeping it from constantly moving right-side up.)

✔ **Notifications:** Designed for people tired of seeing notifications about Instant Messages and other tripe popping up on their Start screen, this button lets you turn them off for one, three, or eight hours so you can get some work done.

✔ **Power:** Tap here to Sleep, Shut down, or Restart your tablet.

✔ **Keyboard:** This lets you switch between different keyboards or languages, depending on how your tablet's manufacturer set it up.

✔ **Change PC Settings:** Tap here to visit the Start screen's PC Settings area, a gold mine of settings for tweaking the Start screen to meet your particular needs. (Visit the PC Settings area's Personalize section, for example, to customize your tablet's Lock screen, Start screen, and your account picture.) I cover the PC Settings area in Chapters 13 and 14.

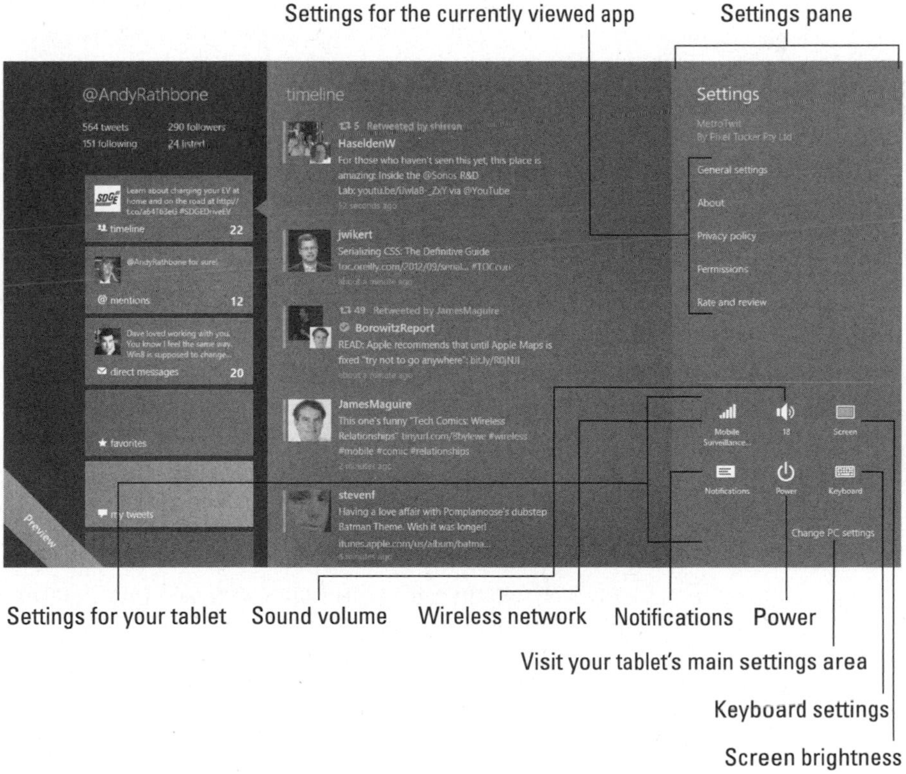

Settings for the currently viewed app

Settings pane

Figure 4-8: The top of the Settings pane lists settings for your currently viewed app; the bottom of the pane lists short-cuts to other popular settings.

Settings for your tablet   Sound volume   Wireless network   Notifications   Power

Visit your tablet's main settings area

Keyboard settings

Screen brightness

Organizing the Start Screen

For some reason, Windows 8 doesn't bother to organize your Start screen. As you add apps from the Windows Store, the Start screen tosses them onto its far right edge, where they're completely out of sight.

To combat the sprawl, organize your Start screen with this Six Step Plan. It organizes your Start screen only as much as you want. If you prefer working with a messy desk, stop after the first step or two. If you sort your pens by color in a tray, then follow these steps to the very end. Doing so will transform your sprawling Start screen into an array of neatly labeled groups.

Follow these steps to organize your Start screen into something you can live with:

1. **Remove tiles for apps you don't want.**

 When you spot an app you'll never use, get rid of it: Slide your finger down the tile slightly to select it. Then, from the App menu that appears along the screen's bottom, tap Unpin from Start (shown in the margin). Repeat until you've removed all your unwanted app tiles.

 Choosing Unpin from Start doesn't *uninstall* the app or program; it only removes the tile from the Start screen. If you accidentally remove the tile for a favorite app or program, you can easily put it back in the next step.

2. **Add tiles that you *do* want.**

 Swipe your finger upward from the Start screen's bottom edge, and then tap the All Apps button along the screen's bottom. The Start screen disappears, showing icons for *all* your available apps listed in alphabetical order.

When you spot an app that you want to appear on the Start screen, select it with a quick downward slide of your finger. (A check mark appears in the app's upper-right corner to show that it's selected.)

 Finally, tap the Pin to Start icon from the Start screen's bottom menu. Windows 8 tosses a tile for that app onto the Start menu's far-right end.

You can select several apps simultaneously and then tap the Pin to Start icon to place them all onto the Start screen.

3. **Move related tiles closer to each other.**

When related tiles appear next to each other, they're easier to find on the Start screen. For example, I like to keep my people-oriented apps — Mail, People, and Calendar — next to each other.

To drag a tile from one place to another, select it first with a little downward drag. Then drag it to its new location. As your finger moves the tile, other tiles automatically move out of the way to make room.

When you've dragged an app's tile to the desired spot, lift your finger, and the tile remains in its new home.

If a rectangular tile consumes too much space, shrink it into a square. Select the tile with a slight downward slide; then tap the Smaller button from the App menu along the Start screen's bottom. (Remember, though, some apps have room to show only live updates on larger, rectangular tiles.)

4. **Move related tiles into groups.**

   Placing related tiles into separate groups makes them easier to relocate. For example, you may want to create one group for tiles you use at home, another for work-related tiles, and a third for tiles that play media — choose whichever groups work for you.

   To begin creating new groups, look closely at your Start menu. Groups have an empty space between them.

   To create a new group, select a tile with a slight downward drag; then drag that tile into the empty space that separates two groups.

   As you position the tile into that empty space, the adjacent groups move farther apart (see Figure 4-9), and a bar appears between the groups. After you've positioned the tile between the two groups, lift your finger to drop the tile into place.

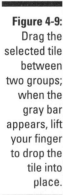

Figure 4-9: Drag the selected tile between two groups; when the gray bar appears, lift your finger to drop the tile into place.

Repeat this step, dragging tiles into new groups until your related tiles live together in their own separate groups.

5. Name the groups of related tiles.

Now that you've created groups or related tiles, give each group a name so you can easily identify its purpose.

Start by pinching the Start screen tiles between two fingers. As you slide your two fingers closer together, the tiles shrink until you're looking at all of your groups onscreen (see Figure 4-10).

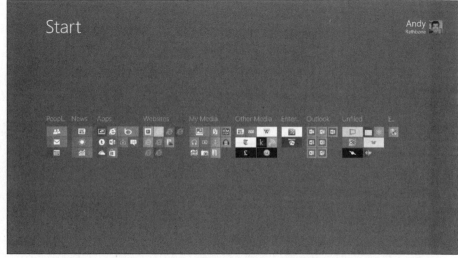

Figure 4-10:
Pinch the Start screen with your fingers to shrink the tiles, bringing all your groups into view.

Select a group with a slight downward slide of your finger. Then, from the bottom menu that appears, tap the Name Group icon. When the Name box appears, type the group's name and tap the adjacent Name button to finish the job.

Repeat, until you've named all your groups.

6. Move groups so your most important ones appear first.

While you're still looking at your groups as miniatures, shown earlier in Figure 4-10, rearrange the groups by dragging them into new positions.

Select a group with a slight downward slide of your finger; then drag and drop the group into a different place.

Repeat until your most frequently accessed groups of tiles appear on the far left.

When you finish dragging, dropping, and naming tiles and groups, your Start screen is customized to the way you use your tablet. Your tiles live in their own neatly named groups, and your most frequently accessed tiles appear first on the screen.

 You can add favorite desktop folders and libraries to the Start screen, as well. While on the desktop, tap and hold your finger on a desired folder or library; when a square appears, lift your finger. Then, from the menu that appears, tap Pin to Start.

Choosing Files with the File Picker

Eventually, you'll need to select a file from within a Start screen app. For example, you may want to open a photo to view in the Photos app. That's where the File Picker comes in. It's not much of a file management tool, but it works fine for selecting a few files or folders when needed.

Oddly enough, the File Picker can't be summoned on its own; there's no way to fetch it and simply browse your files. When you want to browse files, head to the Desktop app and run File Explorer, as I describe in Chapter 5.

No, the File Picker can be summoned only from within a Start screen app. When it appears, you'll see it's a bare-bones program, designed merely to navigate storage areas and find a file or two (see Figure 4-11).

Follow these steps to locate a file on your tablet with the File Picker:

1. **Tap the word *Files* in the screen's upper-left corner and choose the storage area containing your file.**

   When you tap the word *Files*, a menu drops down, listing all the storage areas available on your tablet: your Documents, Pictures, Music, and Videos libraries, for example, as well as your Windows desktop and your Downloads folder. (The Downloads folder contains all the files you download from websites.)

   You can also access places *outside* of your tablet. You can access files shared on your Homegroup by other networked PCs, as well as files stored on SkyDrive, which I cover in Chapter 6.

   Some of your apps may have added their storage spaces to the File Picker's menu, as well.

Move up one folder level

Tap to choose between storage areas

Name of folder being displayed

Toggle sorting by name or date

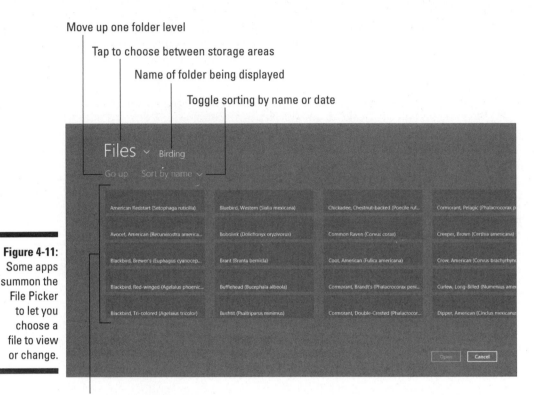

Figure 4-11:
Some apps
summon the
File Picker
to let you
choose a
file to view
or change.

Items within current folder

2. Tap the folder or storage area you want to open, or tap the file you want to select.

When you tap a storage area in Step 1, the File Picker displays all of that storage area's folders and files. (To help you keep track of what you're seeing, the File Picker lists the name of the folder you're currently viewing next to the word Files, as shown earlier in Figure 4-11.)

If you see your file's name, tap it, and you're through: Your app opens it.

Tapped the wrong folder by mistake? Tap the words *Go Up*, just below the Files button, to return.

If you don't see your desired file, keep tapping folders, opening different ones to keep looking.

Still can't find your file? Then summon the Charms bar and tap the Search icon, described earlier in this chapter. The Search feature can find it fairly quickly.

Using the Start Screen with a Mouse and Keyboard

If you plan on using the Desktop app to crank out some serious work, you'll want to plug a mouse and keyboard into your tablet, as I describe in Chapter 5. The mouse and keyboard will feel right at home on the desktop, of course, but the Start screen is a different world.

Even when you work within the desktop app, you'll still find yourself scurrying to the Start screen to open programs, add accounts for new people, and perform other common tasks.

If you want, you can simply use your fingers while navigating the Start menu; plugging in a mouse and keyboard doesn't disable the touch controls. But if you prefer to leave your hands on your mouse and keyboard, Table 4-1 shows how to control the Start screen with a mouse and keyboard.

Table 4-1	Controlling the Start Screen with a Mouse and Keyboard	
How to do this . . .	*Mouse*	*Keyboard*
Open the Charms bar	Point at the screen's upper- or lower-right corner.	Win+C
Return to last-used app	Point at the screen's upper-left corner and click.	Win+Tab, Enter
Return to Start menu	Point at the screen's lower-left corner and click.	Win
See currently running apps	Point at the screen's upper-left corner; then slide the mouse downward.	Win+Tab (then keep pressing Tab to cycle through open apps)

Chances are, though, you'll still use your fingers on your tablet's screen even after plugging in a mouse and keyboard. You'll probably use the keyboard only for typing text and the mouse for pointing at small items on the desktop.

Power users take note: If you right-click any screen's bottommost left corner, a power menu appears (see Chapter 5 for more on the power menu). That menu places many oft-used settings a mouse-click away. (That secret menu is available only with a mouse or a trackpad.)

Chapter 5

Visiting the Windows Desktop

*T*he Start screen and its apps ecosystem excel at letting you consume information on the run. You can find appointments, scan the headlines, check e-mail, browse the web, and listen to music. When you find some downtime, your tablet doubles as an e-book reader, letting you browse books, magazines, and newspapers.

But when you need to create rather than consume, your tablet can transform once again: It can behave just like a desktop PC, ready to either support your own muse or that of your boss.

Just as it does on desktop PCs, your tablet's desktop excels at file management, creating large documents, and manipulating large amounts of information.

When you're ready to set up camp on the tablet's Desktop app, this chapter will help you load the app and make the most of it with your fingers, a stylus, a mouse and keyboard, or — best of all — all four.

Setting Up Camp on the Desktop

To launch the desktop, tap the Start screen's Desktop app. The Desktop app's pretty easy to find. It's not only labeled Desktop, but also its tile looks like a miniature view of your real desktop, complete with the same background.

When loaded (see Figure 5-1), the Desktop app looks and behaves much like the desktop from earlier versions of Windows, including Windows 7 and Windows Vista.

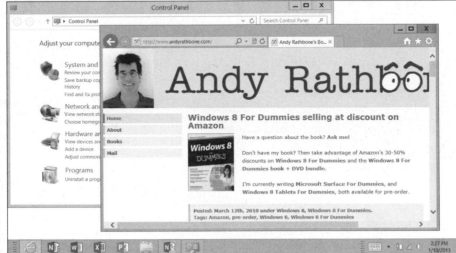

Figure 5-1: Windows 8's Desktop app brings the traditional Windows desktop to your tablet.

 Don't see the Desktop app on the Start screen? Swipe your finger up the screen from your tablet's bottom edge; then tap the All Apps icon (shown in the margin). When your tablet displays a list of all your installed apps, the Desktop app should be listed alphabetically in the Apps section. Tap the Desktop app's tile to launch it.

Your fingers can control much of the desktop. But many parts of the desktop require more pinpoint precision than a fingertip can give. Specifically, you'll have trouble selecting items from lists, editing text, and selecting menu options.

So, if you're ready for some *real* work on the desktop, follow these steps to turn your Windows 8 tablet into a full-fledged desktop PC:

1. **Plug in a keyboard.**

   You may be a speedy typist on your tablet's glass keyboard, but no matter how fast you type, the keyboard always covers half of your tablet's screen. To bring your full desktop back into view, you need a *real* keyboard. You can plug one into your tablet's USB port or connect wirelessly with a Bluetooth keyboard.

Spot an unused desktop computer lying around the office or hotel? Feel free to borrow a keyboard from any of them. (You can attach and detach a USB keyboard from a desktop PC without turning off the PC first.)

Then plug the keyboard into your tablet's rectangular *USB port,* covered in Chapter 2. (I cover wireless keyboard options in Chapter 6.)

2. **Plug in a mouse.**

You can also plug mice into a USB port. If a keyboard already hogs the port, a small Bluetooth mouse comes in handy. Its wireless connection doesn't require a USB port.

Or you can buy a portable USB hub. When you plug the hub into your tablet's lone USB port, your tablet immediately sprouts extra USB ports for your accessories. I cover Bluetooth, portable hubs, and other accessories in Chapter 6.

3. **Plug in an external monitor (optional).**

If your tablet's screen doesn't seem large enough, connect a cable between your tablet's video port and an external monitor, either an HDTV or a desktop PC monitor. Then set up your tablet for dual screens, as I describe in Chapter 6. This way, you can view your notes on your tablet while using the larger desktop monitor to write and edit your document.

4. **Plug your tablet into the wall to recharge the battery.**

When you set up camp at a desk, it's also a good time to plug your tablet's charger into a nearby wall outlet and start recharging your tablet.

Plugging in a keyboard and mouse combines the best of the touchscreen and desktop PC worlds. You can still use touch commands on the tablet, but when a mouse and keyboard handle a job more easily, you can reach for them, too.

True to tablet form, when you're through, you can unplug everything and walk away, taking all of your information with you.

If you'll be using the desktop a lot on your tablet, position the Desktop app in the Start screen's upper-left corner. After you plug in an external keyboard, press Enter at the Start screen to launch the Desktop app.

What's missing from the Windows RT desktop?

The inexpensive and low-power Windows RT tablets, described in Chapter 1, ensure plenty of battery life, but that battery life comes at a price. The Win RT Desktop app isn't powerful enough to run traditional desktop programs. Windows RT tablets still include the Desktop app and Microsoft Office's heavyweights — Microsoft Word, PowerPoint, Excel, and OneNote — wait for you on the desktop.

However, you can't install other programs on Windows RT's desktop. These desktop staples, included in Windows 8 tablets, are also missing from Windows RT tablets: WordPad, Windows Media Player, Windows Media Center, Sticky Notes, and Windows Journal.

Windows RT's desktop still includes File Explorer for managing files, handy when shuttling files to and from flash drives. You'll also find traditional Windows desktop programs like Paint, Notepad, Calculator, Windows Defender, Windows Easy Transfer, and all the Ease of Access programs for physically challenged people.

To fill in any other computing needs in Windows RT, though, you must rely on Start screen apps, available through the Windows Store app.

Making the Desktop Friendlier to Fingers

No doubt about it, the Windows desktop works best with a mouse and keyboard, but that shouldn't stop you from performing the tweaks in this section, as they'll make the desktop a little easier to use with your fingers. You won't be able to work as quickly as with a mouse, but at least your fingers will stand a better chance of tapping the right spots on the desktop.

Down the road, when you don't have a mouse and keyboard handy, you'll appreciate the time you spent here to make the desktop as finger-friendly as possible.

If your tablet includes a stylus, don't underestimate its power on the desktop. It works very well as a makeshift mouse, letting you select files and tap buttons, as well as enter and edit text, as I describe in Chapter 3.

Enlarging the desktop's menus

When you fire up the Desktop app from the Start screen, Windows 8 seems to assume you'll be using a mouse and keyboard. Unlike the Start screen's big buttons and finger-sized controls, the desktop remains rooted in the tiny controls of yesteryear, as shown in Figure 5-2.

Figure 5-2:
The Windows 8 desktop defaults to small letters, tiny buttons, and thin borders, making them difficult to access with your fingers.

You can change that fairly easily, though, by telling Windows to make everything on the desktop *larger*. Once you flip that switch, everything on your desktop expands to resemble the desktop shown in Figure 5-3.

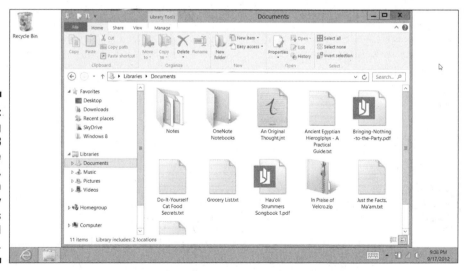

Figure 5-3:
By telling Windows 8 to enlarge the desktop, you can more easily touch its buttons and controls.

Sure, taking these steps will pack less information onto the screen, but you'll at least be able to take advantage of the information displayed there. In addition, they're reversible, so you can always return to the mouse-sized controls.

Before following these steps, save all your open work and close all of your open programs. One of the steps requires you to sign out of your account and then sign back in.

To enlarge everything on the desktop so that it's easier to touch, follow these steps:

1. **Launch the Desktop app from the Start menu.**

   The traditional Windows desktop fills the screen.

2. **Summon the Charms bar by sliding your finger inward from the screen's right edge. Tap the Charms bar's Settings icon to fetch the Settings pane. Then tap Control Panel at the top of the Settings pane.**

   The desktop's Control Panel appears.

3. **On the Control Panel window, tap the Hardware and Sound category; then tap the Display link.**

   The Display window appears, as shown in Figure 5-4.

Figure 5-4:
Choose
Medium
— 125% to
make the
desktop
controls
easier to
touch with a
finger.

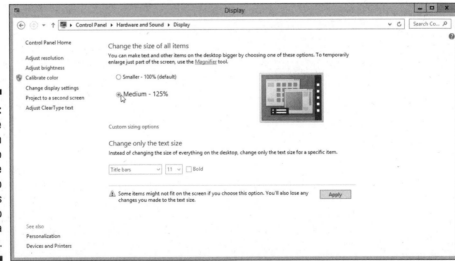

4. **In the Change the Size of All Items area, tap the setting Medium – 125%; then tap the Apply button.**

5. **When Windows asks you to sign out of your computer and apply your changes, tap the Sign Out Now button.**

   If you haven't saved your work, save it before clicking the Sign Out Now button.

Tapping an item from a drop-down menu

When you try to tap an item from a desktop's drop-down menu, you'll rarely hit the desired option with your finger on the first try.

So, when you encounter a drop-down menu — or any scrolling menu, for that matter — aim and tap your finger on the desired item: But *don't* lift your finger.

Instead, slide your finger up or down the list. Windows will highlight different choices as you move your finger. When Windows highlights the choice you were originally aiming for, *then* lift your finger.

This little trick ensures that you make the correct choice, saving you from tapping repeatedly until you eventually stumble upon your desired option.

When Windows restarts, your desktop will be larger and easier to control by touch, as shown earlier in Figure 5-3.

- ✔ The increased size affects *only* the desktop. Your Start screen and apps will remain unaffected. That's a good thing, actually, because the Start screen is already built for touch controls.

- ✔ If your desktop is still too small, make everything even *larger*. In Step 4, tap Custom Sizing Options instead of tapping Medium – 125%. The Custom Sizing Windows opens, with a drop-down menu letting you change the sizing percentage up to 200%. (I don't suggest going past 150%, because the desktop controls may become too large to reach if you increase the size even more.)

- ✔ If a crucial portion of an enlarged window drops off the bottom of your screen, turn your tablet sideways; the desktop automatically rotates, giving you more space along the desktop's bottom edge. That usually lets you access the entire window. (I explain how to maneuver windows with your fingers later in this chapter's "Basic Windows Mechanics" section.)

- ✔ If the settings in the Custom Sizing Options window make the screen look slightly blurry, check the Use Windows XP Style Scaling box.

Turn on the Ribbon menu

Familiar to people who've used the latest versions of Microsoft Office, the Ribbon menu now appears as a staple atop every folder in Windows 8. The Ribbon menu is simply a thick strip of options that dangle from the top menu bar, as shown in Figure 5-5.

Tap the tabs to see menus relating to that subject.

Tap the little arrow to toggle the Ribbon menu on or off.

Figure 5-5:
Windows Explorer, now renamed File Explorer, includes a Ribbon menu. The Ribbon menu's larger buttons provide an easier target for your fingers.

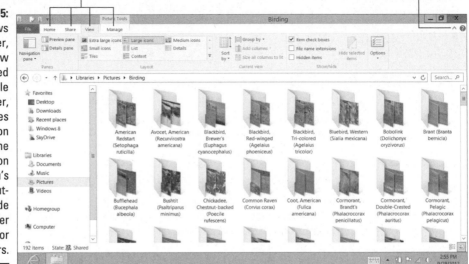

When looking for items on the Ribbon menu, remember to look at the little tabs across the top. Tap a different tab — the View tab, for example — and the Ribbon menu changes to show all the options controlling how you *view* the window's contents. Similarly, tap the Share tab, and the menu changes to show different ways you can share items in the window.

The Ribbon menu's large menus and buttons come in handy on a tablet, and you may miss the Ribbon should it suddenly disappear. If your Ribbon menu falls off the top of your folder, put it back by finding the little arrow shown in Figure 5-5.

That arrow serves as a toggle switch. Tap it to either hide the Ribbon or bring it back into view.

Hiding the menu gives you more workspace, and tapping a tab always brings the hidden Ribbon menu temporarily back into view. Leaving the Ribbon menu turned on, though, makes it faster to tap a menu item.

There's no right or wrong way with this one. Experiment with leaving the Ribbon menu turned on or off, and see which one you prefer. The key here is knowing how to switch between the two modes.

Managing Files and Folders by Touch with File Explorer

In earlier versions of Windows, a program named *Windows Explorer* let you manage your files and folders. By opening Windows Explorer, you could view your computer's files, folders, and storage spaces, and you could shuffle them all to different areas.

In keeping with Windows 8's new spin on things, Windows Explorer is now called *File Explorer.* Thankfully, File Explorer works in almost the same way as Windows Explorer, and it lets you do the same things: manage your tablet's files, folders, and storage areas.

File Explorer is included on the desktop of every Windows 8 tablet, including Windows RT.

To open File Explorer and begin browsing or manipulating your files, open the Desktop app from the Start screen. Then tap the File Explorer icon (shown in the margin), found on the desktop's taskbar — that strip along the desktop's bottom edge.

File Explorer appears, as shown in Figure 5-6. To see your tablet's storage spaces, tap Computer from File Explorer's left pane, which is called the *Navigation pane.* There, you see all the drives accessible by your tablet: its internal hard drive and removable memory card, as well as anything you've plugged into its USB port, including flash drives, portable hard drives, and even digital cameras.

Frequently accessed places

Ribbon menu

Ribbon menu tabs

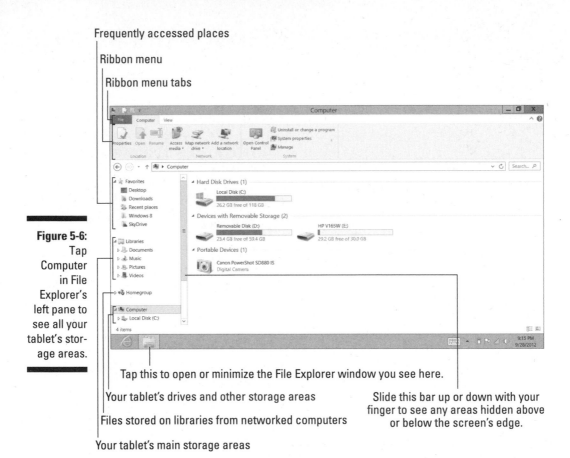

Figure 5-6:
Tap
Computer
in File
Explorer's
left pane to
see all your
tablet's stor-
age areas.

Tap this to open or minimize the File Explorer window you see here.

Your tablet's drives and other storage areas

Files stored on libraries from networked computers

Your tablet's main storage areas

Slide this bar up or down with your
finger to see any areas hidden above
or below the screen's edge.

When you want to copy or move items from one place to another, Windows makes you take two steps: First, you select the items; next, you choose to *Copy* or *Move* them to their new location.

That new location can be a different folder, a flash drive attached to a USB drive, a network location, or just about anywhere else the tentacles of your tablet can reach.

The next two sections explain how to select items and copy or move them to a new destination. (It also explains how to rename or delete selected files.)

Selecting files and folders with a fingertip

To select several items with an attached mouse and keyboard, press and hold the Ctrl key while clicking items with a mouse.

Selecting items or groups of items with your fingers, by contrast, can be one of a tablet's most maddening chores. It's fairly easy to select one item: Just tap it, and Windows highlights it, showing that it's selected. But when you tap a second item, Windows selects *that* item, deselecting the first item.

How do you select more than *one* item? The key is a precisely placed tap under just the right conditions. The following steps show the way to select more than one item using precisely placed taps:

1. **Open File Explorer and navigate to the drive or folder containing the items you want to copy or move.**

   Open File Explorer with a tap of its icon (shown in the margin) on the *taskbar* — that strip running along the desktop's bottom edge. When File Explorer appears, examine the Navigation pane along its left edge. It lists all of your tablet's storage areas.

   Tap the storage area containing your items; that storage area's contents appear in File Explorer. Double-tap a drive, library, or folder to open it. Keep digging until you've found the location of the item to be moved.

2. **Switch to Details view.**

   File Explorer lets you view items in many different ways, and Details view is the easiest way to select things with your fingers. So, tap the View tab along the Ribbon menu's top edge; then tap Details in the Layout section. File Explorer displays the items in Details view: rows of names of files and folders.

3. **To select a file, tap *just to the left of a file's icon*. A check box containing a check mark appears next to the file's icon.**

   This is the trickiest part. With the tip of your pinky, tap just to the left of the file's or folder's name. When you tap in just the right spot, you place a check mark in the box that appears, as shown in Figure 5-7.

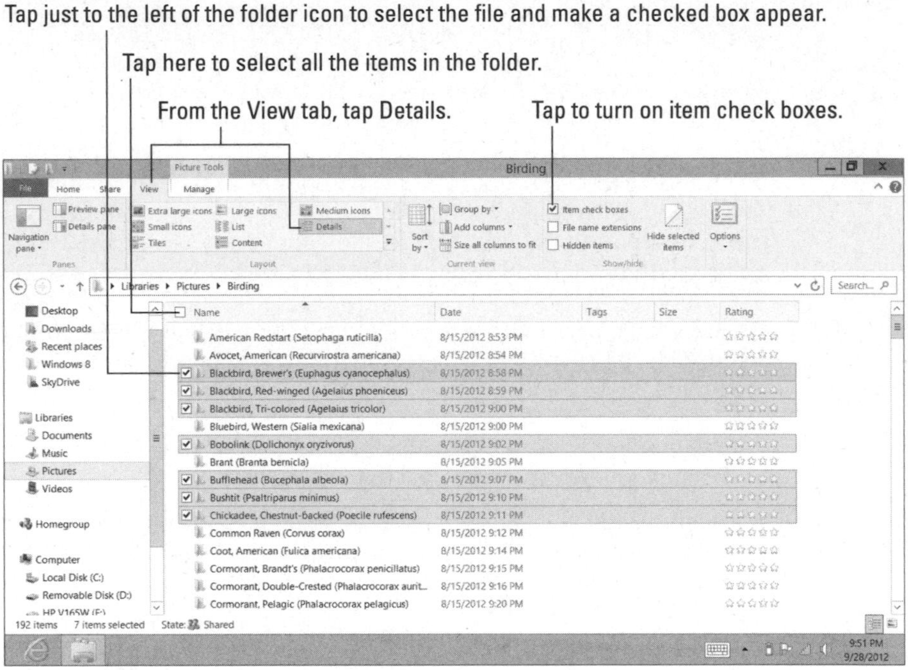

Tap just to the left of the folder icon to select the file and make a checked box appear.

Tap here to select all the items in the folder.

From the View tab, tap Details.

Tap to turn on item check boxes.

Figure 5-7:
Tap just to the left of the file's or folder's icon, and a check mark appears, showing you've selected the file or folder.

As you quickly discover, this takes practice. If just one tap is off, Windows deselects *everything,* and selects only what you've just tapped. Keep trying, and you'll eventually find the sweet spot, just to the left of the file's or folder's icon.

After you select the items you want, move to the next section: copying or moving files and folders.

✔ On the Start screen, a tap opens an item. On the desktop, a tap *selects* an item. The desktop requires a *double-tap* — two quick taps in succession — to open an item.

✔ When selecting many items, it's sometimes easier to check the Select All check mark and then tap to deselect unwanted items.

✔ To delete your selected items, tap the Ribbon menu's Home tab, and tap the Delete icon (shown in the margin).

✔ If your tablet includes a *stylus* — a plastic pen for drawing on your tablet — rejoice! It's *much* easier to select and deselect items by tapping their check boxes with the tip of a stylus.

✔ You can also *lasso* items using your finger or stylus. Draw a rectangle around your desired items, and Windows selects them for you.

✔ After fiddling around with your fingers on the desktop for a few minutes, you'll see why a mouse or stylus can be invaluable for precision desktop operations. I describe how to attach mice, both wired and Bluetooth, in Chapter 6.

Copying or moving files and folders

As you discovered in the previous section, selecting items on the desktop with your fingers can consume a lot of time. But once you've selected them, it's fairly easy to copy or move them to a new location by following these steps:

1. **From File Explorer, tap the Home tab.**

   The Ribbon menu changes, showing file management icons that you see in Figure 5-8.

Copy to

Move to   Delete

The Home tab   Rename

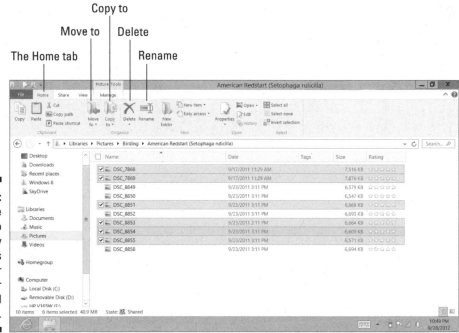

Figure 5-8:
Tap the
Move To
or Copy
To icons
to move or
copy your
selected
files.

2. **Tap the Move To or Copy To icons.**

   A menu drops down from your tapped icon, listing locations where you've previously saved items. If you spot your destination, tap it to complete the process.

   Don't spot the destination on the menu? Then choose the entry at the list's bottom: Choose Location.

   The Copy To or Move To Window appears.

3. **Select the items' destination from the window; then tap the Copy or Move button to send your items to their new destination.**

   The Copy Items or Move Items window, shown in Figure 5-9, works much like a tiny Navigation pane that you see along the left edge of every folder. Tap Libraries to send your items to your Documents, Music, Pictures, or Videos libraries, for example.

Figure 5-9:
Tap a location; then tap the Copy or Move buttons to send your items to their final destination.

Or to send items to a flash drive, tap your flash drive from the drives listed in the Computer section.

When you've chosen your items' resting place, tap the Copy or Move button in the bottom of Figure 5-9. (The button's name depends on whether you tapped the Copy To or Move To icons in Step 2.)

 Adding File Explorer to your Start screen lets you jump to the program with a quick tap. I explain how to add destinations to your Start screen in Chapter 4's Organizing your Start screen section.

When a program *isn't* a program

Eager to promote its new Start screen system of computing, Windows 8 refers to its Start screen programs as *apps*. However, Windows 8 also refers to desktop programs as apps. In the world of Windows 8, the word "program" no longer exists.

However, because the entire computer industry will take some time to scrub the word "program" from its menus, software boxes, and websites, this book isn't scrubbing away the history of computing.

In this book, programs that run on the desktop are called *programs*. Programs that run on the Start screen are called *apps*.

Launching Desktop Programs

Although the Desktop app may seem like a self-contained world, it's not. The Desktop app tosses you back onto the Start screen on several occasions, most noticeably when you want to load a program.

Because the Windows 8 desktop lacks the Start button of yesteryear, you load a desktop program by following these steps:

1. **Return to the Start screen.**

   You can return to the Start screen by pressing your tablet's Windows button, pressing the Windows key on a keyboard, or swiping in from your tablet's right side and tapping the Windows icon.

2. **Tap your desired program's icon from the Start screen.**

   I describe how to load programs from the Start screen in Chapter 4, but here are some quick tips:

   - If your desired program doesn't have a tile on the Start screen, swipe up from the bottom of your tablet's screen and tap the All Apps icon. That lists icons for all of your installed apps and programs.

   - When looking at the Start screen's All Apps view, desktop programs appear along the screen's far right edge.

When you tap the desktop program's icon, Windows 8 returns you to the Desktop app and begins running the program on the desktop.

Adding desktop programs to the taskbar

To skip some trips to the Start screen, add your favorite desktop programs to the desktop's taskbar — that strip along the desktop's bottom edge. To stock your taskbar with your favorite programs, follow these steps:

1. **From the Start screen, slide your finger up from the bottom edge to reveal the App bar; then tap the All Icons icon.**

   The Start screen reveals icons for every app and program installed on your tablet.

2. **Select a favorite desktop program by sliding your finger up or down slightly on its icon.**

A check mark appears next to the program's name, and the menu along the screen's bottom changes.

3. **From the bottom menu, tap the Pin to Taskbar icon.**

   The next time you visit the desktop, that program's icon will be waiting on the taskbar, where you can launch it with a tap. By stocking the taskbar with your favorite programs, you can minimize your trips to the Start screen.

Basic Window Mechanics

The key to maneuvering windows on the desktop with your finger is to think of your finger as a mouse pointer. Then follow these rules:

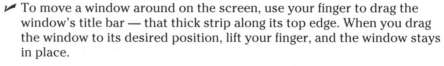

✔ To move a window around on the screen, use your finger to drag the window's title bar — that thick strip along its top edge. When you drag the window to its desired position, lift your finger, and the window stays in place.

✔ To close a window, tap the X in its upper-right corner.

✔ To minimize a window, tap the little line icon near the window's upper-right corner.

✔ To shift your focus from one window to another, tap anywhere on the window you want to begin using.

Snapping an App Alongside the Desktop

Windows 8's Start screen and Desktop app live in very separate worlds. The Start screen is modern, while the Desktop app is traditional. They look and behave nothing alike, and for the most part, they work apart from each other.

Sometimes, though, it's helpful to mix the two. For example, wouldn't it be nice to see your Calendar app at the same time as your desktop, so you could see your next appointment?

Windows 8 lets you do that with a feat called *snapping an app,* and the result looks like Figure 5-10.

Figure 5-10: Snapping an app places a Start screen app to the side of your desktop for reference.

Follow these steps to snap any Start screen app to the side of your desktop:

1. **Open the Desktop app; then open any Start screen app.**

   To reach the Start screen from the desktop, press the Windows key at the bottom of your tablet's screen. Find the app you want to see alongside the desktop, and tap the app to bring it to the screen.

2. **Switch back to the desktop.**

   Slide your finger inward from the screen's left edge, dragging the desktop back onto the screen.

3. **Snap the app against your desktop.**

   Slowly drag your finger from the left edge of the screen inward; your most recently opened app appears, following along with the motion of your finger. When a vertical strip appears onscreen, lift your finger, and the app snaps itself to the screen's left edge.

When the app snaps against the desktop's left edge, a small vertical bar separates it from your desktop. The snapped app stays in place, even if you head back to the Start screen and run a few apps. When you return to the desktop, your snapped app will still stick to the side.

App-snapping works well for a few tasks, but it includes more rules than a rebate coupon:

✔ You can't snap an app to the side of the Start screen or any Smart screen apps. The hoggy Start screen and its apps always consume the entire screen. Apps can snap only to the side of your desktop.

✔ You can't snap an app onto each side of your desktop. You can snap only one app on one side.

✔ To unsnap the app, use your finger to drag that vertical bar back toward the screen's closest edge.

✔ You can snap apps only on a screen with a resolution of at least 1366 x 768. In human language, that means an extra-wide computer screen, which you won't find on most netbooks or older laptops. You will find that resolution, however, on all Windows 8 tablets.

✔ If you love instant messages, snap the Messaging app to your desktop, so you can always procrastinate.

The Desktop's Hidden Power Menu

You can't summon this menu with your fingers. But when you plug in a mouse or trackpad and right-click in the secret spot, you'll wonder why this menu wasn't in *every* version of Windows.

Right-click in any screen's bottommost left corner, and the menu shown in Figure 5-11 appears. Tablet owners will find these options the most useful:

Figure 5-11:
Right-click
in any
screen's
bottommost
left corner
to fetch the
Windows
8 power
menu.

✔ **Programs and Features:** Click this to see the Control Panel's Programs and Features window, which lists all your installed desktop programs. From that window, click an unwanted program and click the Uninstall button to remove it, a process I cover in Chapter 9.

✔ **Mobility Center:** This desktop program (which I cover in Chapter 13) offers quick access to frequently accessed features for laptops and tablets.

✔ **Power Options:** This takes you to the Control Panel's Power Options window. There, you can choose between the existing battery saving plans or customize your own plan, a task I cover in Chapter 13.

✔ **System:** This takes you straight to your Control Panel's System page, where you can see your tablet's Windows version, amount of memory, and CPU type. You'll also need to visit here to add the Windows Media Center program. (To do that, choose the link called *Get More Features with a New Edition of Windows.*)

✔ **Task Manager:** This shows a list of your computer's currently running programs. There, you can shut down misbehaving ones by clicking their names and clicking the End Task button.

✔ **Control Panel:** This mammoth panel of switches (which I cover in Chapter 13) lets you fine-tune how your tablet behaves.

✔ **File Explorer:** This program, which I talk about earlier in this chapter, lets you manage your tablet's files and storage areas.

✔ **Desktop:** Choose this to jump to the desktop.

Part II
Connecting, Playing, and Working

Discover more on how to control a tablet through touch at www.dummies.com/extras/windows8fortablets.

In this part . . .

✔ Find out how to connect to the Internet, wireless networks, printers, monitors, storage, and more.

✔ Navigate websites with the Internet Explorer app.

✔ Stay in touch with people through the Mail, People, Calendar, and Messaging apps.

✔ Load apps on the Start screen and programs on the desktop.

Chapter 6

Connecting to the Internet, Printers, Monitors, Storage, and More

. . . .

In This Chapter

▶ Connecting to the Internet or a printer

▶ Connecting to accessories

▶ Connecting to a monitor or HDTV

▶ Connecting to storage

▶ Connecting to networked PCs

. . . .

*Y*our tablet strips computing down to the bare essentials: your data, a screen, and your fingers to control it all. You end up carrying a package weighing less than two pounds.

Yet, tablets can still adapt to meet your needs. Need to leave a paper trail? Plug in a printer. Windows 8 automatically recognizes most of them.

Need to crank out some Excel spreadsheets or a Word document? Plug in a mouse and keyboard and fire up the Desktop app. Screen too small? Plug in an external monitor.

Need more storage space? Plug in a flash drive, or even a portable hard drive. The list goes on: To watch high-definition movies in style, plug in an HDTV.

When you're through with all the accessories, unplug them and walk away. You've returned to minimalist mode, carrying all of your data with you.

That's the beauty of a Windows 8 tablet.

Connecting to the Internet

Windows 8 lives and breathes through the Internet, and if you're not connected, your programs will start to complain. Some Internet-starved programs offer helpful messages like "You're Not Connected." Other apps simply freeze, hoping you'll notice the tiny word *Offline* in the upper-right corner.

All Windows tablets can connect to a *wireless network* (known as *Wi-Fi*), and almost all networks offer Internet access. Your tablet isn't limited to Wi-Fi Internet connections, though.

With the right tricks, tablets can also connect to the Internet through wired networks, dial-up networks, cellular data plans, and by tethering to a smart- phone.

This section explains each way your tablet can connect to the Internet.

Connecting to wireless networks

All Windows 8 tablets can connect to the Internet *wirelessly* — they already contain a built-in wireless network adapter. To connect, you and your tablet need only be within range of a wireless network. (Wireless networks sometimes go by the name of "hotspots" or "mobile hotspots.")

Today, that's easier than ever. You'll find Wi-Fi networks in airports, coffee shops, hotels, and many homes. (I describe how to set up a wireless network in *Windows 8 For Dummies,* published by John Wiley & Sons, Inc.)

These steps explain how to find out when you're within range of a Wi-Fi network, as well as how to connect to it and start browsing the Internet.

1. **From any screen, summon the Charms bar by sliding your finger inward from the screen's right edge.**

   When the Charms bar appears along the screen's right edge, look at the dark rectangle that also appears near the screen's bottom left. A glance at the icon in the rectangle's upper-left corner, shown in Figure 6-1, shows when you're within range of a wireless network.

   If you're within range, move to Step 2. Not within range? Move to another spot, hopefully one with clusters of people huddled over their tablets and laptops.

A Wi-Fi network is available

Figure 6-1:
When you
summon the
Charms bar,
this icon lets
you know
whether
you're
within range
of a Wi-Fi
signal.

9:26 Friday
September 21

No Wi-Fi network available

9:26 Friday
September 21

2. **Tap the Charms bar's Settings icon. When the Settings pane appears, tap the Network icon.**

   The bottom of the Settings pane, shown in Figure 6-2, shows six icons. The icon in the top left represents networks. The Networks icon toggles between Available and Unavailable depending on whether you're currently within range of a wireless network.

Figure 6-2:
Amid the
cluster of
icons at the
bottom of
the Settings
pane, tap
the one in
the top-left
corner. (The
icon usu-
ally says
Available.)

Tap this icon to connect to a wireless network.

- **Available:** When the icon says Available (shown in the margin), you're within range of a wireless network. Move to Step 3 to begin connecting.

- **Unavailable:** When the icon says Unavailable (shown in the margin), you're out of range and out of luck. (Wi-Fi signals rarely reach more than 300 feet from their transmitter.) Try moving to a different location or ask somebody if there's a Wi-Fi signal available. Then return to Step 1.

3. **Tap the Available icon, if it's present.**

   The Settings pane turns into the Network pane, shown in Figure 6-3, listing the names of all the wireless networks around you. Depending on your location, you may see several listed. Windows ranks the wireless networks by signal strength, placing the strongest (and usually closest) network atop the list.

Figure 6-3: Your tablet lists all the Wi-Fi networks within range. To connect to a network, tap its name.

A wireless network's name is known as its *SSID* (Service Set *ID*entification). The SSID represents the name that you (or the network's owner) chose when originally setting up the wireless network.

4. **Tap the name of the network you want to connect to, and tap the Connect button that appears.**

If you'll be connecting to this network frequently, tap the Connect Automatically check box before tapping the Connect button (both shown in Figure 6-4), which tells your tablet to connect automatically whenever you're within range — a convenience you'll enjoy in your home, office, or favorite coffee shops.

Figure 6-4:
When your tablet lists names of all the Wi-Fi networks within range, connect to one by tapping its name and tapping the Connect button.

If Windows connects to the network, you're finished: You've connected to an *Open network*, meaning it's unsecured and requires no password. (Don't do any shopping or banking on an unsecured network.)

If Windows asks you to enter a password, though, move to Step 5.

5. **Enter the password for the wireless network and tap the Next button.**

If Windows asks you to Enter the Network Security Key when you tap the Connect button, you're trying to connect with a *secured*, or password-protected, network. So, you must type the network's password, as shown in Figure 6-5.

If you're in your own home, here's where you type the password you created when setting up your wireless network. (On some wireless routers, you can simply press a button on the router at this point, which proves you're in the same room.)

If you're connecting to somebody *else's* wireless network, by contrast, you need to ask the network's owner for the password. (Or whisper "What's the Wi-Fi password?" to the person next to you at the coffee shop.)

Windows hides the password as you type it, keeping it secure from nearby eyes. Think you've made a typo? Then tap and hold the eyeball icon, shown earlier in Figure 6-5, and Windows displays your password. (That handy eyeball icon appears whenever you type hidden passwords into a Start screen app.)

Tap and hold the "eyeball" icon to reveal your password.

Figure 6-5:
Type the
network's
password,
and tap
Next.

6. **Choose whether you want to share your tablet's files on the network.**

This important choice, shown in Figure 6-6, depends on whether you're connecting in a public location like a hotel or coffee shop, or in a private setting like your home or office.

Figure 6-6:
Turn on
sharing only
if you're
connecting
to your own
network.

- **Private:** If you're at your home or office, tap Yes, Turn on Sharing and Connect to Devices. That lets you connect with networked printers and swap files with other people on the network.

- **Public:** Because you don't want strangers to access your files, tap No, Don't Turn on Sharing or Connect to Devices. That lets you access the Internet, but keeps other people on the network away from your files.

When you finish the steps, Windows connects to the network, and your Internet connection begins flowing. If the Internet remains dry, however, try these things:

✔ Move closer to the transmitter. This often difficult maneuver cures 90 percent of Wi-Fi connection problems. Ask somebody where the Wi-Fi transmitter is located, or look for the small plastic box with two pencil-sized antennas sticking up from it. (They're often mounted on walls, or atop cabinets.)

✔ Try connecting to an unsecured network. They work fine for casual browsing.

 ✔ You can also connect to a wireless network from the Windows desktop. When the taskbar's right corner shows a wireless network available icon (shown in the margin), tap it. That takes you to the preceding Step 4 to choose a network and tap the Connect button.

✔ To disconnect from a wireless network, simply walk out of range; Windows disconnects automatically. Or if you want to disconnect while still in range, summon the Charms bar, tap the Settings icon, tap the Network icon, tap the network's name, and tap the Disconnect button.

Connecting to a wired or dial-up connection

You may find a hotel that offers only *wired* Internet access. This worked fine a few years ago because all laptops had network jacks. To connect with the Internet, you connected a network cable between the hotel room's network jack and the jack in your laptop. A few seconds after plugging in the cable, your computer sniffed out the Internet connection and connected automatically.

Although few people still use those network jacks, they still work. And they're often faster than the hotel's overcrowded Wi-Fi connection.

To connect to a wired network on your tablet you need an accessory shown in Figure 6-7: a USB cable with a traditional network jack on the end. You probably won't need it often, but if you're trapped in an old-school hotel that offers only wired access, it's a lifesaver.

TIP

✔ Look for the network jack near the desk in your hotel room. Sometimes it's built into the phone.

✔ A different but similarly shaped adapter lets your tablet connect to the Internet through phone lines, as well. You can still buy dial-up network access through NetZero (`www.netzero.net`) and Juno (`www.juno.com`). (Both companies offer ten hours of free dial-up access each month.)

Figure 6-7:
A USB
adapter
with a wired
network
jack lets
your tablet
connect
to network
jacks found
in some
hotel rooms
and offices.

✔ During power outages, phone lines often provide the only Internet source. You can not only stay up to date on the emergency, but you can also tweet about your slow dial-up connection.

✔ Another solution for dealing with wired networks is to carry a portable router often called a *pocket router*. Plug the pocket router into the hotel room's network jack, and set it to Bridge mode. The router then creates a Wi-Fi network that fills your hotel room. It's quite a wallet saver in hotels that charge per device for Wi-Fi access.

Buying a data plan for your tablet

Some tablets include a built-in cellular radio and a data plan from a wireless carrier like Verizon, Sprint, or AT&T. The tablets access the Internet much like a cellphone does — through neighboring cellphone towers.

You'll know if your tablet includes a data plan, because the carrier will ask you to sign up for it when you buy the tablet. (In most cases, the carrier won't let you cancel the data plan for two years without having to pay a steep penalty.)

Connecting to a dial-up network

Very few people still connect to the Internet through dial-up networks. Accordingly, Microsoft buried Windows 8's dial-up networking options in a very dark corner of Windows 8. To connect to a dial-up network with your tablet, fetch a flashlight, and walk slowly down these steps:

1. **Plug a dial-up adapter into your tablet's USB port; then connect a phone cable between the adapter's phone jack and the phone jack in the wall.**

2. **From the Start menu, tap the Desktop app and load Internet Explorer.**

3. **When Internet Explorer appears, tap the Settings icon near the program's upper-right corner. (The icon looks like a gear.)**

4. **When Internet Explorer's Settings menu appears, tap Internet Options from the list.**

5. **When the Internet Options window appears, tap the window's Connection's tab.**

6. **Tap the Setup button to begin entering the dial-up number, name, and password given to you by your dial-up Internet service provider.**

When you tap the Connect button, Internet Explorer dials the number, enters your name and password, and leaves you with a working Internet connection. Just like any connection, the dial-up connection lets you work with both desktop and Start screen apps. Be prepared for long waits, though, as dial-up Internet connections are v-e-r-y slow. But it's better than nothing.

Most carriers track the information you upload and download, limiting you to a certain amount per month. If you go over, you pay more. (If you don't use all of your allotted monthly amount, you don't get a discount, though. Funny how that works.)

✔ Even if your tablet has a data plan, you can still connect to the Internet using Wi-Fi. In fact, Windows 8 automatically connects to Wi-Fi networks whenever possible, helping you to avoid extra charges.

✔ If you decide to cancel your data plan, you can still connect to the Internet using Wi-Fi. You're not stuck with a useless tablet.

✔ If your tablet doesn't include a built-in cellular chip, then you can't buy a data plan for it. However, you can rent a portable hotspot from a cellular carrier, described in the next section.

✔ Tablets that include built-in cellular radios usually include a *GPS* (Global Positioning System) chip, as well. GPS lets you track your current position on a map, which is handy for driving from Point A to Point B, while stopping at Point C for sandwiches along the way.

Connecting to a smartphone or portable hotspot

Today, many people buy *smartphones:* cellphones that serve as mini-computers, complete with web browsers and Internet access. Most cellular carriers also offer *tethering plans:* a way to turn your phone into a portable Wi-Fi network — for an extra monthly fee, of course.

When your smartphone begins broadcasting its Wi-Fi signal, you can connect your tablet to your phone's Wi-Fi network, just as you'd connect with any other Wi-Fi network.

You may be able to download an app for your phone to turn it into a Wi-Fi hotspot *without* paying your carrier an extra monthly fee. And some apps let you share your phone's Internet connection through a USB cable or *Bluetooth,* another type of wireless connection I cover later in this chapter.

If you don't have a smartphone, or don't want to overload your phone's data plan with your tablet's web browsing, some cellular carriers sell portable *hotspots.* These battery-powered boxes work like a Wi-Fi network you can carry with you. Whenever you're within range of a cellphone tower, the hotspot begins broadcasting a Wi-Fi signal, and your tablet automatically connects to the Internet.

Disconnecting for airplane mode

Airplane mode is shorthand for disconnecting completely from the Internet. You'll want to turn on Airplane mode under any of three conditions:

- You're on an airplane. Most flights prohibit Internet access while you're flying.

- You're on a data plan with cellular access, and you're afraid of going over your monthly allotment of Internet access.

- You want to prolong your battery life. Putting your tablet in Airplane mode tells the tablet to stop searching for available Wi-Fi connections. That lets you save battery life while you're doing something that doesn't require Internet access.

To put your tablet in Airplane mode, follow these steps:

1. **Summon the Charms bar by swiping your finger in from the screen's right edge; then tap the Settings icon.**

2. **When the Settings pane appears, tap the Network icon.**

3. **When the Network pane appears, tap the Airplane Mode toggle switch along the pane's top edge. (A tap will toggle any tablet's toggle switch. You don't need to slide your finger.)**

The Settings pane's Network icon shows that you're in Airplane Mode. To turn off Airplane mode and return to a lifestyle of searching for Internet connections, repeat the three steps.

Connecting to Networked PCs

Tablets come with tiny hard drives, at least by desktop PC standards. Since you probably can't fit all of your information onto your tablet, keep an eye out for other places to stash files, perhaps storing a few videos here, and a few CDs there.

One of the easiest places to stash your files may be on your home or office network. To browse the files on those huge hard-drive-stuffed PCs, you need to connect to the same wireless network that connects them.

To connect to PCs on a home or office network, follow the steps in the previous section to connect to their wireless network. In the last step, though, be sure to tap the button Yes, Turn on Sharing and Connect to Devices.

But what if you forgot to tap that Sharing and Connect button?

You can turn it on by following these steps. These steps also let you connect to a *homegroup* — a simple way for Windows 7 and Windows 8 computers to share files.

1. **Summon the Charms bar by sliding your finger in from your tablet's right edge; then tap the Settings icon.**

2. **Tap your wireless network icon.**

3. **When the Network pane appears, listing your connected wireless network, hold your finger on the network's name until a circle appears; then lift your finger.**

   Holding your finger on an item until a menu appears is the equivalent of right-clicking with a mouse. In this case, the right-click menu appears, shown in Figure 6-8.

4. **Tap Turn Sharing On or Off (see Figure 6-8).**

   The permission screen you saw earlier in Figure 6-6 presents itself again.

   That right-click menu offers other handy options, which I describe in the "Changing a Wi-Fi network's settings" sidebar later in this chapter.

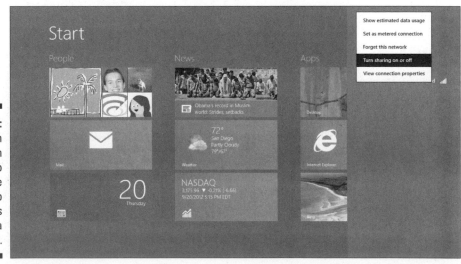

Figure 6-8:
Tap Turn Sharing On or Off to either share files or stop sharing files on a network.

5. **Tap the button, Yes, Turn on Sharing and Connect to Devices button.**

   Now that you've turned on sharing, join your network's homegroup, if you have one.

6. **Tap the Start screen's Desktop app; then tap the File Explorer icon.**

   You'll find the icon for File Explorer (shown in the margin) near the left end of the *taskbar* — the strip along the bottom of the desktop. (I cover File Explorer in Chapter 5.)

7. **When File Explorer appears, tap the word *Homegroup* from the Navigation pane that clings to every folder's left edge.**

   The Homegroup window appears.

8. **Tap the Join Now button, shown in Figure 6-9, and follow the steps to enter the homegroup's password.**

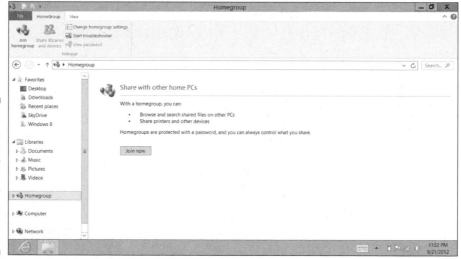

Figure 6-9: Tap the Join Now button and follow the steps to enter the home-group's password.

Don't know the homegroup's password? To find it, visit any computer on the homegroup, open any folder, and right-click the word *Homegroup* from the Navigation pane. When the pop-up menu appears, choose View the Homegroup Password, which is the password you need to enter into your tablet.

✔ In the preceding Step 8, tapping the Next button at each window lets you conncct to the homegroup and begin sharing the contents of your Pictures, Videos, and Music libraries. It also lets you connect any networked devices (usually, printers). Your Documents folder remains private and not shared.

✔ Store things you want to share in your tablet's libraries: Music, Pictures, and Videos. They'll be available to all the other Windows 7 and Windows 8 PCs on the network's homegroup.

✔ To share any other items, either on your tablet or from the other networked PCs, place them in your *Public* folders. For example, double-tap the Documents library on your tablet, and you'll see two folders: My Documents and Public Documents. To share items with other people on the homegroup, place them in the Public Documents folder. (You'll find similar Public folders inside your other libraries, as well.)

✔ Although Windows Vista and Windows XP PCs can't join homegroups, you can access their files from your tablet in another way. Tap the word *Network*, at the bottom of any folder's Navigation pane. The Network window appears, listing every networked PC. Tap any PC's name to open it, and browse its shared files.

Changing a Wi-Fi network's settings

Windows 8 offers many handy ways to change or keep track of your Wi-Fi network's settings. However, it's difficult to find the right switches until you follow these steps:

1. **Summon the Charms bar by sliding your finger in from your tablet's right edge; then tap the Settings icon.**

2. **Tap your wireless network icon.**

3. **When the Network pane appears, listing your currently connected wireless network, hold your finger on the network's name until a square appears; then lift your finger.**

The equivalent of right-clicking with a mouse, that action accesses a pop-up box with these options:

✔ **Show Estimated Data Usage:** Designed for people with metered cellular data plans, this toggle switch displays how many megabytes of data have flowed through your connection. To return your counter to zero, tap the Reset button.

✔ **Set as Metered Connection:** Choose this if you're on a *tiered* data plan, which limits the amount of data you can upload or download. Enter your limit in this area, and Windows will warn you when you're about to surpass your limit. Plus, Windows automatically switches to Wi-Fi when possible, saving you money.

✔ **Forget this Network:** If you accidentally log on to an unwanted network, choose this option to forget the network. Doing so stops Windows from logging on again automatically when you're within range. (It also lets you start over if you think you've somehow botched the settings.)

✔ **Turn Sharing On or Off:** Described elsewhere in this chapter, this option lets you toggle sharing, a handy way to either stop or start sharing your files and devices with other people on the network.

✔ **View Connection Properties:** This switches to the Desktop app's Wireless Network Properties window to change advanced settings.

Connecting to a Printer

Windows 8 tablets can connect with just about any printer that works with your desktop PC.

Most printers connect either through a USB port or through a wired-or-wireless network.

- ✔ **USB:** The simplest way to connect with a USB printer is to plug the printer's USB cable directly into your tablet's USB port. Your tablet will connect with Windows Update, download any drivers, if needed, and automatically set up the printer to work with your programs.

- ✔ **Network and wireless:** Once you create a network, as I describe in the previous section, your tablet will have access to all the printers shared on that network.

To see if your tablet recognizes a networked printer, follow these steps:

1. **Open the Charms bar by sliding your finger inward from the screen's right edge.**

2. **Tap the Settings icon; when the Settings pane appears, tap the words Change PC Settings.**

   The PC Settings screen appears.

3. **Tap Devices from the PC Settings screen.**

   The PC Settings screen shows every device attached to your printer. They're listed alphabetically, and attached printers have the icon seen in the margin.

If you don't see a networked printer, add it by following the steps in the sidebar, "Finding missing printers."

Not every Start screen app can print, and there's no way to know if your app is print-worthy until you try. So, open any Start screen app and try to print by following these steps:

1. **From within any app, open the Charms bar by sliding your finger inward from the screen's right edge; then tap the Devices icon.**

   The Devices pane appears, listing all the devices capable of working with your app. (Their icons look like the one in the margin.) If you see a printer listed, move to Step 2. No printer listed? Your app isn't able to print, unfortunately.

2. **Tap the desired printer's name and make any final adjustments.**

The Start screen's Printer window, shown in Figure 6-10, sums up exactly what's going to the printer. It shows a preview and the number of pages required. To see all of the pages you're printing, slide your finger across the preview image from right to left.

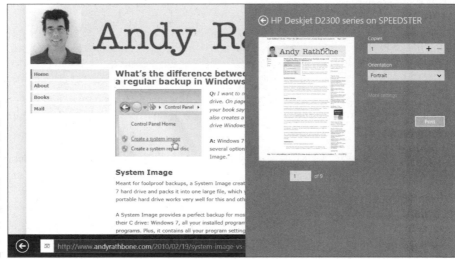

Figure 6-10: The Start screen's Printer window offers minimal adjustments to your print job.

To see even more options, tap the More Settings link. There, you can choose the type of printer paper you want to use, an essential step when using photo paper on a color printer.

3. **Tap the Print button.**

Your tablet sends your information to the printer. But the Start screen's emphasis on speed rather than details leaves out some details:

- Many apps can't print. You can't print a day's itinerary from your Calendar app, for example, or even a monthly calendar.

- When printing from the Start screen's Internet Explorer app, you're stuck printing the entire web page — advertisements, comments, and everything in between. There's no way to print selective portions.

- If you need more control over your print jobs, it's time to head for the desktop and its cadre of more full-featured programs.

Finding missing printers

Sometimes the Start screen's Devices pane takes too long to locate all your available printers, especially after you're connected to a network. When you tire of waiting, hand the flashlight to the Desktop app, and let it search for the printers. To locate printers, open the Desktop app and follow these steps:

1. **Summon the Charms bar by sliding your finger in from the screen's right edge; then tap the Settings icon.**

2. **At the top of the Settings pane, tap the words *Control Panel*.**

3. **From the Control Panel's Hardware and Sound category, tap View Devices and Printers.**

4. **Near the top of the Devices and Printers window, tap Add a Printer.**

   When the Add a Printer window appears, Windows searches for all the printers available to your tablet, including wireless printers, and printers attached to other PCs on your network.

5. **When the list of printers appears, tap the printer you want to add, click Next, and follow the steps.**

The steps walk you through adding the printer and printing a test page, if you want. After you add the printer, it appears in the Charms bar's Devices area, where you can select it with a tap when you want to send a print job its way.

Connecting to Portable Accessories

Once you finally sit down at a desk with your tablet, you can plug in a few strategic accessories to give your tablet extra powers. This section describes some gadgets you may want to stuff into your gadget bag; a few well-packed accessories let you transform your tablet into whatever you need, whenever you need it.

If your tablet came with a stylus, *always* carry it with your tablet. The size of a pen, the stylus comes in really handy for tapping the desktop's buttons, as well as editing text, as I describe in Chapter 3.

Connecting to a USB hub

Most accessories plug into your tablet's USB port. Windows 8 usually recognizes them on the spot and downloads any necessary drivers through the nearest Wi-Fi connection.

Unfortunately, most tablets include a *single* USB port. That limitation brings us to the first accessory on the list: *a portable USB hub*, like the one shown in Figure 6-11. Small, flat, and easily packable, a portable hub plugs into your tablet's lone USB port and offers two or more USB ports in return.

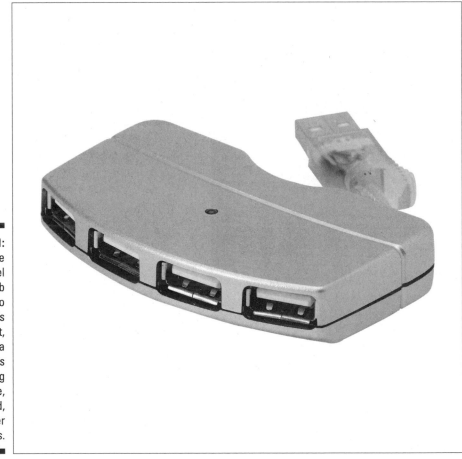

Figure 6-11: A portable or travel USB hub plugs into your tablet's USB port, adding extra USB ports for plugging in a mouse, keyboard, and other accessories.

When choosing a USB hub, stick with these tips:

- ✔ Portable hubs are inexpensive. If you're paying more than $15, look around for something cheaper. They often sell for under ten dollars.

- ✔ Choose the smallest, flattest hub you can find, so it will lie as flat as possible in your tablet's case.

- ✔ Buy a hub with an attached cable. Hubs without cables will protrude awkwardly from your tablet's side. If inadvertently knocked, the force can damage your tablet's lone USB port.

- ✔ You don't need a *powered* USB hub — one that plugs into a wall outlet — unless you'll be plugging in heavy- duty accessories, like a portable DVD drive. Most USB accessories, including many portable hard drives, work fine on a regular, unpowered USB hub.

- ✔ Some tablets include the newer and faster USB 3.0 ports rather than the standard USB 2.0 ports. If your tablet includes USB 3.0, spend a little extra money for a USB hub that supports the faster USB 3.0 speeds.

- ✔ When you're not using USB accessories, unplug them from your tablet to preserve battery life. (If your tablet's plugged into a wall outlet, feel free to leave all your USB accessories attached.)

Is my tablet's USB port 2.0 or 3.0?

Although all Windows 8 tablets include a USB port, the ports come in two main types: the traditional USB 2.0 found on desktop PCs for years and the newer, faster USB 3.0 ports. (USB 3.0 ports are ten times as fast as their predecessors.)

The USB 3.0 ports fall back to slower speeds when working with your older USB gadgetry. But if you plug in a newer, USB 3.0 accessory, you can take full advantage of the faster speeds.

How do you tell which type of USB port is in your tablet? If you're shopping, look at the tablet's list of specifications. For example, the Microsoft Surface RT tablet includes a USB 2.0 port, but the more expensive Microsoft Surface Pro tablet includes a USB 3.0 port.

Or if you have the tablet in your hands, look at the USB port on the tablet's side: The USB 2.0 ports are usually black; the newer USB 3.0 ports are almost always blue.

Connecting a mouse or keyboard

When you open your tablet's Desktop app, you'll probably want to grab a mouse and keyboard, as well. Your fingers can still control the desktop, as I describe in Chapter 5. But a mouse and keyboard let you work about ten times as fast. Plus, plugging in a keyboard lets you see your entire tablet screen — the virtual keyboard won't be hogging half of it.

Mice and keyboards come in two types:

✔ **Wired:** These plug straight into your USB port. Any mouse or keyboard that works with a desktop PC will also work with your tablet. To plug in both a mouse and keyboard, though, you'll need to buy an inexpensive USB hub, described in the previous section. Or you can plug in one mouse or keyboard and use a *wireless* model for the other, described next.

✔ **Wireless:** All Windows 8 tablets include *Bluetooth* — a way of connecting to nearby gadgets without wires. You'll find plenty of Bluetooth mice and keyboards on the market.

When shopping for a mouse and keyboard for your tablet, keep these tips on your checklist:

✔ Since you may pack your mouse and keyboard when traveling, look for flat, lightweight models. For example, Microsoft's Arc mouse flattens completely for storage and then curls up into a mouse shape when needed.

✔ Before buying a mouse or keyboard, try one out in your own hands. They're highly personal items, and only you can tell if it feels right for you.

✔ Almost all mice and keyboards created for iPads will also work with a Windows 8 tablet. The biggest exceptions are keyboards with built-in stands to prop up the tablet. Many are designed to fit only an iPad.

Connecting Bluetooth accessories

When you're running out of room to plug in USB accessories, Bluetooth is your friend. Bluetooth works much like Wi-Fi, but it specializes in connecting gadgets that live less than ten feet apart. If you add a Bluetooth mouse and Bluetooth keyboard to your tablet, it's USB port remains free for other items.

Bluetooth can also link your tablet with some cellphones to provide Internet access, described earlier in this chapter.

To add a Bluetooth item to your tablet, follow these steps:

1. **Turn on your Bluetooth device and, if necessary, make it *discoverable*.**

   Most Bluetooth devices include an Off switch to save power. Sometimes turning it on is as simple as flipping an On/Off switch; others sense movement, automatically turning on and off when needed.

   Making a device *discoverable* makes it available to be detected by a computer, usually for a period of 30 seconds. Some devices automatically become discoverable when turned on. Others make you press a button until their light begins blinking.

2. **Fetch the Charms bar by sliding your finger inward from the screen's right edge. Tap the Settings icon to fetch the Settings pane; then tap the words *Change PC Settings*.**

   The Start screen's PC Settings screen appears.

3. **From the Devices category, tap the Add a Device icon.**

   The PC Settings' Devices screen appears (shown in Figure 6-12) listing all of your tablet's recognized devices, whether they're currently plugged in or not. When you tap the Add a Device icon, your computer begins searching for adjacent Bluetooth devices that are in "discoverable" mode.

   If Windows doesn't find and list your device by name, head back to Step 1 and make sure your Bluetooth gadget is still turned on and discoverable. (If it's been longer than 30 seconds, your device may have given up.)

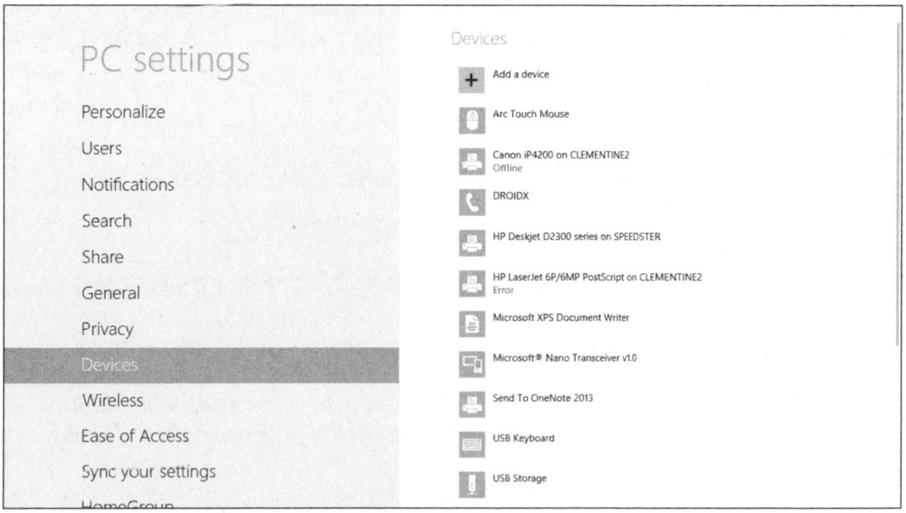

Figure 6-12: The Devices screen lists all of the devices your tablet recognizes. Tap the Add a Device button to add a new device.

4. **When your Bluetooth device's name appears in the Devices list, tap the device's name so Windows knows to connect to it.**

5. **Type your device's code if necessary and, if asked, click the Pair button.**

Everything usually works pretty smoothly until Step 5, where Bluetooth's security measures kick in. Windows needs you to prove that you're controlling both your computer *and* your Bluetooth device, and that you're not somebody sitting three rows back on the bus trying to break in.

To clear that security hurdle, different Bluetooth devices offer slightly different tactics. Sometimes you need to type a *passcode* — a secret string of numbers — into both your device and your computer. (Pull out the device's manual to find the passcode.) Adding to the tension, if you don't type in the passcode quickly enough, both gadgets stop waiting, forcing you to start over.

Some Bluetooth gadgets let you press and hold a little push button at this step, proving you're holding it in your hand.

When in doubt, type **0000** on your tablet's keyboard. That's often recognized as a universal passcode for frustrated owners of Bluetooth devices who are trying to connect their gadgets.

Once your new gadget successfully pairs with your tablet, its name and icon appear in the Devices category of the PC Settings screen, shown earlier in Figure 6-12.

To remove a device shown in the Devices list in Figure 6-12, tap its name; then tap the minus sign that appears to the right of its name. Finally, tap the Remove button that appears.

Connecting a digital camera and importing your photos

Nobody likes viewing photos on a camera's tiny screen. Thankfully, Windows makes it easy to import your camera's photos onto your tablet, where they shine on the big screen. And you can do it all from the Start screen, making it an easy task to perform while in the field.

Best of all, you needn't install any of the software that came with the camera; Windows handles it all.

To import your camera's photos into your tablet, follow these steps:

1. **Plug the camera's cable into your computer.**

   Plug the small end of your camera's cable into your camera. The cable's larger end plugs into your tablet's USB port, usually found on the tablet's side.

2. **Turn on your camera and wait for Windows 8 to recognize it.**

   Wait for a little announcement in your computer screen's top-right corner. The announcement, called a *toast* in some manuals, lists your camera's name and asks you to Tap to Choose What Happens with This Device.

   Tap the announcement; then move to the next step. (If the announcement disappears before you can tap it, turn off your camera, wait a second and then turn it on again; the announcement reappears.

3. **Choose how to import your photos.**

   The next announcement, shown in Figure 6-13, offers three options on how to handle your newly recognized digital camera:

Figure 6-13: Choose Import Photos and Videos to import your photos with the Start screen's Photos app.

- **Import Photos and Videos:** This is the easiest method. Choose it to import your photos with the Start screen's Photos app; then move to Step 4.

- **Open Device to View Files:** If you prefer to import your files from the desktop, choose this option. The desktop offers more control, but works better with a mouse and keyboard than your fingers. This option fetches File Explorer (refer to Chapter 5 for more on File Explorer), where you can manually copy the photos from the camera to a folder of your choosing.

- **Take No Action:** This option simply cancels the importing process, which is handy if you decide to postpone importing your photos.

After you chose an option, Windows remembers it, automatically taking the same route the next time you plug in your camera.

4. **When the Photos app appears, choose your options; then click or tap the Import button to import your camera's photos and videos.**

The Start screen's Photos app, shown in Figure 6-14, tries to keep things simple. It offers to import all your camera's photos and videos into a folder named after the current date. To make a quick-and-easy transfer, tap the Import button to copy the photos onto your tablet.

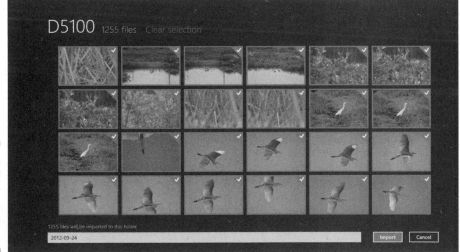

Figure 6-14:
Copy all of your camera's photos into your tablet.

But if you don't want to import every photo, or you want to change the name of the folder, you can change those options:

- **Pictures:** The Photos app selects *all* of your camera's photos and videos for importing. To leave behind any blurry ones, tap the ones you don't want. Want just a few photos? Tap the words Clear Selection from the screen's top-right corner to deselect all of them. Then tap the photos you want to import.

- **Folder name:** To change the incoming folder's name, tap the folder's current name in the white strip along the screen's bottom, shown in Figure 6-14. Then type a different name for the incoming folder.

When you tap the Import button, the Photos app imports your camera's photos and videos. When the Photos app announces that it's finished importing the photos, click the announcement box's Open Album button to see your photos.

The Photos app only imports your camera's photos; it doesn't delete them from the camera. You can manually delete them from the camera by telling the camera to format its memory card.

Connecting a TV tuner

The Internet provides plenty of distractions, but many people still turn to television for entertainment. By adding a TV tuner to your tablet, you can not only watch live TV but also schedule automatic recordings of upcoming shows to watch later.

To connect a TV tuner to your tablet and begin watching or recording TV, follow these steps:

1. **If necessary, upgrade your tablet's version of Windows 8 to include Windows Media Center.**

   Few tablets include Windows Media Center, Microsoft's optional TV recording package. (Windows Media Center also lets you watch DVDs if you connect a portable DVD drive to your tablet's USB port.)

   To add Windows Media Center to Windows 8, open any folder on the Windows desktop, tap and hold the word *Computer* in the folder's Navigation pane, and choose System from the pop-up menu.

   When the System window appears, tap the link Get More Features with a New Edition of Windows. The window Add Features to Windows 8 appears, which walks you through buying or entering a product key for Windows Media Center.

2. **Buy a USB TV tuner and plug its USB port into your tablet's USB port.**

   USB TV tuners, like the one shown in Figure 6-15, look much like thick flash drives, and they plug into your tablet the same way: Push the connector into your tablet's USB port. Most USB TV tuners cost less than $100.

Importing photos from the desktop

Taken a lot of photos on a multiday trip?: Then importing them all might warrant a trip to your tablet's Desktop app. Whereas the Start screen drops all your photos into one folder, the desktop can automatically separate your photos by shooting session, placing each session of photos into a differently named folder.

To import your photos from the desktop, follow these steps:

1. **Open the Desktop app from the Start screen. Then connect your camera through your tablet's USB port and turn on your camera. Then tap the File Explorer icon on the taskbar.**

2. **When File Explorer appears, tap Computer in the Navigation pane along File Explorer's right edge.**

3. **When File Explorer lists all of your tablet's storage areas, find your camera listed in the Portable Devices section. Right-click your camera's icon and choose Import Photos and Videos.**

Windows then offers you an advanced option called Review, Organize, and Group Items to Import. As you click the Next button within each window, the option walks you through sorting your photos into different groups, sorted by the time or date you shot them.

When you're done, you've separated photos from different sessions into differently named folders, making them much easier to locate later. It's time-consuming and difficult to do with fingers, but it keeps your photo shoots much more organized — and easier to locate down the road.

---

3. **Connect an antenna or your TV cable to the TV tuner.**

   Your TV cable or HDTV antenna — sometimes bundled with the tuner — feeds a source of TV signals to your tuner, so you can view or record the channels available in your area.

4. **Run Windows Media Center.**

   Windows Media Center walks you through setting up the program, your incoming TV signal, and the TV tuner. Then it begins downloading TV listings for the channels in your area.

After it's installed, Windows Media Center automatically keeps its program schedule up-to-date.

What Windows Media Center can't do, though, is record *scrambled* TV signals. These typically include channel 100 and higher, including high-definition content and pay channels offered by your cable or satellite TV company.

The tuner can, however, record high-definition TV signals using an antenna. Some tuners even include a portable antenna for you to record high-definition content available in your area.

Figure 6-15:
Insert the
TV tuner's
USB port
(top) into
your tablet's
USB port;
on the other
end (bot-
tom), screw
on the cable
from your
TV signal.

Connecting to a Monitor, HDTV, or Digital Projector

Your tablet's screen rarely matches the size of your desktop PC's monitor. That doesn't mean you're stuck with your tablet's small screen, though. Your tablet includes a video port that lets you plug in desktop monitors, HDTV sets, and many digital projectors used for PowerPoint presentations.

Since all three of those potential monitors plug in the same way, this section refers to them all as *monitors*.

Plugging in a monitor not only gives you a larger screen, it also gives you *two* screens: Your tablet's screen stays active, as well.

This section explains how to connect a monitor to your tablet, as well as how to tell the monitor to begin displaying your tablet's input. Finally, it tells you exactly how the monitor should display your tablet's screen: Windows 8 can send its signal four different ways.

Connecting your tablet to a monitor

In theory, connecting your tablet to a monitor is quite simple: Connect a cable between your tablet's video port and your monitor's input port.

The challenge is finding the *right* cable. No single cable works in every situation. That's because tablets and monitors contain different types of video ports, and your cable needs the correct jack on each end, or it won't work.

Most tablets come with a Micro HDMI port, and most PC monitors and HDTVs include a full-size HDMI port. So, you connect a cable as shown in Figure 16-16.

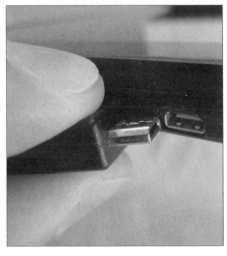

Figure 6-16: The cable's small Micro HDMI plug pushes into your tablet's port (left); the cable's larger HDMI plug pushes into your monitor or TV's HDMI port (right).

But if those ports don't resemble the ones on your tablet or external monitor, read on.

Most tablets come with one of two types of video connectors: HDMI or miniDisplayPort.

 ✔ **HDMI:** By far the most popular, HDMI ports appear on most high definition TV sets (HDTVs), computer monitors, and even cellphones. Most tablets include a *Micro HDMI* port, shown in the preceding Figure 6-16 (left). It's the same type of video port found on many cellphones today.

✔ **miniDisplayPort:** Launched on Apple computers and slowly moving to some PCs, the miniDisplayPort now appears on some tablets.

TVs and monitors also include one or more different types of video adapters.

✔ **HDMI:** Shown in Figure 6-16 (right), this port is the same as the ones found on many tablets, but it's full-size — more than twice as large.

✔ **DVI:** The next most popular, this port appears mostly on PC monitors rather than on TVs.

✔ **VGA:** This old chestnut appeared on monitors for more than a decade, so it's still around on a lot of equipment as a last resort connector. Cables and adapters with VGA connectors cost more, because they need more circuitry to translate between the types of signals flowing through the cable.

After you identify the video ports on your tablet and your monitor, buy a cable with a plug for your tablet on one end and the plug for your monitor on the other.

There's another method, as well: If you already have a cable that fits into the video port on either your tablet or your monitor, head to Amazon (www. amazon.com), Newegg (www.newegg.com), or your local electronics store to buy an *adapter* for the cable's other end. An adapter can turn a cable's HDMI plug into a miniDisplayPort plug, for example, letting it plug into a tablet's miniDisplayPort.

✔ Depending on the variety of external monitors you plan to connect to your tablet, you may need to collect several types of cables or adapters.

✔ Don't pay more than ten or fifteen dollars for a cable. The higher-priced ones don't make the video signal any better.

Windows 8's four different ways of using an attached monitor

After you connect your tablet to your external monitor, you need to tell the tablet how to send its image. Windows 8 offers you four options, and you can see them by following these steps:

1. **Swipe your finger inward from any screen's right edge to fetch the Charms bar; then tap the Devices icon.**

2. **Tap the Second Screen icon and choose how your tablet should send its signal.**

   It offers the following four choices (also shown in Figure 6-17).

Figure 6-17:
Choose how
Windows 8
should
handle
your newly
connected
monitor.

- **PC Screen Only:** This option recognizes the second monitor, but keeps it blank, displaying only your tablet's screen. It's an asset mostly when connecting to a projector at a meeting or conference. You can get everything set up on your tablet without everybody having to watch on the projector. Then, when you're ready to wow the crowd, switch to one of the other modes, described next.

- **Duplicate:** This is perhaps the easiest way to use two monitors. It simply duplicates your tablet's screen onto the second monitor or projector. It's great for presentations, and it lets you control what you see on either screen with whatever seems natural at the time. When your fingers touch the tablet, you'll see the effect on both screens.

- **Extend:** This extends your tablet's screen across your second monitor, giving you an extra- wide desktop. Or you can keep the Start screen on your tablet and run the desktop on the second screen, which is probably larger. (The Extend mode adds several complications, which I cover in the "Fine-tuning an extended desktop," sidebar elsewhere in this chapter.)

- **Second Screen Only:** This blanks the tablet and displays its screen only on your second monitor. It's a simple way to connect a larger monitor, but you lose the benefits of your touchscreen tablet. Unless you're trying to mimic a desktop computer, use the Duplicate feature, instead.

After you tap your choice, your tablet usually makes the screen blank as it looks for and connects to the second screen. A second or two later, your tablet's screen appears on the second screen.

Working on two different monitors simultaneously can be confusing at first. The following tips will help you adjust to this strange new configuration:

- ✔ Your tablet's sound piggybacks along with its video through both an HDMI and a miniDisplayPort cable. However, the sound will play through the speakers built into your monitor or TV set. If you want better sound, route your tablet's sound separately through a stereo or external speakers, described in the next section.

- ✔ When setting up the second monitor for the first time, choose Duplicate. Doing so makes it a lot easier to see if your monitor is recognizing your tablet.

- ✔ When you choose Extend, Windows makes the screen extend off your tablet's right edge and onto the second monitor. To change that, visit the Desktop app's Control Panel. In the Appearance and Personalization category's Adjust Screen Resolution section, you can tell Windows which way to extend the desktop: left, right, up, or down.

- ✔ The Adjust Screen Resolution section's Detect and Identify buttons help you figure out which monitor is which, and then position the two screens to meet your needs.

- ✔ Head for the Desktop Control Panel's Mouse settings, and toggle on Display Pointer Trails. The mouse pointer displays long trails as it moves, allowing you to spot it more easily as it moves from one screen to another.

- ✔ The hot corners on Windows 8's desktop, described in Chapter 4, work on both monitors. Point and click in either monitor's lower-left corner to fetch the Start menu, for example.

Making your monitor recognize your tablet

After you connect the correct cable between your tablet and the monitor and tell the tablet to send its signal to the monitor, you face one last challenge. You must convince the monitor to *recognize* your newly plugged-in tablet.

Doing so isn't as easy as it sounds. Most monitors let you keep several things plugged into them: DVD players, game consoles, cable boxes, home stereos, or other PCs.

Your job is to make your monitor display your *tablet's* video signal rather than the signals from the other items. The solution here works a little differently, depending on whether you're connecting your tablet to a HDTV or a PC monitor.

Make sure your tablet's turned on and set to Duplicate mode, described in the previous section, so your tablet sends a constant video signal to your monitor. When you see the tablet's screen on the monitor, you'll know you've found the right combination.

✔ **HDTV:** On your TV's front panel or handheld remote control, look for a button for switching between Video Inputs. Keep pressing the remote's Video Input button, and your tablet's screen will eventually appear.

✔ **Monitor:** If your monitor is already connected to another PC, unplug the second PC. (You can plug the cable back in when you're through.) Your monitor should sense your tablet's signal and automatically begin displaying it. (Sometimes turning the monitor on and off again will help it switch to the right signal.)

It might take a little fiddling, but you'll eventually see your tablet appear on the big screen.

Connecting to external speakers or a home stereo

If you're watching your tablet's movies on an external monitor — perhaps even on a wide-screen TV — you'll want to route your sound to your home stereo rather than the tinny speakers built into most monitors and TVs.

You may have already followed these steps to connect a portable music player to your stereo. If you haven't or you want a refresher, follow these steps to route your tablet's sound to your home stereo:

1. **Buy a cable with a single ⅛-inch stereo jack on one end and two RCA jacks on the other end.**

   Shown in Figure 6-18, this same handy cable can be used to connect any portable music player like an iPad, iPod, or cellphone to a home stereo.

2. **Plug the cable's small end into your tablet's earphone jack.**

   Most tablets place tiny pictures of headphones and a microphone next to this jack.

3. **Plug the cable's two RCA jacks into your stereo's Audio Input or Line In jacks.**

   You can plug the cable into any unused Audio Input jack on your home stereo. The red jack plugs into the audio jack labeled Right. The other end plugs into the audio jack labeled Left.

Fine-tuning an extended desktop

Windows 8's Extend mode uses the second monitor to extend your desktop. Although a larger work area sounds wonderful, that extra room complicates many things you've taken for granted.

First, the Extend option initially places the second monitor to the *right* of your tablet, which means your mouse pointer will disappear off your tablet's right edge and reappear on your second monitor's left edge. Until you've done it a few times, you'll lose track of your mouse pointer as it disappears off your tablet's screen and reappears on the second screen.

Second, because the second monitor will probably be larger than your tablet's screen, your mouse pointer will move more quickly on the second monitor. There's no way to control

this, unfortunately, because Windows doesn't offer separate mouse speed controls for each monitor. Again, you'll eventually grow used to it.

Finally, when you start running a program on your tablet, the program appears on the *tablet's* desktop, not the larger, external monitor's desktop. You'll have to manually drag the windows over to the second screen using a mouse. (Once you open and close a program on the second screen, the program will reopen on that screen the next time you launch it.)

It's often easier to leave your tablet running the Start screen, while the desktop runs on your second monitor. That way you can watch your Start screen's tiles update with new e-mail while you work on your desktop.

Figure 6-18:
Push the cable's small end into your tablet's headphone jack (left); push the cable's other two ends into your stereo's Audio In or Line In jacks (right).

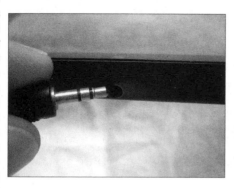 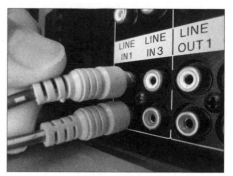

Now that you've connected your tablet's sound to your stereo, make sure it works. Play some music or a video on your tablet and turn its volume up about a third of the way.

Routing the sound to an external monitor

HDMI cables carry video *and* sound to your second monitor. If your monitor doesn't have speakers, you've effectively muted your tablet. To switch back to the tablet's speakers (or its headphone jack, which lets you plug in external speakers), head for the Desktop app.

Then tap the little speaker icon on the taskbar's right edge. When the sliding volume control appears, tap the word *Mixer.* The Volume Mixer window appears, showing every device able to play sounds. Tap the drop-down menu next to the word *Speakers* listed in the Device section, and choose Speakers rather than your model of monitor.

That routes the sound back to your tablet rather than to your mute monitor.

Then turn on your home stereo, turn down the volume, and switch your stereo to play music from the audio input jacks you used in Step 3. As you turn up the stereo's volume, you should hear your tablet playing through your home stereo speakers.

Adding Portable Storage

By nature, tablets include small hard drives. The drives are quite quick, letting your tablet come to life a few seconds after you press the On button. But the drives in most tablets hold only from 16GB to 128GB of storage. That's tiny compared to today's desktop PCs, which usually include more than 300GB of storage space.

If you need more storage, tablets offer you several options, each serving different needs:

- ✔ **Hard drive:** Your tablet's hard drive stores Windows 8, along with your desktop programs, your apps, and essential files. Just that information can consume your tablet's entire hard drive. That leaves you the next three options for storing more files.

- ✔ **Memory slot:** This slot in your tablet's side accepts a tiny memory card that holds between 32 and 64 GB, with higher capacity cards on their way. You can swap memory cards to access different batches of files, but memory cards can be expensive and cumbersome to move around.

- ✔ **Portable hard drive:** Essential for people who collect a lot of information in the field, portable hard drives let you tote a huge number of files. Today's portable hard drives can hold 3TB (terabytes) of information: That's about *3000GB*, which should be more than enough space until you return to your desktop PC.

✔ **Flash drives:** Flash drives work best for quick file transfers between PCs or tablets. When you need to copy files onto your tablet, copy them to your flash drive first. Then insert the flash drive into your USB port and copy the files to your tablet's hard drive.

The rest of this section describes these storage spaces in more detail. If that's not enough room, drop by the following section: "Connecting to the Cloud with SkyDrive."

Connecting to built-in memory cards

Almost all Windows tablets include a special slot for sliding in a tiny memory card. Shown in Figure 6-19, they're much like the cards that people slide into digital cameras and cellphones every day.

Figure 6-19: Most tablets accept microSD cards (top left), microSDHC cards (middle left), and microSDXC cards (bottom left).

The slots and cards are so tiny, in fact, that you should buy a large-capacity card, push it into your tablet's slot, and leave it there.

I explain how to copy information to and from cards and other storage spaces in Chapter 5.

✔ Most Windows 8 tablets can use three types of cards shown in Figure 6-19. The microSDHC cards can hold up to 32GB, whereas the newer microSDXC cards come in capacities of 64GB, with higher capacity SDXC cards on the way.

✔ Before buying a microSDXC card, make sure your tablet can handle that type of card. (Check the fine print on the tablet's box.)

✔ For best results, buy the largest capacity card your tablet can use. Insert it into your tablet, and use it as a backup space with Windows 8's new FileHistory backups. Covered in Chapter 14, FileHistory makes your backups both automatic and easy to access.

Connecting to portable hard drives

If you carry around a lot of information — perhaps a large music or video collection — then your tablet's hard drive won't be nearly large enough. Only one gadget can handle the job: a portable hard drive, like the one shown in Figure 6-20.

Plug the cable from one of these tiny hard drives into your tablet's USB drive. After a few moments, the drive shows up in File Explorer, covered in Chapter 5.

Most portable hard drives draw their power directly from your tablet's USB port. Some still work when plugged into a hub; others need to be plugged directly into the tablet's USB port. Still others require a powered USB hub, and some portable drives need their own power adapter.

The problem with portable DVD drives

Portable CD/DVD drives have been around for years, but they rarely work well on a tablet. Most of them require a lot of power to both spin the disc and light the laser required to read or burn the disc's information.

Because a single USB port can't put out enough electricity to power the drive, most DVD drives include a cable that plugs into *two* USB ports simultaneously. Most tablets can only offer one USB port, ruling out the majority of drives.

If you must use a DVD drive on the road, look for one that plugs into a wall outlet for power. That ensures the drive will work, but it reduces the drive's portability.

Figure 6-20:
Plug a portable hard drive into your tablet to carry a huge number of files, songs, or videos.

Portable hard drives can hold up to 3TB of information, which is about 3000GB. That should be enough to last most people while on the road.

Connecting to flash drives for file transfers

Flash drives are essential additions to your gadget bag. They are tiny memory sticks that plug into the USB drive on your tablet's side. Once inserted, the drive appears in File Explorer, just like your tablet's hard drive.

Flash drives are the simplest and fastest way to copy files to or from your tablet. In fact, they're why Windows 8 tablets beat many competing tablets — few competing tablets even include a USB port, much less let you copy files to and from a flash drive.

I explain how to copy files to and from drives in Chapter 5.

Connecting to the Cloud with SkyDrive

Today, it seems every company wants you to save your files on the *cloud*. That's technospeak for an online storage place to stash your files. Microsoft, Amazon, Google, and a host of other companies offer free Internet storage spaces for you to fill with your files.

All Windows 8 tablets include an app to access Microsoft's cloud, called *SkyDrive*. Depending on when you signed up, SkyDrive offers you from 7GB to 25GB of space for you to stash your files. Once you fill up that space, Microsoft offers you two choices:

- ✔ Delete some old files to make room for your newer, incoming files.
- ✔ Pay up. For a larger space, Microsoft charges a yearly fee that increases as your storage space grows.

SkyDrive holds many advantages, especially for storage-starved tablets. Once you stash files on SkyDrive, you can access them from *any* Internet-connected tablet, computer, or phone.

You can access your SkyDrive-stashed files several different ways: from your Start screen's SkyDrive app, the Windows desktop's SkyDrive folder, or even through a web browser. Also, if you lose your tablet, your SkyDrive files stay safe and password-protected in the cloud.

Now, the odd parts about SkyDrive: The Start screen's SkyDrive app lets you access your SkyDrive files. It even lets you upload files. But it won't let you upload *folders,* making it awkward for mass operations, and when you're setting up SkyDrive for the first time, you usually want to stuff it full of files you'll need while traveling.

So, to stock your SkyDrive more quickly, install Microsoft's SkyDrive for Windows program, described in the next section.

Installing SkyDrive for Windows and uploading files to SkyDrive

For the easiest access to SkyDrive, install Microsoft's SkyDrive for Windows program on your tablet *and* on your desktop PC.

To keep things simple, SkyDrive for Windows places a handy SkyDrive folder in the Navigation pane of every folder on your Windows desktop.

Anytime you add folders or files to your computer's SkyDrive folder, SkyDrive automatically synchronizes them with your SkyDrive space on the Internet. That makes those files available to *all* your computers, tablets, and phones.

To download and install the desktop's SkyDrive for Windows program and begin stocking your SkyDrive account with files, follow these steps:

1. **From the Windows desktop, download and install SkyDrive for Windows.**

   Open Internet Explorer on the Windows desktop; then visit the SkyDrive for Windows website (`http://windows.microsoft.com/skydrive`). Follow the instructions to download and install SkyDrive for Windows onto your tablet, as well as onto your desktop PC.

   That same website also offers apps for your Android, Apple, and Windows phones, so they can access your SkyDrive-stored files, as well.

   Windows RT tablets can't install SkyDrive for Windows on the desktop. Instead, install SkyDrive for Windows on your home PC; then move to Step 2.

2. **Decide whether to make your PC or tablet's files available to other devices; then tap the Done button.**

   SkyDrive's installation program tosses you an odd option before closing: Make Files on this PC Available to Me on my Other Devices.

   The answer to this proposition takes some serious thought, so I cover it in the upcoming "Turning your desktop computer into a cloud" sidebar. For now, though, uncheck the box before tapping or clicking the Done button. (You can turn it back on later.)

3. **When asked, sign in with your Microsoft account.**

   As SkyDrive finishes installing on your desktop, it asks you to sign in with your Microsoft account. Here, you type the same e-mail address and password you use when signing on to your tablet with a Microsoft account.

4. **Open the SkyDrive folder.**

   When you finish downloading, installing, and signing on to SkyDrive, the program places a SkyDrive folder in the Navigation pane of every folder on your desktop (see Figure 6-21).

5. **Copy files and folders to the SkyDrive folder.**

   The SkyDrive folder works like any other folder on your PC. You can drag and drop folders and files into it. Or you can copy and paste files into the SkyDrive folder. (I describe how to copy and move files and folders in Chapter 5.)

Feel free to add files you might need while on the road: favorite photos, for example, favorite music, and backups of important files.

The SkyDrive folder in the Navigation pane

Figure 6-21:
SkyDrive for
Windows
places a
SkyDrive
folder
in every
folder's
Navigation
pane that
auto-
matically
synchro-
nizes with
the web's
SkyDrive.

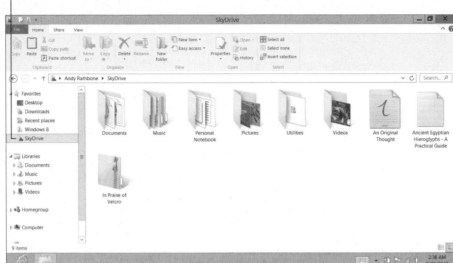

You can do many things with SkyDrive by right-clicking its folder in the Navigation pane. To right-click with your finger, tap and hold the word *SkyDrive*; when the little square appears, lift your finger. The right-click menu appears, offering these special SkyDrive options:

- ✔ **Include in Library:** Choose this to stash your SkyDrive contents into one of your libraries. This comes in handy mainly for backup systems that automatically copy your libraries' contents.

- ✔ **SkyDrive Pro:** This offers extra features for paying customers.

- ✔ **Open Folder Location:** Windows keeps a copy of your SkyDrive account's contents on your own computer. Choose this option to see that folder's contents.

- ✔ **Open in New Window:** This opens a new window showing your SkyDrive contents, handy when you want to drag and drop files into it from another window.

- ✔ **Pin to Start:** This places a Windows for SkyDrive tile on the Start screen, so you can jump to your desktop's SkyDrive folder quickly.

Downloading files with the SkyDrive app

After you stock SkyDrive with files, you can access those files quickly and easily from your tablet's SkyDrive app.

Can't find your tablet's SkyDrive app? Download it for free from Microsoft's Store app, which I cover in Chapter 9.

When you want to upload or download files using the SkyDrive app, follow these steps:

1. **From the Start screen, tap the SkyDrive app.**

   The SkyDrive app fills the screen, shown in Figure 6-22, showing all of your folders and files uploaded to your SkyDrive account. Although they're the same folders and files shown in the preceding Figure 6-21, the app shows them in a slightly different style.

Figure 6-22:
Shown here in Thumbnail view, the SkyDrive app lets you upload or download files on your SkyDrive storage space.

If the SkyDrive app doesn't show your files, make sure you're connected to the Internet; otherwise, you can't connect to SkyDrive.

2. **Tap what you want to open.**

   Tap a folder, and it opens to display the files and folders inside.

   Tap a file, and a program appears to show the file's contents and let you view or edit it. If a file *doesn't* open, you don't have a program or app on your tablet that's capable of opening the file.

3. **To upload new files, fetch the App menu bar and tap the Upload icon.**

   To fetch any app's App menu bar, slide your finger up from the screen's bottom edge.

   The File Picker appears, described in Chapter 5, ready for you to select the file or files you want to upload. (The SkyDrive app lets you upload only *files*, not folders.)

   You can select several files within a folder by sliding your finger downward on their tiles. To select them all, tap the words Select All along the top of the File Picker.

Fetching SkyDrive's App menu bar in Step 3 reveals more than just the Upload icon. The App menu bar also offers these options:

 ✔ **Refresh:** Tap this to tell SkyDrive to refresh its list of files and folders, which is handy if you're waiting for something to be uploaded from another computer.

 ✔ **New Folder:** This creates a new folder in SkyDrive, an essential task when organizing files.

 ✔ **Upload:** Covered in this section, this option lets you choose files to store on SkyDrive.

 ✔ **Details/Thumbnails:** This switches SkyDrive from Thumbnail view (shown earlier in Figure 6-22) to Details view, which lets you fit more information on the screen.

 ✔ **Select All:** This selects everything on the screen — files and folders. Once they're selected, you can tap either of the two new icons that appear: Clear and Delete. (You probably won't use this much.)

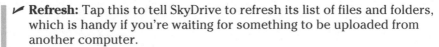

Turning your desktop computer into a cloud

When you finish installing SkyDrive for Windows on your desktop PC, the program leaves you looking at a check box next to this odd sentence: *Make Your PC or Tablet's Files Available to Other Devices.*

If you uncheck the box, the program simply installs SkyDrive for Windows, letting you stock your SkyDrive storage space with files and folders.

If you leave the check mark in place, however, Windows adds something extra to SkyDrive: It lets you access *that entire PC* from the SkyDrive website (`https://skydrive.live.com/`). That's right: All of your PC's files, folders, libraries, and drives will be available through SkyDrive.

Leaving that check mark in place automatically expands your tablet's storage space to include your entire desktop PC. Naturally, Microsoft took some security precautions with such a bold move. Before letting you access a new PC for the first time, SkyDrive asks you to type a code.

In the background, Microsoft sends a text message with a code to the cellphone associated with your Microsoft account. When you receive the message, you type the code into the computer you're using to access the PC. When Microsoft receives the matching code, it adds that PC to your list of accessible PCs.

You can access only PCs you've left turned on, so you'll need to leave your desktop PC turned on to access it from the road.

If you're planning on using this handy SkyDrive feature, be sure to enter your cellphone number when setting up your Microsoft account.

Chapter 7

Visiting Websites

. . . .

In This Chapter

▶ Visiting websites with the Start screen's browser

▶ Browsing with your fingers or a mouse

▶ Keeping several sites open in tabs

▶ Browsing in private

▶ Downloading files

▶ Saving favorite sites for revisits

▶ Changing your browser's settings

. . . .

*T*he Internet-hungry Windows 8 includes *two* web browsers. The Start screen's nimble browser works easily with your fingers. The old-school browser on the Desktop app provides extra power, by contrast, but works best when you plug in a mouse and keyboard.

Although the two browsers behave quite differently, they're oddly intertwined: They share your home page, logon passwords, browsing history, and your list of Favorites sites, among other things. Adding to the confusion, both browsers bear the same name: *Internet Explorer*.

This chapter covers your tablet's two versions of Internet Explorer. It explains how they work, how they differ, and which one works best in which situations.

Not yet connected to the Internet? Flip back to Chapter 6, where I explain four different ways your Windows 8 tablet can connect with the Internet.

Opening the Start Screen's Internet Explorer App

 To open the Start screen's browser, tap its icon (shown in the margin) on the Start screen. The browser opens, filling the screen as shown in Figure 7-1.

Figure 7-1: Like all Start screen apps, the Internet Explorer app hides its menus, filling the screen with your website.

When opened, the Start screen's browser will show one of these three things:

- ✔ **Your home page:** When opened for the first time, the Start screen's browser displays your *home page:* a favorite site you've chosen to display whenever you open Internet Explorer. If you haven't chosen a home page, as I describe later in this chapter, Microsoft fills the screen with one of its own websites.

- ✔ **Your last-visited site:** Unless you specifically *closed* the browser after your last visit, the browser will display the same site you last visited. (I explain how to close apps in Chapter 4.)

- ✔ **You're not connected:** When the browser displays this alarming message, it means your tablet isn't receiving an Internet connection. (I explain how to connect with the Internet in Chapter 6.)

But no matter which page your browser displays upon opening, notice how the page completely fills the screen. That makes the page easier to read, but it also highlights the Internet Explorer app's greatest weakness: The browser hides all of its menus.

You probably won't miss the menus much, though. The browser loads quickly, and you can easily tap one page's links to jump to another page. The fast-loading browser excels at serving up quick bits of information, which is what most people need from the Start screen. If you need more power, head for the desktop version of Internet Explorer, covered in this chapter's "The Desktop's Browser" section.

The rest of this section explains everything you need to know about the Start screen's nimble browser: how to find and open its menus, load websites, jump quickly to favorite sites, simultaneously browse several sites, share and download files and information, and adjust your browser's settings — all with your fingertips.

Open the Start screen browser's menus

Like most Start screen apps, the browser app hides its menus. That lets you concentrate on the picture rather than the frame.

When you need the menus, you can reveal them using the same trick that summons the menus from any Start screen app: Just slide your finger inward from the screen's top or bottom edges. As you slide your finger, it drags the menu into view, snapping it along the screen's top or bottom edges, as shown in Figure 7-2.

Each icon on the App bar performs a different task with a tap of your finger:

 ✔ **Back arrow:** Tap this to revisit your previously viewed web page.

✔ **Address bar:** To type a new web address, tap inside the address bar. The touch keyboard appears, ready for you to type the address of the website you want to visit. (As you type, the area above the address bar lists matching names of previously visited sites. Spot the name of the site you want to visit? Tap its name to load it.)

 ✔ **Cancel/Refresh:** As you view a site, this becomes a Refresh button; tap it to reload the page, retrieving the latest content. The Refresh button turns into a Cancel button while a web page loads; if the site takes too long to load, tap the Cancel button to stop trying to load the sluggish site.

 ✔ **Pin to Start:** Tap this to pin the site's name and icon to your Start menu. Doing so not only makes for easier launching from the Start screen but also makes it easier to launch from within the browser itself, as I explain in the next section.

 ✔ **Page tools:** When a page doesn't load properly, tap this little wrench icon. When the pop-up menu appears, choose View on the Desktop, and the site opens in the *desktop* version of Internet Explorer. (A wrench icon sprouting a plus sign means that the site offers an app for easier access.)

Currently open sites in tabs   Close tab

Open new tab

Tab menu

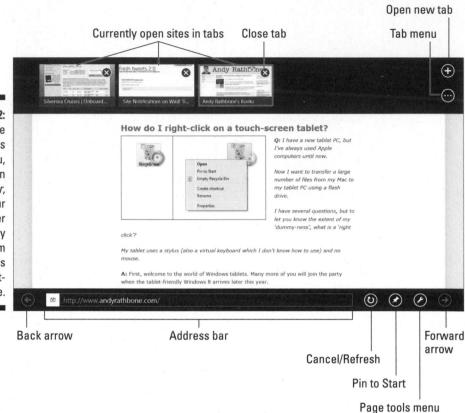

Figure 7-2:
To see the browser's menu, called an *App bar*, slide your finger slightly inward from the screen's top or bottom edge.

Back arrow   Address bar

Cancel/Refresh

Pin to Start

Page tools menu

Forward arrow

➤ **Forward arrow:** After clicking the Back arrow to revisit a site, click the Forward arrow to move back to the site you left.

➤ **Tabbed sites:** Along the top edge, the browser lists other sites currently open in your browser. To revisit one, tap it. To remove one from the list, tap the X in its upper-right corner.

➤ **Open new tab:** A tap of the plus sign icon in the top right lets you open a blank new tab, which lets you open a new web page, handy when you want to compare two websites. (You can jump between the sites by tapping their thumbnails on the top menu.)

➤ **Tab menu:** Dedicated to the tabbed sites shown on the top row, this icon brings a pop-up menu with two options: Close tabs, which closes all the open tabs, and New InPrivate tab, which opens a new tab for browsing in private (covered in the Browsing in Private sidebar, later in this chapter).

Browsing in private

Most websites leave lasting impressions long after they've left your eyes. Days or months later, the sites' names can still pop up in your address bar as you begin typing a few letters. They appear in your browser's history of visited websites. They often leave behind *cached* photos (copies of viewed photos) on your computer's hard drive. And they leave behind *cookies* (small files that help the website track your visits).

When you want to visit a website without leaving so many footprints, head for the Start screen browser's InPrivate mode from the Tab menu. InPrivate mode lets you shop for holiday presents, visit controversial websites, or browse on a public computer without letting the next person know your business.

To turn on InPrivate mode on the Start screen's browser, follow these steps:

1. **From the Start screen's Internet Explorer, slide your finger down slightly from the screen's top edge to reveal the menu.**

2. **Tap the Tab menu (it looks like three dots) and, when the pop-up menu appears, tap New InPrivate tab.**

A blank InPrivate window appears in the browser, ready for you to browse without leaving traces.

Entering the InPrivate mode in the desktop's version of Internet Explorer requires different steps:

1. **Tap the browser's Tools icon in its upper-right corner. (The icon resembles a gear.)**

2. **When the drop-down menu appears, tap Safety.**

3. **When the Safety pop-out menu appears, tap InPrivate browsing.**

A new version of Internet Explorer opens, showing a window that reads InPrivate is On.

To leave InPrivate mode and return to normal, close Internet Explorer, or just close the browser's InPrivate window.

The Start screen browser may look lightweight, but it's actually fairly full-featured, providing everything you need for casual browsing. As shown earlier in Figure 7-2, the browser lets you open several sites simultaneously, each in its own tab.

I describe how to close the Internet Explorer app in Chapter 4, but there's really no need to close Internet Explorer or any other Start screen app. They're designed to stay open constantly, letting you switch between them as needed (which I also describe in Chapter 4).

Navigating a website with your fingers or with a mouse

Designed specifically for your fingers, the Start screen's version of Internet Explorer works quite well with touch controls. When browsing a website, you can easily do any of these tasks with a touch of a finger:

- ✔ **Scroll through a web page:** When viewing a web page, remember the "sliding a piece of paper" rule: Slide your finger up or down the page, and the web page travels along the screen with your finger. By sliding your finger up or down the page, you can read the entire page, skipping up or down a few paragraphs at your own pace.

- ✔ **Enlarge tiny text:** When the text is too small to read, place two fingertips on the screen, then spread them. As your fingers move, the information expands, enlarging the text. Pinching the screen between two fingertips shrinks the page. By stretching and pinching, you'll find the sweet spot for easy visibility of both text and photos. (A quick double-tap makes the page as large as possible, letting you then pinch it down to your preferred size.)

- ✔ **Fetch menus:** Slide your finger up slightly from the screen's bottom, or down slightly from the screen's top. A menu pops up along the screen's top edge, bottom edge, or both.

- ✔ **Open a link in a new tab:** Tap and hold your finger on the link until a square appears. Lift your finger, and a pop-up menu appears. Then tap Open Link in New Tab. (To access pages open in tabs, slide your finger down slightly from the screen's top edge; then tap the thumbnail of the page you want to revisit.)

The Start screen's Internet Explorer and a mouse

Most of the time, you'll be using the Start screen's Internet Explorer with your fingertips. But if you plug in a mouse, the app tosses these new moves your way:

- ✔ **Back/Forward:** As you browse between a string of websites, hover your mouse pointer over the current page's left or right edges. An arrow appears along the edge, letting you click to move backward or forward, revisiting previously viewed pages.

- ✔ **Opening menus:** To fetch the menus from Internet Explorer and any Start screen app,

right-click a blank portion of the web page, away from words and pictures.

- ✔ **Dragging:** As you drag a mouse across a map on the Google maps website, Google automatically fills in the formerly off-the-edge portions. It's handy, for example, to see what's just north of the currently viewed screen. When you try dragging with a finger, though, Windows thinks you're trying to move the entire screen; it doesn't limit your movements to the map's contents. Moral: The mouse works much better when viewing Google Maps.

Visiting websites

You don't always have to open Internet Explorer to begin browsing. If you spot a web link inside a piece of e-mail, for example, tap the link. The Start screen's Internet Explorer app automatically rears its head, automatically displaying that website.

Tap a link on a web page, and the browser obligingly opens that link, as well, letting you see its contents. And if you've pinned a favorite site to the Start screen with a tap of the App bar's Pin icon, a quick tap of that site's Start screen tile brings it to the forefront.

The app lets you visit sites several other ways, as well:

✔ **Return to your last visited site:** Slide a finger up from the screen's bottom until a menu appears; then tap the left-pointing arrow. (Conversely, a tap on the Forward arrow returns to the site you left.)

✔ **Type a site's address:** Slide your finger up from the page's bottom edge to fetch the menus, and begin typing the site's name in the address bar, shown earlier in Figure 7-2.

✔ **Revisit a favorite site:** When you tap in the address bar, look directly above the address bar. There, Windows lists three categories of sites: Pinned (sites you've pinned to the Start menu), Frequently Visited, and Favorites (sites you've marked as favorites). To scroll through them all, slide your finger from right to left. Tap a site's name to revisit it.

✔ **Revisit a favorite site:** As you begin typing a site's name in the address bar, the browser checks your list of favorite sites, listing sites that match what you're typing. If you spot your desired site's name before you finish typing, tap the site for a quick revisit.

Windows remembers quite a bit about what you do on Internet Explorer. It remembers every term you've searched for, as well as every site you've visited. Although that sometimes comes in handy when trying to relocate information, some view it as an invasion of privacy.

To please everyone, Windows offers you two ways to control what your browser remembers about the time you spend online:

✔ **Delete your search history:** To delete your search history from the Start screen's version of Internet Explorer, fetch the Charms bar and tap Settings. When the Settings pane appears, tap Internet Options. Finally, when the Internet Explorer Settings pane appears, tap the Delete button beneath the words *Delete Browsing History*.

> ✔ **Stop Windows from saving searches:** To tell Windows not to remember items you've searched for, fetch the Charms bar and tap Settings. When the Settings pane appears, tap Change PC Settings at the bottom of the pane. When the PC Settings window appears, tap Search from the left pane. Finally, turn off the Let Windows Save My Searches As Future Search Suggestions toggle switch.

Managing several sites in tabs

It's not obvious, but the Start screen's version of Internet Explorer often keeps several sites open at the same time. For example, you may be viewing a website and then switch to the Mail app and tap a link somebody e-mailed you.

The Start screen's Internet Explorer appears, displaying the e-mailed website. What happened to the web page you were viewing previously? The browser places it on a hidden *tab* — a storage place the browser uses to juggle several open sites simultaneously.

The browser often opens new tabs on its own, but you can open a link into a new tab, too, a handy trick when you want to visit a page, but keep the first page open for reference.

To open a link in a new tab, tap and hold your finger on a link. When a pop-up menu starts to appear, lift your finger. Then from the pop-up menu, tap Open Link in New Tab, as shown in Figure 7-3.

To see your currently open tabs, slide your finger down slightly from the top edge of the Internet Explorer app. When the menus appear, the top menu lists all the sites currently open in tabs, as shown earlier in Figure 7-2.

To revisit a site, tap its name; the browser switches to that tab.

After a site lives on a tab, it stays there, even if you restart your computer. In fact, tabbed sites close only if any of these three things happen:

> ✔ You manually close a tabbed site by clicking the X in the thumbnail's upper-right corner.

> ✔ You close the browser manually, usually by swiping your finger from the screen's top edge all the way to the bottom. (The next time you open the browser, only your home page will appear.)

> ✔ You open more than eight tabs. The browser only has room for eight tabbed sites. If you open a ninth, your oldest tab disappears to make room for the newcomer.

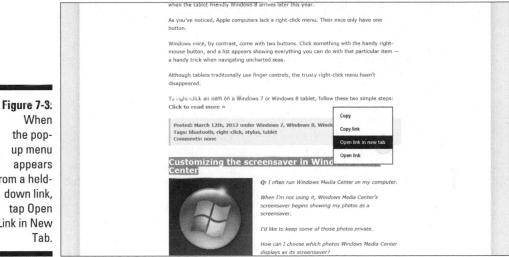

when the tablet-friendly Windows 8 arrives later this year.

As you've noticed, Apple computers lack a right-click menu. Their mice only have one button.

Windows mice, by contrast, come with two buttons. Click something with the handy right-mouse button, and a list appears showing everything you can do with that particular item — a handy trick when navigating uncharted seas.

Although tablets traditionally use finger controls, the trusty right-click menu hasn't disappeared.

To right-click an item on a Windows 7 or Windows 8 tablet, follow these two simple steps:
Click to read more »

Posted: March 12th, 2012 under Windows 7, Windows 8, Wind
Tags: bluetooth, right-click, stylus, tablet
Comments: none

Copy
Copy link
Open link in new tab
Open link

**Customizing the screensaver in Wind
Center**

Q: I often run Windows Media Center on my computer.

When I'm not using it, Windows Media Center's screensaver begins showing my photos as a screensaver.

I'd like to keep some of those photos private.

How can I choose which photos Windows Media Center displays as its screensaver?

Figure 7-3:
When the pop-up menu appears from a held-down link, tap Open Link in New Tab.

Making sites available with one tap

Eventually, you'll run across a site you don't want to forget. When that happens, "pin" the site to your Start screen. Seeing that tile on the Start screen jogs your memory that you haven't visited for awhile, which you can remedy with a tap on the tile.

To pin a site to the Start screen, follow these steps:

1. **While viewing the site, slide your finger up from the screen's bottom to see the app menu.**

   The app menu rises from the screen's bottom, shown earlier in Figure 7-2.

2. **Tap the Pin to Start button.**

   The browser quickly creates a new tile based on the website's dominant colors and then sticks that tile on the Start screen's far-right edge. (The tile also bears the website's name.)

When you want to revisit the site, tap its icon from the Start menu. Or open the browser's bottom menu and tap the address bar; a list of pinned sites appears above the address bar, enabling you to revisit one with a tap on its name.

The Start screen always tacks new items onto its far-right edge. To help you manage your Start screen's inevitable sprawl, I describe how to organize the Start screen into groups in Chapter 4.

Sharing sites and their information

Eventually, you'll stumble upon something worth sharing with friends. It may be an entire web page; it may be just a recipe's ingredients and instructions from a cooking site.

In Windows versions, you'd probably reach for the age-old copy-and-paste trick to shuttle the information to your friends.

 Windows 8's apps update that maneuver with the easier-to-use Share icon. Sharing items begins with a trip to the Charms bar. Fetch the Charms bar by sliding your finger in from the right edge; then tap the Sharing icon, shown in the margin.

When the Sharing pane appears, shown in Figure 7-4, you see every app capable of sharing your screen's current contents. For example, tap the Mail icon, and the Sharing pane shows the Mail app, letting you type an e-mail address and send the page on its way.

Recently e-mailed person

Link of current web page

Apps capable of receiving onscreen information

Share pane

Figure 7-4:
Tap the Charms bar's Share icon to see how to share your currently viewed or selected item.

The Share pane shows these items, from top to bottom:

- ✔ **Link's name:** The web link you're sending appears at the top.

- ✔ **Previous recipients:** The Share pane lists the last five people you've shared things with previously, and the app you used to share them. For example, a tap of an e-mail address shares the item with that person again, saving you the bother of typing the address.

- ✔ **Apps capable of sharing:** Here, the program lists all of your apps that are capable of sharing web links. Tap an app to load the app and share the link.

When you spot the People app (see Figure 7-4), tap it to share the web link with your social networks. You can send the link via a Twitter post or a Facebook app, for example.

Not all apps can share. If you don't see an app listed, it's not able to share that particular content.

Downloading files

The Start screen's Internet Explorer app can download files, just like its full-sized cousin on the desktop. To download a file from a website, tap the website's Download button. A permission bar appears along the screen's bottom, as shown in Figure 7-5.

Figure 7-5: From the menu along the site's bottom edge, tap Run to download and run the file or tap Save to save the file to run later.

The permission bar offers three options:

- ✔ **Run:** Tap this option if you're downloading a program to install on your tablet. The browser downloads the program and then automatically installs it, saving you some time.

- ✔ **Save:** This option saves the file in your Downloads folder, which is handy when you're downloading something you want to access later.

- ✔ **Cancel:** Tapped a Download button by mistake? A well-placed tap on the Cancel button stops the download.

To find your Downloads folder, open the Desktop app; then open any folder. Tap the Download folder's name, found in the Favorites section of every folder's Navigation pane along the left edge.

I explain how to install saved program files in Chapter 9.

Changing settings

The Start screen browser, like nearly all apps, lets you tweak its settings to meet your particular needs, and, just as with all apps, opening the settings area begins with a trip to the Charms bar, as described in the following steps:

1. **Fetch the Charms bar by sliding your finger inward from the screen's right edge. Then tap the Settings icon.**

   The Settings pane appears.

2. **Tap the words Internet Options, near the top of the Settings pane.**

   The Internet Explorer Settings pane appears (see Figure 7-6).

   The Internet Explorer app is built for speed rather than power, so it lets you change only these things:

   - **Delete Browsing History:** Don't want anybody to see websites you've browsed? Tap the Delete button to delete them all. (The desktop's Internet Explorer lets you delete specific entries, as I describe later in this chapter's "The Desktop Browser" section.)

   - **Permissions:** Some sites ask for your physical location, usually to either tell you about your surroundings or send you targeted advertising. Leave the toggle set to On, and the browser politely asks permission before revealing your location to a nosy website. Toggle it off, and all sites automatically know your location. (Tap the Clear button to revoke location permission from sites that have previously had access.)

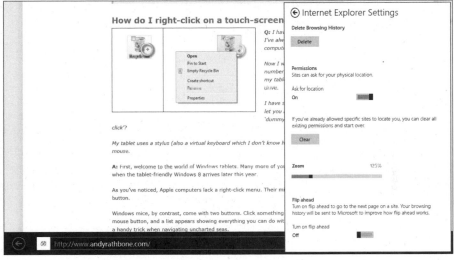

Figure 7-6:
To see the
menus, slide
your finger
slightly
inward
from either
the top or
the bottom
menu.

- **Zoom:** Handy when you can't read the tiny text on websites, this sliding bar lets you choose the magnification level to view sites. If you've set up the desktop to enlarge the screen by 125 percent, as I describe in Chapter 5, this will be set at 125. That's fine for most websites, as you can pinch or stretch them to the size that best displays their content.

- **Flip Ahead:** Described in the upcoming "Turning on Flip Ahead" sidebar, this lets you read websites like reading a book, flicking the pages from right to left. To turn it on or off, tap the toggle switch. (The word On or Off appears next to the toggle switch, letting you know which way it's switched.)

- **Encoding:** Rarely used, this area lets you change how the browser displays sites containing foreign languages.

3. **Tap anywhere on the web page to close the Internet Explorer Settings pane and return to browsing.**

Your changes to the Internet Explorer app's settings take place immediately.

Sending a site to the desktop's browser

Not all sites display properly in the Start screen's minimalist, finger-friendly browser. Some sites can't play Flash videos, for example; other sites protest with cryptic error messages about Java that leave you with frustration rather than solutions.

Turning on Flip Ahead

Windows 8's Start screen apps usually move their pages across the screen *horizontally*. That lets you swipe your finger in from left to right to move to the next page, much like you do when reading a book.

Websites, by contrast, expect you to move *down* the page, which is contrary to Windows 8's natural movements.

The solution? Microsoft's new *Flip Ahead* technology purports to fix things. When you turn on Flip Ahead, Microsoft reformats web pages in the background as they flow onto your screen. To scroll down the page, just flip your finger from right to left, just like turning a book's page: The website's next page appears.

While this makes web browsing more like flipping magazine pages, the cost is a loss of privacy. Turning it on sends Microsoft a link to every web page you visit, which allows it to format the pages in advance. If you're not concerned about privacy, though, Flip Ahead might enhance your web browsing experience.

It can also break the natural flow of some websites, leaving awkward page breaks. To try out Flip Ahead, visit the Internet Explorer app's Settings pane.

Beware, though, because the Flip Ahead feature won't work for every site, even when turned on.

Instead of giving up and moving on to another site, try routing the site to the desktop's more powerful browser, which specializes in coddling cranky websites.

To route a misbehaving site to the desktop's web browser, follow these steps:

1. **Swipe your finger up from the screen's bottom to fetch the browser menu.**

2. **From the browser's bottom menu, tap the Settings icon.**

   It's a little wrench with a plus sign, shown in the margin.

3. **Choose Send to Desktop.**

   The Desktop app appears, Internet Explorer in tow. Internet Explorer's savvier tools usually help the site display its wares to its fullest capacity.

The desktop version of Internet Explorer found on Windows RT tablets doesn't offer much more power than the Start screen's version. You still won't be able to play Flash videos nor run Java applets. This means that many Facebook games won't run well, if at all.

The Desktop's Browser

The desktop browser works much like the one in earlier Windows versions. In fact, it's almost identical to the one in Windows 7. On a tablet, you'll probably find yourself opening it mostly when you plug in a mouse and keyboard, open the Desktop app, and pretend you're working at a desktop PC. (Windows 8 tablets are pretty good at that, actually.)

 To open the desktop browser, tap the Start screen's Desktop app; then tap the Internet Explorer icon (shown in the margin) from the taskbar along the screen's bottom edge.

The desktop browser offers many more settings than the Start screen's browser. Because some of those settings also affect your Start screen's browser, you'll find yourself heading there periodically just to change the settings described in the rest of this section.

Setting your home page

The Start screen's browser doesn't offer a way to set a *home page* — the page your browser display shows when first opened. Instead, it merely piggybacks on the home page you set in the desktop's version of Internet Explorer.

So, to set your home page on *both* browsers, load the desktop version of Internet Explorer and follow these steps:

1. **With the desktop version of Internet Explorer, visit the site you want both sites to display when first opened.**

   Visit your favorite site by typing its address into Internet Explorer or clicking a link.

   When you're looking at the site you want to see when Internet Explorer opens, move to Step 2.

2. **Click the Tools icon in the program's upper-right corner. (It looks like a gear.)**

3. **When the drop-down menu appears, tap Internet Options.**

4. **When the Internet Options page opens to the General tab, tap the Use Current button.**

That sets your currently viewed page as your home page in both versions of Internet Explorer.

✔ Because both browsers can show several sites simultaneously in separate tabs, you can also open different sites in the desktop version of Internet Explorer. Tapping the Use Current button in Step 4 adds *all* of those sites to your home page; they'll each open in their separate tabs every time you open either version of Internet Explorer.

✔ To open a new tab in the desktop version of Internet Explorer, tap and hold your finger on the taskbar's Internet Explorer icon (shown in the margin). When a menu begins to appear, lift your finger. When the pop-up menu appears, tap Open New Menu. A new tab appears, letting you type a website address you want to visit.

Removing unwanted sites from Browsing History

Both versions of Internet Explorer remember *everything* you search for on the Internet. You can delete your past searches while in the Start screen's browser, but it strips away *everything*. You lose your list of visited websites, as well as your saved passwords, your cookies, and all other temporary files created while browsing.

To prune your past searches more selectively, fire up the desktop's browser and follow these steps:

1. **Open the desktop version of Internet Explorer and click the Tools icon in the program's upper-right corner. (It looks like a gear.)**

2. **When the drop-down menu appears, tap Internet Options. Then tap the Delete button in the Browsing History section.**

   The Delete Browsing History window appears (see Figure 7-7), letting you choose exactly what to delete.

3. **Tap the Delete button.**

   The browser deletes what you've chosen, preserving the rest.

For best results, leave the first option checked. Doing so preserves the settings from your favorite sites.

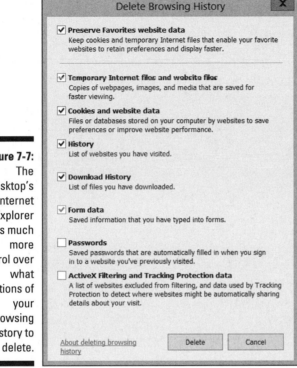

Figure 7-7:
The desktop's Internet Explorer offers much more control over what portions of your browsing history to delete.

Chapter 8

Keeping in Touch Through the Mail, People, Calendar, and Messaging Apps

....

....

*N*obody enjoys typing their contacts' names and addresses into Yet Another New Computer. And typing them all on a glass tablet makes an unwieldy chore even worse.

Taking mercy on a new tablet owner, Windows 8 *automatically* enters your friends into your contacts list and stashes upcoming appointments into your calendar. Windows even collects many photos you've posted online, so you can show off all of your photos right from your tablet. And how does Windows find this information?

You tell it where to look. Your friends are probably already listed on your social networks. When you tell Windows about your Facebook, Twitter, LinkedIn, Google, and other accounts, your tablet's People app automatically grabs your friends' names and contact information. As it grabs names, phone numbers, and e-mail addresses, the app scoops up your friends' latest status updates, too.

Similarly, your tablet's Calendar app automatically copies any appointments you've created on calendars from Google or Microsoft's online services. When you open your Contacts and Calendar apps, they're already stocked.

Yes, after 25 years, computers are finally making things easier.

Adding Your Social Accounts to Windows 8

Before you can run Windows 8's core apps — Mail, People, Calendar, and Messaging — you need a Microsoft account. (I explain Microsoft accounts in Chapter 2.) Without a Microsoft account, the apps simply display a notice with the words Sign Up for a Microsoft Account. Tap those words to sign up for a Microsoft account on the spot.

Before the apps can do their job, they need something else, too: your username and password information from Facebook, Google, Twitter, LinkedIn, Hotmail, and other accounts you may use.

Although handing over your password sounds fishy, it's actually safe, secure, and quite convenient. Armed with your social networking information, Windows 8 dutifully fills out your tablet's People app with everybody's contact information and stashes your Facebook and Twitter photos in your tablet's Photos app.

To let Windows 8 copy and stash the information that's currently scattered across your social networks, follow these steps:

1. **From the Start screen, open the Mail app.**

   From the Start screen, tap the Mail app's tile, and the Mail app fills the screen, listing any mail you've received from your Microsoft account.

2. **Tell the Mail app about your other accounts.**

   To add your accounts to the Mail app, head for the Charms bar's Settings icon: Summon the Charms bar by swiping your finger inward from the tablet's right edge, and tap the Settings icon (shown in the margin).

   When the Settings pane appears, tap the word Accounts, and the Accounts pane appears. From the Accounts pane, tap the Add an Account link, and the Mail app lists the accounts you can add (see Figure 8-1).

   For some accounts, Windows 8 simply adds the information and then collects any waiting mail. For others, like Google, Windows 8 visits a secure area on Google's website where you can authorize the transaction.

   Repeat these steps for other e-mail accounts you want to add to the Mail app. (Microsoft constantly tinkers with the apps, so don't be surprised if you see a few other accounts listed on your own tablet.)

   Don't see your e-mail account listed? I explain how to add missing e-mail accounts in the "Adding other e-mail accounts to Mail" sidebar, later in this chapter.

Figure 8-1:
The Mail app lets you enter e-mail accounts from different services.

As of this writing, the Mail app doesn't accept POP mail servers. To add IMAP servers, tap the Other Account option and enter your username, password, and IMAP server.

3. **Return to the Start screen, tap the People tile, and enter your other accounts.**

   When the People app first opens, you may already see a few of your friends, grabbed from online contact lists associated with the e-mail accounts you entered in Step 1.

   To stock the app with more of your friends, tell the People app about your social networking sites, like Facebook, Twitter, LinkedIn, and others.

   Your importing experience will vary from account to account. For some accounts, you simply need to enter your username and password. Other accounts, like Facebook, take you straight to their website, where you enter your information to authorize the action, as shown in Figure 8-2.

After you enter your account information, Windows 8 finishes the job, filling your Mail app with e-mail, stocking the People app with your friends' contact information, and adding any appointments to your Calendar app.

 ✔ Your contacts list updates automatically, constantly reflecting your relationships on Facebook, Twitter, or LinkedIn. If you manually add a contact to one of your online networks from any computer, that person's information automatically appears in your tablet's People app, as well.

 ✔ If somebody unfriends you from Facebook, or if you stop following somebody on Twitter, your People app silently erases them without notice.

✔ In addition to collecting contact information, the People app collects your friends' latest updates from *all* of your social networks. When you visit the People app's What's New section, you can read everyone's updates from every network, without having to visit all of them.

✔ You can still visit Facebook and other networks to read your friends' updates. The People app simply provides an alternative way of keeping track of your friends, quickly and easily.

Figure 8-2:
Enter your Facebook e-mail account and password to import your friends into your People app.

Sending and Receiving E-Mail

Windows 8's Mail app does a no-frills job of sending and receiving e-mail. It's free, preinstalled on every tablet, includes a spell checker, and if you follow the steps in the previous section, it's already filled with the e-mail addresses of your friends.

In fact, you don't even need to open the Mail app to see what's new. The Mail app includes a *live* tile, meaning it constantly updates with the latest information. When you glance at the Start screen, you'll see your Mail tile turn into a mini-billboard, displaying the first few lines of your unread e-mails and their senders.

The rest of this section explains how to open the Mail app, send and receive e-mail, switch between folders and accounts, and send and receive files to friends or coworkers.

Adding other e-mail accounts to Mail

The Mail app receives e-mail only from the accounts listed in the Accounts pane, which includes e-mail from Hotmail, Google's Gmail, America Online, Outlook.com, and Yahoo!. If you want to read mail from other sites, you have two options:

✔ **Read it online:** Launch the Internet Explorer app with a tap of its Start screen tile. Then visit your mail's website and read your e-mail online. It bypasses the Mail app, but it's an easy solution.

✔ **Import it to Google, Hotmail, or Outlook:** In this rather convoluted process, you must set up a *supported* account to import the e-mail from your *unsupported* account. Visit the settings area on Outlook (www. outlook.com), Hotmail (www. hotmail.com), or Gmail (www.

google.com/mail). Find the setting where you can import mail from another account. There, enter your e-mail account's username and password. You may also need to enter more complicated information like the site's POP3 and SMTP addresses, found on your mail company's website or technical support staff.

After a supported account imports your other account's e-mail, that supported account will route that account's mail to the Mail app, letting you read everything in one place.

Microsoft eventually plans to support more mail services in its Mail app, sparing you from jumping through these admittedly uncomfortable hoops.

Switching between the Mail app's accounts, folders, and e-mail

A tap on the Mail app's Start screen tile brings the Mail app to the screen (see Figure 8-3). Even if the app's already running in the background, a tap on its tile brings it front and center.

The Mail app splits the screen into three columns:

✔ **Left column:** The name of your currently viewed e-mail account appears at the top; that account's folders appear below its name. (The highlighted folder is the one you're currently viewing.) At the bottom of the column, you see names of any other e-mail accounts you've set up. To see mail from another account's mail, tap that account's name.

✔ **Middle column:** Tap a folder from the left column, and a list of that folder's e-mails appears in the middle column. There, you see the sender's name, the e-mail's arrival date, and the subject name.

✔ **Right column:** Tap an e-mail listed in the middle column, and its contents spill out in the right column.

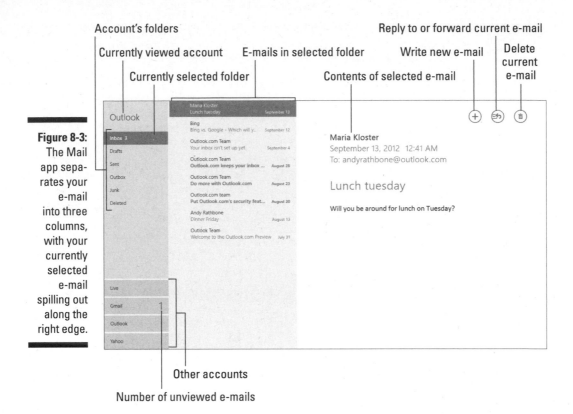

Account's folders

Currently viewed account   E-mails in selected folder

Currently selected folder   Contents of selected e-mail

Reply to or forward current e-mail

Write new e-mail

Delete current e-mail

Figure 8-3:
The Mail app separates your e-mail into three columns, with your currently selected e-mail spilling out along the right edge.

Other accounts

Number of unviewed e-mails

To browse your mail, follow these two steps:

1. From the left column, tap the account and then the folder you want to browse.

When you tap the folder, its contents appear in the middle column.

2. From the middle column, tap the e-mail you want to read.

The message's contents spill out into the right column.

Can't read an e-mail's tiny letters? Then put two fingers on the tablet to stretch or pinch it until it's the right size.

In Figure 8-3, shown earlier, for example, you see an Outlook account in the left column. Beneath it, you see other available accounts, including ones from Windows Live, Google's Gmail, Outlook, and Yahoo!. (If you set up only one account, you see only one account listed.)

Mail accounts from different accounts often include different folders. If you've set up customized folders in Gmail, for example, those same customized folders appear in the Mail app. But every account always contains these basic folders:

✔ **Inbox:** When you open the Mail app or switch between accounts, you always see the contents of your *Inbox* — the holding tank for newly received messages.

✔ **Drafts:** Started a heartfelt e-mail but can't finish it through your tears? Store it in the Drafts folder to finish later: Tap the Close icon shown in the margin; when the drop-down menu appears, tap Save Draft. Later, when you want to finish the e-mail, tap this folder to see it waiting for completion. (I cover sending e-mail in the next section.)

✔ **Sent Items:** Previously sent e-mail lives in here, letting you reference it later. Some accounts, like Gmail, only show your last two weeks of sent messages. I show how to change that time frame in the "Changing an account's settings" sidebar later in this chapter.

✔ **Junk:** The Mail app drops suspected junk mail into this folder. Although the app's Junk filter works well, occasionally visit here to salvage any e-mail that lands there by mistake. (Some Yahoo! accounts call this a Bulk Mail folder.)

✔ **Deleted:** Deleted something by mistake? Look in here to find it. To delete something permanently from the Deleted Items folder, select it and tap the Delete icon.

✔ **Outbox:** The Mail app immediately tries to connect to the Internet and send your message. If your Internet connection isn't working correctly, your message lounges comfortably in this folder. Once you're connected with the Internet, tap the Sync button, if necessary, to send the message on its way.

Like all apps, the Mail app hides its menus, and, like all apps, you reveal those menus by sliding your finger upward from the bottom edge of the screen. The App bar appears, as shown in Figure 8-4, with all the app's menus in tow. The App bar is context-sensitive, meaning it changes to show icons relevant to what you're currently viewing.

Composing and sending an e-mail

To write, spell-check, and send an e-mail from your tablet's Mail app to a friend's Inbox, follow these steps:

1. **From the Start screen, tap the Mail app's tile and tap the New icon in the program's top-right corner.**

   An empty New Message window appears, ready for you to fill with your words of glory. If you've set up several e-mail accounts in the Mail app, your e-mail will be sent from the account you last viewed.

Figure 8-4:
Slide your
finger up
from the
bottom
edge of the
screen to
reveal the
Mail app's
menus.

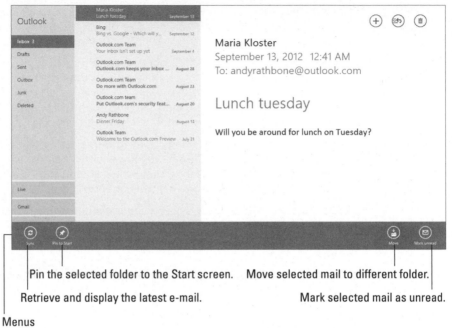

Pin the selected folder to the Start screen.   Move selected mail to different folder.

Retrieve and display the latest e-mail.   Mark selected mail as unread.

Menus

Changing an account's settings

Most e-mail accounts let you change how they handle your mail. For example, a Gmail account usually contains hundreds, if not thousands of e-mails. That's a *lot* of e-mail to sort through. To keep things simple, Gmail displays only your last two weeks' worth of sent and received e-mail.

To change that time frame — or to change the settings of any mail account — open the Mail app and follow these steps:

1. **Fetch the Charms bar by sliding your finger in from the screen's right edge; then tap the Settings icon.**

2. **When the Settings pane appears, tap Accounts; when the Accounts pane lists your e-mail accounts, tap the account you want to change.**

The settings for your chosen account appear, and the keyboard rises, ready for you to make your changes. (You can slide your finger up or down the Settings pane to bring more of it into view.)

3. **Tap in the area you want to change and then change the setting by either tapping the adjacent toggle switch, tapping an item from a menu, or typing words.**

Your changes take place immediately; you don't need to tap a Save button. To remove accounts you no longer use, tap the Remove Account button at the bottom of the account's Settings pane.

To close the Accounts pane, tap anywhere within the Mail app.

To send e-mail from a different account, tap the downward-pointing arrow next to your e-mail address in the screen's upper-left corner. When the menu drops down, tap the name of the account you want to use for sending that particular mail.

2. **Type your friend's e-mail address into the To box.**

   Tap the plus sign to the right of the To box. The People app appears, letting you tap the name of everybody you want to receive the e-mail. Tap the Add button, and the Mail app automatically fills in everybody's e-mail address — a very handy thing on a tablet.

   Or you can tap inside the To box; the keyboard pops up for you to begin typing in the recipient's name or e-mail address. With each letter you type, the Mail app scans the contacts listed in your People app, constantly placing potential matches below the To box. If the app happens to guess the right name, tap the name to place it in the To box.

3. **Tap inside the Subject box and type a subject.**

   Tap the words Add a Subject along the message's top. Those words quickly vanish, and the keyboard rises from the screen's bottom edge, ready for you to type your own subject, shown at the top of Figure 8-5.

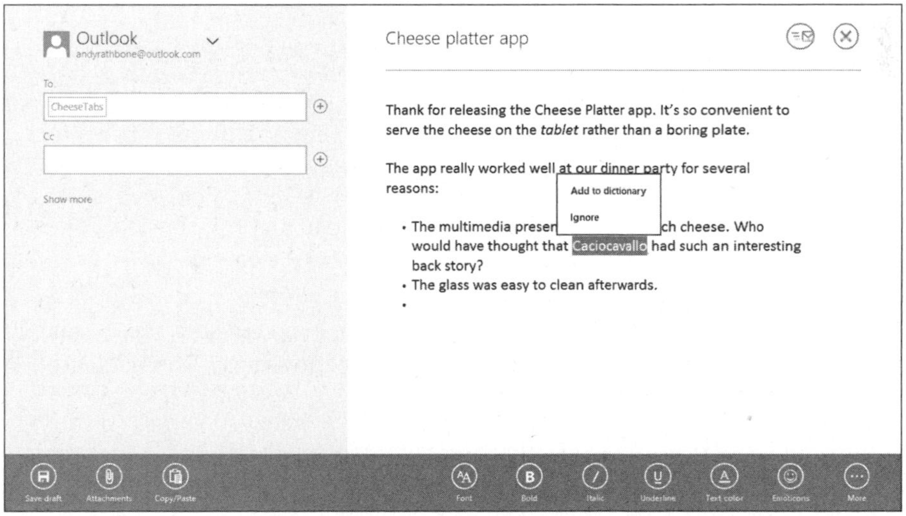

Figure 8-5:
Type your message, keeping a watchful eye for any spelling errors caught by the built-in spell checker.

> Outlook ⌄
> andyrathbone@outlook.com
>
> To
> CheeseTabs ⊕
>
> Cc
> ⊕
>
> Show more
>
> Cheese platter app   ⊟🖊 ⊗
>
> Thank for releasing the Cheese Platter app. It's so convenient to serve the cheese on the *tablet* rather than a boring plate.
>
> The app really worked well at our dinner party for several reasons:
>
> Add to dictionary
>
> Ignore
>
> • The multimedia presen...   ...ch cheese. Who would have thought that Caciocavallo had such an interesting back story?
> • The glass was easy to clean afterwards.
> •
>
> 🖫 Save draft   📎 Attachments   📋 Copy/Paste   AA Font   B Bold   I Italic   U Underline   A Text color   ☺ Emoticons   ⋯ More

4. **Type your message into the large box beneath the Subject line.**

   I share tips on typing on your tablet's glass keyboard in Chapter 3. The Mail app watches as you type, automatically underlining words it doesn't recognize. To correct a misspelled word, tap the underlined word. A pop-up menu appears (refer to Figure 8-5), letting you choose the correct spelling.

To embellish your prose, change the text's formatting by swiping your finger upward from the bottom of the screen to fetch the App bar. There, you can change fonts, add italics, create numbered lists, and add other flourishes by tapping the appropriate icon.

To save an e-mail in progress, tap the Save Draft button at the App bar's far left. The Mail app saves your e-mail in the Drafts folder of the account you're using to send the e-mail.

5. **Attach any files or photos to your e-mail, if desired.**

You find more about attaching files in the section, "Sending and receiving files through e-mail," later in this section, but here's a spoiler: Tap the Attachments icon on the Mail app's App bar.

6. **Tap the Send button, located in the screen's top-right corner.**

The Mail app shuttles your e-mail through the Internet to your friend's mailbox. Depending on the speed of your Internet connection, mail can arrive anywhere from within a few seconds to a few days, with a minute or two being the average. (All of your sent mail appears in your Mail app's Sent folder, so check there to make sure your tablet has sent your message.)

If you find yourself at a loss for words, tap the Close button, shown in the margin. A drop-down menu appears, letting you tap Delete to delete the message. Or tap Save Draft, and the Mail app stashes your unfinished e-mail in your current account's Drafts folder to finish later.

Reading an e-mail

Every time your tablet finds an Internet connection, it automatically grabs any new e-mails it can find. Proud of its background work, the Mail app's Start screen tile updates itself, listing the sender, subject, and first line of your latest e-mails.

To respond to a particularly enticing e-mail, follow these steps:

1. **Tap the Start screen's Mail tile.**

The Mail app appears, displaying the first e-mail in your last-viewed account's Inbox (refer to Figure 8-3). Below that, older e-mails appear, listed chronologically.

2. **Open a message by tapping its name.**

The message's contents fill the window's right edge.

3. **Tap an option from the buttons along the e-mail's top edge:**

- **Do nothing:** If the message doesn't warrant a response, move on to something more interesting by tapping a different message from the Mail app's middle column.

- **Respond:** To reply to a message, tap the Respond button in the screen's top-right corner. When the menu drops down, tap Reply. A new e-mail appears, already addressed with the recipient's name and subject, and containing the original message for you both to reference.

- **Reply All:** When an e-mail arrives that's been addressed to several people, tap the Respond button, but choose Reply All from the drop-down menu. That sends your response to everybody who received the original e-mail.

- **Forward:** Tap Forward from the Respond button's drop-down menu to send a copy of your friend's must-see cute cat photo to your own friends.

- **Delete:** A tap of the Delete button moves the message to your Deleted folder. To permanently delete a message, tap the Deleted folder, tap the unwanted message, and tap the Delete button. The message, having no place left to hide, vanishes.

You can print a message the same way you print from any other app: Open the message, fetch the Charms bar, tap the Devices icon, tap your printer from the list of devices, and tap the Print button.

Even though the Map app gathers your e-mail, you can still view your e-mail from your mail service's website in Internet Explorer. Your same e-mails will still appear in Gmail (www.google.com/gmail) or Hotmail (www.hotmail.com), for example.

Sending and receiving files through e-mail

E-mailed files, referred to as *attachments* by computer linguists, can be tucked inside an e-mail message. You can send or receive nearly any file, but with a few stipulations:

- ✔ Most mail servers can't handle files totaling more than 25MB. That's enough for a song or two, a handful of digital photos, and most documents. That's usually *not* enough to send videos, though.

- ✔ If you send a file you've created in Microsoft Word and the recipients don't have Microsoft Word, they won't be able to open or edit your Word file. To avoid confusion, let the recipient know what program you used to create your file.

With those two stipulations out of the way, plunge onward into this section, which explains how to open, save, and send attachments.

Viewing or saving a received attachment

To conserve your tablet's precious storage space, the Mail app doesn't automatically download attached files and save them to your tablet. Instead, the Mail app shows attached files using a faintly colored icon, like the one shown in the margin.

Whether you want to open or save the attachment, follow these steps:

1. Tap the word *Download* next to the attached file.

Tap Download, and the Mail app downloads the file to your tablet. Once the Mail app finishes downloading the file, its icon regains its normal coloring, shown in the margin.

If you just want to view the attached file (or play an attached song), tap the file's icon and choose Open from the drop-down menu. If your tablet has an app or program capable of opening the file, that program opens the file, letting you see or listen to the attachment.

Once you've seen or heard the file, you may be done, and ready for different adventures. But if you want to edit the file, or access it later, extract the file from your e-mail and save it in a more permanent location by moving to Step 2.

2. Tap the attached file's icon and tap Save from the drop-down menu.

Windows's File Picker appears (see Figure 8-6) — I cover the File Picker in Chapter 4. The File Picker serves as the Start screen's equivalent of the desktop's File Explorer: It lets you shuttle files from one location to another.

3. Choose a folder to receive the saved file.

Tap the word *Files* in the File Picker's top-left corner and then choose which library to receive the incoming file: Documents, Pictures, Music, or Videos.

Windows constantly indexes the contents of your four libraries: Documents, Pictures, Music, and Video. Saving your file in one of those libraries makes it easier to find it again later by using the Charms bar's Search icon, and searching the Files area.

Don't know where to put it? Choose the Documents library, which serves as a catchall for anything that's not a photo, song, or movie.

4. Tap the Save button in the File Picker's bottom-right corner.

Once you've chosen the file's destination, the File Picker places a copy of the e-mailed file in that location.

Figure 8-6:
To save a
file sent
through
e-mail, tap
Files, select
a location to
save the file,
and then
tap the Save
button.

5. **Repeat these steps to save any other attached files.**

   Unfortunately, the Mail app doesn't allow you to select multiple files and save them in the same place. So, you must repeat these steps for every attached file you want to save.

Windows 8's built-in virus checker, Windows Defender, automatically scans your incoming e-mail for viruses, worms, and other malware. Keep these tips in mind when using the Mail app:

✔ Even after you save a file to a folder, it remains in your e-mail. If you somehow lose your saved file, head back to the original e-mail and repeat these steps to save a fresh copy.

✔ You can download attached files only when connected to the Internet. That's why it's important to save files you may need to access in areas without WiFi coverage.

✔ To avoid hogging space on your tablet, many e-mail accounts display only your last *two weeks* worth of messages in the Mail app. After two weeks, those files will scroll off your tablet's Mail app.

✔ If you need an attachment you received *three weeks* ago, it's not lost forever, even if it's scrolled off the Mail app. Visit your e-mail's website. From the website, you can find all your e-mails, no matter how old they are.

Sending a file as an attachment

Sending a file through the Mail app works just the opposite of saving an attached file, which I cover in the preceding section. Instead of finding a file in an e-mail and saving it into a folder or library, you're finding a file in a folder or library and saving it in an e-mail.

To send a file to somebody through the Mail app, follow these steps:

1. **Open the Mail app and create a new e-mail, as described earlier in the "Composing and sending an e-mail" section.**

   Choose the recipient, and write your message.

2. **Open the Mail app's App bar and tap the Attachments icon.**

   Open the App bar by sliding your finger up from the screen's bottom edge. (You can do this even if your tablet's keyboard fills the screen's bottom half.)

   Tap the Attachment icon from the App bar, and the Windows 8 File Picker window appears (refer to Figure 8-6).

3. **Navigate to the file you want to send.**

   Tap the word *Files* to see a drop-down menu listing your computer's major storage areas. Most files live in your Documents, Pictures, Music, and Videos libraries.

   Tap any folder's name to see a list of the files stored inside. Don't see the files you want? Tap the File Picker's Go Up link to retreat from that folder and try again with a different folder.

4. **Tap the name of each file you want to send; then tap the Attach button.**

   A tap selects a file; tap a file again to deselect it. As you tap files, their color changes to show they're selected.

   A tap of the Attach button returns to the Mail app and attaches the file or files to your e-mail.

5. **In the Mail app, tap the Send button.**

   The Mail app sends your mail and its attached file or files to the recipient. Depending on the size of your attached files, this may take from several seconds to several minutes. Because it all takes place in the background, feel free to switch to another app, browse the web, or grab another bagel at your free WiFi spot.

Retrieving lost mail from the pile

Instead of envelopes piling up on your desk, e-mail now piles up in your Inbox. Actually, that could be *Inboxes,* if you've set up several e-mail accounts in the Mail app. You can relocate a wayward e-mail with the same tactic used to find things in any Windows 8 app: Summon the Search pane.

From within Windows Mail, tap the account holding the e-mail you want to search through; then slide your finger inward from the screen's right edge. When the Charms bar appears, tap the Search icon.

When the Search pane and keyboard appear, type a word from the lost e-mail — even the person's name will do — and then tap the Search key to see a list of matching e-mail.

At the time of this writing, the Mail app doesn't provide a way to search through all your e-mail accounts simultaneously. To search through all of your accounts, you must use the Search command on each individual account.

When your recipient receives your attached files, he can save them onto his own computer, no matter what type of computer or e-mail program he owns.

- ✐ If you try to attach too many large files, the Mail app warns you with a message across the mail's top: The Attachments Might Be Too Large to Send This Message. Try Selecting Send Using SkyDrive Instead.

- ✐ If you spot that message, tap Send Using SkyDrive Instead. The Mail app then uploads those files to a new folder on your SkyDrive account and sends the recipient a link to that folder where he can view or download them.

Managing Your Contacts in the People App

This chapter's first section explains how to link the People app with your online social networks. After you follow those steps, your People app stocks itself with your favorite people, whether they're on Facebook, Twitter, LinkedIn, or other networks.

Open your People app with a tap on its Start screen tile, and the People app appears, as shown in Figure 8-7, listing all of your friends it grabbed online. In keeping with the latest computing trend, People alphabetizes your contacts by their first names. Your friend Adam Zachary *finally* appears first.

Access your account photo or profile, write updates, or view photos posted online.

Return to the last viewed contact.   Edit an account's settings.

Available for instant message   View your contacts.

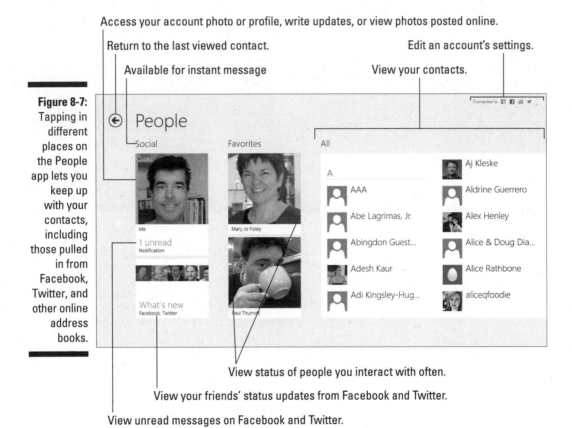

Figure 8-7: Tapping in different places on the People app lets you keep up with your contacts, including those pulled in from Facebook, Twitter, and other online address books.

View status of people you interact with often.

View your friends' status updates from Facebook and Twitter.

View unread messages on Facebook and Twitter.

The People app keeps itself updated automatically, adding and dropping people as they enter or leave your social networks.

However, some people don't share their lives through a social network, which leaves them out of the People app's virtual reach. Also, networks like Facebook contain huge switchboxes full of privacy controls. Some of your friends may have flipped a Facebook switch that keeps their information sequestered in Facebook's walled garden, and away from the clutches of the People app.

The point? You'll eventually need to remove your gloves and manually add or edit entries in the People app. This section explains the details of a job that can't be sloughed off to the People app's robot crawler.

✔ Tapping your way through the People app can lead you to friends, their adventures, and even the adventures of your friends' friends. If you're feeling lost in a sea of people, slide your finger up from the tablet's bottom edge and tap the Home button. That takes you back to the front page.

✔ When anybody is available to receive an instant message, a thin green bar appears along their picture's left edge. To make yourself *Invisible* — unavailable for instant messaging — open the Messaging app and change your status to Invisible, a task described in this chapter's last section.

Keeping track of your friends' updates

To see *everything* that's happening with your friends, tap the People app's What's New section in the app's bottom-left corner (shown in Figure 8-7). The app fetches all of your friends' latest updates from Facebook and Twitter, and then it places them in chronological order for your scrolling pleasure.

If that's information overload, see one friend's updates by tapping her name in the People app. When her name and information appears, her latest update appears on the page's right side. To see more of her updates, tap the View All link next to the headline What's New. There, you'll see your friend's stream of updates from Twitter and Facebook, including the comments left by Facebook friends.

If your What's New feed is overcrowded with updates from friends, acquaintances, and even interesting strangers you follow on twitter, you can whittle it down with the People app's *filtering* capacity. With a flick of a switch, you can tell People to display updates from only your Facebook friends or only your Twitter friends.

To filter an account from People's What's New feed, follow these steps:

1. **Open the People app and tap the What's New feed.**

2. **When the What's New feed appears, slide your finger up slightly from the screen's bottom edge.**

3. **When the App bar appears, tap the Filter button.**

   A menu appears, listing your social accounts, including Facebook and Twitter.

4. **Tap the account you want to filter.**

   Tap Twitter, for example, and you'll see status-only updates posted by your Facebook friends. Or tap Facebook, for example, to see only Twitter updates.

To return to seeing *everything* in the What's New feed, follow the preceding steps, but tap All in Step 4.

Adding contacts

For people who don't appear in your People app, you can add them in either of two ways:

- ✔ Using any computer, add the missing people to the contacts list of one of your online accounts, like Gmail (www.google.com/gmail), Hotmail (www.hotmail.com), or Outlook (www.outlook.com/). Befriending them on Facebook does the trick, too. Once a person appears in a social network or one of your online contacts lists, the People app will automatically pull that person's details into your tablet.

- ✔ Manually type your contact's information into the People app. This isn't a one-way street, either; the People app will add your hand-typed information to the online account of your choice, too.

To add a new contact to the People app, follow these steps:

1. Tap the Start screen's People tile to load the People app.

   When the People app appears, make sure you're on the Home page: Slide your finger up from the screen's bottom edge and tap the Home icon.

2. Slide your finger up slightly from the screen's bottom edge to fetch the App bar. Then tap the New icon.

   A blank New Contact form appears, ready for you to type the contact's details.

3. Fill out the New Contact form.

   As shown in Figure 8-8, type your contact's details, including name, address, e-mail, and phone. To add other information, tap the Other Info button. There, you can add tidbits such as a job title, website, significant other, or notes that don't fit anywhere else.

   If you entered more than one online account into the People app, the Account field in the top-left corner lets you choose which account should also be updated with the new contact. Android phone owners should choose their Google account, which will update your phone, as well.

   Microsoft phone owners should choose their Microsoft account associated with their phone, so the person will appear there.

4. Tap the Save button.

   The People app saves your new contact, both on your tablet and on the account you choose in Step 3. Spot a typo? The "Deleting or editing contacts" section, later in this chapter, explains how to edit an existing contact.

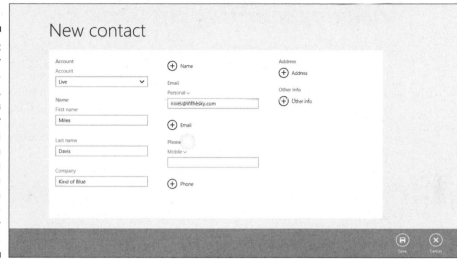

Figure 8-8:
Add your
new con-
tact's name,
as well as
any other
details you
have on
hand. Then
tap the Save
button to
add the per-
son to your
People app.

Adding easy access to favorite people

The People app can be unwieldy when filled with several hundred contacts. You can flip your finger through dozens of pages before finding the one you want, especially if a contact's first name begins with Zeke.

To make it easier to find somebody you frequently deal with, call up his contact page in the People app. While looking at his contact page, summon the App bar by sliding your finger up from the screen's bottom edge.

The App bar offers two buttons to help you stay in touch more easily.

✔ **Pin to Start:** Tap this button to turn the person into a tile on your Start screen. The tile constantly changes, showing either the person's photo or last few status updates. Tap the person's tile to jump quickly to the People app, opened to that person's contact page.

✔ **Favorite:** Tap this to place the person at the front of your People app, as shown earlier in Figure 8-8. A tap of the person's photo fetches his contact page, which shows his contact information as well as his latest status updates.

Like anything else added to the Start screen, a person's tile ends up on the Start screen's far right. If you add a lot of people to the Start screen, consider organizing their tiles into their own group, a process I describe in Chapter 4.

Here's one more trick for dealing with a crowded People app: When swimming in a sea of people's names, pinch the screen: The People app responds by quickly shrinking into an alphabet. Tap the letter W, and the People app opens back up, but this time, starting with people whose names begin with Wanda.

Deleting or editing contacts

As our social and professional relationships change, the People app automatically takes care of the paperwork. When somebody unfriends you on Facebook, they simply drift off your People app without notice. Similarly, if you stop following somebody on Twitter, the People app trims the person off your list.

But if you need to edit or delete a contact you've added manually, it's fairly easy to do by following these steps:

1. **Tap the People tile on the Start screen.**

   The People app appears, as shown earlier in Figure 8-7.

2. **Tap a contact.**

   The contact's page appears full-screen.

3. **Slide your finger up slightly from the screen's bottom edge to fetch the App bar.**

   The App bar appears as an icon-filled strip along the screen's bottom.

4. **Tap the Delete button to delete the contact; tap the Edit button to update a contact's information. Then tap the Save button to save your editing changes.**

   Tapping Delete removes the person and all his information. No Delete button? That means the People app pulled in his information from a social network. To remove him from the People app, you must first delete him from your social network.

   Tapping the Edit button returns you to the screen shown earlier in Figure 8-8. There, you can update or add information. Finished? Tap the Save button to save your changes.

   Described in the previous section, the Pin to Start button transforms a contact into a Start screen tile, giving you easy access to her contact information and latest status updates.

You can send e-mail from within the People app by tapping a person's name. When her contact information appears, tap the Send Email button. The Mail app appears, bearing a previously addressed New Message window, ready for you to type your message and tap Send. (This trick works only if you have that contact's e-mail address.)

If the People app imported contacts from your Facebook or Twitter accounts, you can't delete any of their imported contact information. But you can *add* information to their contacts page.

Seeing too many contacts in the People app? Filter out the social networks you *don't* want included by fetching the Charms bar, tapping Settings, and tapping Accounts from the Settings pane. There, you can tap check boxes next to the social networks you want to see, leaving the others unchecked.

Managing Appointments in Calendar

If you manage your appointments on Google's online Calendar or one of Microsoft's accounts, you're in luck: Windows 8's Calendar app will harvest that information automatically, just like the People app. The Calendar app also picks up any birthdays it finds on Facebook.

Then it neatly packages all the past, present, and future activity into the Calendar app, shown in Figure 8-9.

Figure 8-9:
The Calendar app stocks itself with appoint-ments added from your online social networks, as well as those you add manually.

Don't keep your appointments online? Then you'll need to add everything by hand. Even if your appointments *are* online, you occasionally need to edit old entries, add new ones, or delete ones that conflict with new engagements. This section explains how to keep your appointments up-to-date.

To add an appointment to your Calendar app, follow these steps:

1. **Tap the Calendar tile on the Start screen.**

The Calendar appears (refer to Figure 8-9).

2. Open the App bar and tap the New icon.

Slide your finger up from the screen's bottom edge to reveal the App bar and its icons, including the New icon for creating new appointments.

3. Fill out the Details form.

Shown in Figure 8-10, most of the choices are pretty easy to figure out: Date, Time, Duration, Title, and *Message* — a space where you can add notes about what to bring to the potluck.

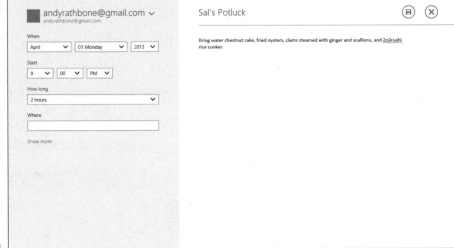

Figure 8-10:
Add your appointment's date, start time, duration, and other details.

The Calendar app will send your appointment to your online calendar, as well, if you have one. To see your options, tap the downward-pointing arrow next to your calendar's name in the top left corner. A menu appears, letting you choose which online calendar should receive the appointment.

Android phone owners should choose their Google account, so their appointment also appears on their phone. Microsoft phone owners, of course, should choose their Microsoft account.

Microsoft's apps don't coordinate well with Apple's online products. But Apple people all own iPads, anyway.

4. Tap the Save button.

The Calendar app adds your new appointment to your tablet's Calendar, as well as to the calendar of the online account you chose in Step 3.

When browsing the Calendar app, these tips will help you find your way around:

- ✔ The Calendar opens to show the view it last displayed, be it day, week, or month. To switch to other views, slide your finger up from the screen's bottom edge to fetch the App bar. Then tap one of the buttons: Day, Week, or Month (shown in the margin).

- ✔ To delete an appointment, open it from the Calendar. Then tap the Delete button (shown in the margin) in the appointment's upper-right corner.

- ✔ To edit an appointment, simply open it with a tap on its entry in the Calendar app. Make your changes, and save your edits with a tap on the Save icon.

- ✔ When browsing the Calendar app, flip through the appointments by flipping your finger across the calendar as though you were paging through a book. Slide your finger to the left to move forward in time; slide to the right to move backward.

- ✔ To jump immediately to the current date, slide your finger up from the bottom to fetch the App bar; then tap Today.

Sending Messages with the Messaging App

True to its name, instant messaging programs let you swap messages with friends almost *instantly*. A tap on the Enter key, and your carefully crafted sentence flies across the Internet and onto your friend's screen. Your friend replies, returning the volley with another tap of the Enter key.

Windows 8's friendly Messaging app lets you type back and forth with any contact listed in your People app. It even handles the mechanics of facilitating interprogram banter: Your friend could be typing in Facebook's instant messaging window, while you're typing back in the Messaging app's window.

To type messages back and forth to an online friend, follow these steps:

1. **From the Start screen, tap the Messaging tile.**

   The Messaging app fills the screen (see Figure 8-11).

2. **Tap the plus sign at the right of the Start a Conversation box.**

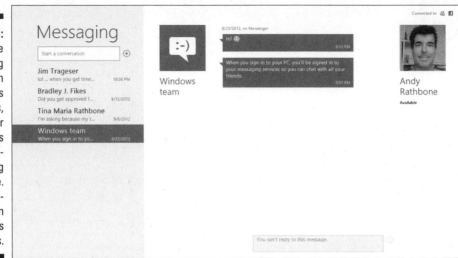

Shown in the top-left corner of Figure 8-11, the plus sign fetches the People app's Online mode, which lists only friends who are currently online and available for chatting. If a friend doesn't appear here, he's either not online, not available for chatting, or not listed in your People app.

3. **Tap the name of the person you want to chat with.**

When the messaging window appears, begin typing, as shown in Figure 8-12. Your friend's own messaging system, whether it's on Facebook, a cellphone, or a different system, will load, letting her know you're starting to chat with her.

4. Type your message; then press Enter.

As you type, feel free to edit your message. Your message isn't sent until you press Enter. When you press Enter, your message appears in your friend's messaging program. When you both finish chatting, simply stop typing, and move onto something else.

Even when closed, the Messaging app keeps an archive of your conversation, and if you two chat again, the archive will grow longer.

And that brings us to these tips regarding instant messaging etiquette and technique:

✔ To delete a conversation, tap it; it becomes highlighted. Slide your finger up from the bottom of the Messaging app to fetch the App bar. Then tap the Delete icon, shown in the margin.

✔ Don't want to be bothered for awhile? Tap the App bar's Status icon, shown in the margin, and choose Invisible from the pop-up menu. That keeps you from showing up as available in your friends' messaging programs. To reappear to your circle of friends, tap the Status icon and choose Online from the pop-up menu.

✔ Don't be too eager to type. Conversations flow best if you wait for a response before sending another message. Flurries of quick messages make for a disjointed conversation, like a debate full of interruptions.

✔ To monitor who's online and ready to chat, open the People app and slide your finger up from the bottom to unveil the App bar. Tap the Online Only button (shown in the margin) to see friends available for chatting.

✔ Extended chats on a virtual glass keyboard can be difficult, because the keyboard covers half of the screen. Switching to a USB or Bluetooth keyboard lets your sparkling wit shine through that much more easily. I cover tablet accessories in Chapter 18.

✔ At the time of this writing, the Messaging app works only with MSN and Facebook's messaging services. But Microsoft updates its apps regularly, so don't be surprised to see other messaging services added.

Chapter 9

Working with Apps and Programs

*W*indows 8 brings many changes, but one of the most baffling is that it no longer likes the word *program*. Programs — software for writing letters or playing games — are now called *apps* in the world of Windows 8.

This holds true for both Start screen apps and those programs, *er*, apps, that run on the traditional Windows desktop.

But because the word "program" still appears on your software boxes and installation discs, this chapter refers to Windows desktop software as *programs*.

Mini-programs that run on the Start screen are called *apps*. With that bit of wordplay taken care of, this chapter tackles a more important topic: Just what can a person *do* with the darn things?

Mini- cheat sheet for apps

The Start screen serves up a smorgasbord of apps that perform different tasks. But no matter how much the apps differ, they all share the same basic commands. These tips work in *every* app, whether it's bundled with Windows 8 or added from the Store app:

✔ **Open an app:** From the Start screen, tap the app's tile with a finger. (You can return to the Start screen with a tap of your tablet's Windows key.)

✔ **Close an app:** Apps needn't be closed, as I explain in Chapter 4. But if you *really* want to close your currently viewed app, slide your finger all the way down the tablet's screen, from the top edge to bottom edge.

✔ **Change an app's settings:** Fetch the Charms bar by sliding your finger inward from the screen's right edge. Then tap the Charms bar's Settings icon.

✔ **Search an app's contents:** Fetch the Charms bar, tap the bar's Search icon, and type your search term in the Search box.

✔ **Print from an app:** Fetch the Charms bar, tap the bar's Device's icon, and tap your printer's name. (Not all apps can print.)

✔ **View an app's menus:** Slide your finger up from the screen's bottom edge or down a bit from the top edge.

✔ **Return to your last-used app:** Slide your finger from the screen's left edge to the right edge; your last-used app drags into view.

✔ **See currently running apps:** Slide your finger in slightly from the screen's left edge and then back to the left edge. A strip appears along the left edge, displaying thumbnails of your currently running apps. To return to an app, tap its thumbnail.

Making the Most of Windows 8's Apps

You can download and install new apps, covered later in this chapter's "Downloading new apps from the Windows Store" section, but Windows 8 comes with more than a dozen built-in apps. Most of them live right on the Start screen for easy access. Although your tablet's manufacturer may add or remove a few apps to your tablet, the following apps usually appear on every tablet:

✔ **Bing:** You can search for websites directly from Internet Explorer, but Microsoft's Bing search engine app brings a more finger-friendly interface, with its larger buttons and handy autocomplete of search terms.

✔ **Calendar:** This handy app lets you enter your upcoming appointments, of course, but it can also automatically fetch appointments you've made in online calendars created through accounts with Google or Microsoft. The app then blends appointments from several sources into one calendar. I cover the Calendar app in Chapter 8.

✔ **Camera:** All Windows 8 tablets include a camera, and often two. Your tablet's front camera works best for vanity shots, whereas the back camera is more suited for scenic vistas, if you don't mind looking dorky while holding up your tablet to frame the wonders of nature. I explain how to use your tablet's camera in Chapter 11's "Snapping photos or videos" section.

✔ **Desktop:** A tap of the Start screen's Desktop tile fetches the traditional Windows desktop (covered in Chapter 5). There, you'll find most of Windows usual accessories. The Desktop app lets you run all of your old, traditional Windows programs. (Windows RT tablets include the desktop, but those tablets can't install your older Windows software.)

✔ **Finance:** This tile shows a 30-minute delay of the Dow, NASDAQ, and S&P. Tap the tile to open the Finance app, filled with charts, indices, news, rates, and stocks you've added to your personalized Watchlist.

✔ **Games:** A tap of the Games app brings the Xbox Games app, a link to your Xbox game console. Here, you can see your friends and gaming achievements, as well as watch game trailers and buy new Xbox games. (The app also lists a few free games to play on your tablet.)

✔ **Internet Explorer:** I cover this stripped-down version of Internet Explorer in Chapter 7. This no-nonsense browser site fills the screen with your currently viewed website, with no messy menus or tabs to get in the way. (To see the app's menus, slide your finger up from the screen's bottom edge.)

✔ **Mail:** Described in Chapter 8, this simple app lets you send and receive files and e-mail. It works in conjunction with your People app, automatically filling in e-mail addresses as you begin typing in a person's name.

✔ **Maps:** The Maps app brings up a version of Microsoft Bing Maps. If your tablet lacks a *Global Positioning System* (GPS) chip, the Maps won't find your exact location or offer turn-by-turn navigation. (Tablets sold with cellular data plans usually contain a GPS; tablets without cellular rarely do.)

✔ **Messaging:** This universal instant message program (covered in Chapter 8) lets you swap text messages to friends through Facebook, Microsoft's Instant Messenger, and other instant messaging programs.

✔ **Microsoft SkyDrive:** This app lets you stash files online. In addition to letting you share files with other computers, it's also a convenient way to add storage to a space-deprived tablet. I cover SkyDrive and other storage solutions in Chapter 6.

✔ **Music:** This music player (covered in Chapter 12) plays music stored on your tablet or stashed away on SkyDrive (Chapter 6). It's also a gateway to Xbox Live Music, which offers an array of streaming music options to owners of an Xbox game console.

✔ **News:** Drop by here to read news pulled from a wide variety of sources, from ABC News to WorldCrunch.

- **People:** The People app (covered in Chapter 8) contains your friends' contact information. You can enter or edit the details yourself, or let the app automatically harvest your friends' information from your Facebook, Twitter, Google, or other online networks.

- **Photos:** The Photos app (covered in Chapter 11's "Viewing photos" section) lets you show off your photos, whether they're stored on your tablet or on accounts from Facebook, Flickr, SkyDrive, or even other Windows computers on your network. It can even import photos from your digital camera.

- **Reader:** Many downloadable documents and manuals come stored in Adobe's *Portable Document Format* (PDF), and this app opens them for easy reading.

- **Sports:** Sports fans drop by here to see the latest team scores and game news. Open the App bar and tap Favorite Teams to create a mini-newspaper devoted to your favorite team's news and statistics.

- **Store:** To download new apps, visit the Windows Store, covered later in this chapter's "Downloading new apps from the Windows Store" section.

- **Travel:** Designed around people who keep their suitcase packed, this app caters to impulse buyers. It's filled with tempting panoramic photos of travel hotspots, maps, reviews, and of course, links for booking flights and hotels.

- **Video:** This plays videos from your tablet and its storage areas, and also provides a portal to Xbox Video, covered in Chapter 11's "Watching movies" section.

- **Weather:** This personalized weather station grants you a weeklong glimpse into your city's future weather patterns. (Load the App bar and tap Places to add other cities to your crystal ball.)

Don't see all of the preceding apps listed on the Start screen? Then slide your finger up from the Start screen's bottom edge and tap the All Icons button. The Start screen then shows *all* of its available apps, including the ones not currently on the Start screen.

I explain the mechanics of the Start screen in Chapter 4, including tips on adding, removing, and organizing apps on the Start screen.

You can customize the News, Finance, Sports, and Weather apps to display information about your current interests, needs, or location, described in the next section.

Customizing apps to meet your needs

Microsoft's built-in apps come preset to cater to the widest audience. But once they're living on *your* tablet, take some time to make sure they cater to your own needs, rather than those of the masses.

In fact, these customization tricks apply to most apps, whether they came bundled with Windows 8 or through the Windows Store app.

To customize an app, follow these steps:

1. **Fetch the App bar by sliding your finger up slightly from the screen's bottom or down slightly from the screen's top.**

   Different apps treat their App bar differently. Some place their menus along the bottom; others drop them down from the top. Some do both.

2. **When the App bar appears, tap its buttons to customize the app to your needs.**

   Fetch the App bar in the News app, for example, and the top App bar offers three options (see Figure 9-1).

Figure 9-1: To customize an app, swipe your finger up from the screen's bottom or down from the top edge to fetch that particular app's App bar.

Here are the three options:

- **Bing Daily:** The equivalent of a browser's Home button, a tap of this button returns you to the News app's front page. (It's called Bing Daily because Microsoft's search engine, Bing, stocks it with news found on the Internet.)

- **My News:** Tap here to personalize your news with topics of interest to you. To start, tap the plus sign within the Add a New Section box; when the Add a Section screen appears, type a favorite topic. Tap the Add button, and the My News section collects stories on that topic. Revisit here to see the latest news about that specific subject.

Place quotes around your topic to include more than one word. For example, type **"brussels sprouts"** to see news only about today's trendy vegetable. Without the quotes, the app fetches news about Belgium and salad toppings.

- **Sources:** Want to read information from one favorite source? Tap the Sources option to read news from a particular new outlet, including *The New York Times, USA Today, Time Magazine, Fox News,* and the major networks.

After customizing the News app to meet your own interests, try these other tips to personalize your tablet's other apps:

✔ Traveling to a particular city? Open the Travel app, fetch the Charms bar with an inward swipe from the screen's right edge, and tap the Search icon. Type your destination and tap the Search key. When the travel guide shows your destination, swipe up from the screen's bottom edge and tap Pin to Start to place your personalized travel guide on the Start screen.

✔ Add your stock portfolio to the Finance app by fetching its App bar, tapping the Watchlist button, and tapping the plus sign to add stock symbols. After you add your portfolio, tap any of the stock's symbols to see detailed information about a stock's historical value.

✔ The Weather app normally knows your current location, but fetch the App bar, tap Places, and tap the plus sign button to add other cities. It's handy to know the weather where your relatives live, or where you travel frequently.

✔ Fetch the App bar in the Sports app, and you can add your favorite teams, as well as jump to news dedicated to football, basketball, baseball, hockey, golf, racing, or soccer. Don't care about a particular sport? Tap the App bar's All Sports button, select the sports you dislike, and tap the Remove button to nix that sport's coverage.

✔ If you don't see any way to customize your app on its App bar menu, fetch the Charms bar and tap the Settings icon. When the Settings pane appears, check the list near the top edge. Some options let you change or personalize your app's behavior.

Organizing your apps

Microsoft sets up your Start screen so it looks pretty in magazine ads. When first set up, it's designed to appeal to a mythical consumer, not you.

So, personalize your Start screen to meet your own needs. As I explain in Chapter 3 (in a section on organizing the Start screen), you can remove tiles for apps you don't use, add tiles for apps you *do* use, move related tiles into groups, and move oft-used tiles to the far left, so they're easy to tap. As a result, Microsoft's tablet will start looking a lot more like *your* tablet.

Downloading new apps from the Windows Store

Windows 8 comes with a plenty of built-in apps, described in this chapter's first section. But sooner or later, those won't be enough. When you need to beef up your tablet with more features, you have an app for that: the Windows Store app.

Apps downloaded from the Store let you build Windows 8 around your own interests. Birdwatchers can download bird-watching tools. Sailors can download tide prediction apps. Cooks can download recipe collections.

As programmers write more apps to fill in different niches, Windows 8 keeps growing, and best of all, most of the apps are free.

Because Windows RT tablets can't run desktop programs, they're limited to apps downloaded from the Store app.

To add new apps to your tablet, follow these steps:

1. **Open the Store app.**

   If you're not already on the Start screen, head there with a tap of the Windows key. Tap the Store app's tile, and the Store app fills the screen, shown in Figure 9-2.

Figure 9-2:
In its upper-
right corner,
the Store
app lets you
search for
new apps,
and it lists
how many
updates are
available for
your apps.

If any of your apps have available *updates* — newer versions that add features or fix problems — the store lists them in its upper-right corner. (I cover updates in this chapter's next section.)

The Store app never shows you *all* of its apps. Some apps are limited to people living in certain countries, for example, and Windows RT tablet owners won't see apps that run only on Windows 8 tablets. (Windows 8 tablet owners see both types of apps.)

2. **Browse for apps, tapping interesting apps to read their description, details, and reviews left by others.**

   You can search for a specific app, as I describe in the next step. But if you feel like browsing, the Store app offers many ways to window- shop its app collection.

   As you browse, watch for the left-pointing arrow in the screen's top-left corner. Tap that arrow to return to the Store page you just left.

   To explore the apps, drop by these places in the Store:

   • **Top Free:** Be sure to tap the Top Free tile, as it lets you see the most popular apps that won't cost a penny to try out. Each Store category offers its own Top Free tile, which lets you limit your search to that particular category.

   • **New Releases:** Although a tap of this tile fetches the latest stuff, it's a mixed bag. There's no filter, so expect to see apps written for other languages or countries. Few shoppers will be interested in an app devoted to another country's railroad timetables, for example.

- **Categories:** As you scroll toward the Store app's right side, the Store's categories appear: Games, Social, Entertainment, Photo, Music & Video, Sports, Books & Reference, News & Weather, Health & Fitness, Food & Dining, Lifestyle, Shopping, Travel, Finance, Productivity, Tools, Security, Business, Education, and Government.

Tap any category's name to browse apps in that category. Some categories offer subcategories. Tap the Games category, for example, shown in Figure 9-3, and you can sort the apps by their game type (adventure or playing card, for example), price, rating, and more.

Figure 9-3: When browsing app categories, tap the drop-down menus along the top to sort the offerings in different ways.

If you spot the app of your dreams, head to Step 4 to install it onto your tablet. If you still can't find the right app, move to the next step and search for it.

3. **Search for an app.**

When you can't find what you want by browsing, try searching. Like every other search in Windows 8, searching for an app begins with a trip to the Charms bar:

1. Slide your finger inward from the screen's right edge, and tap the Search icon.

2. When the Search pane appears, type a keyword or two that describes your app in the Search box, then tap the keyboard's Search key.

Windows searches the Store, shown in Figure 9-4, listing all the matches.

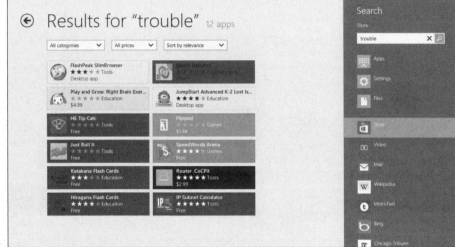

Figure 9-4:
Tap the Charms bar's Search icon to search the Store by subject.

4. **Tap an app's name to read more about it.**

The app's page in the Store appears, shown in Figure 9-5, offering three ways to see more about the app.

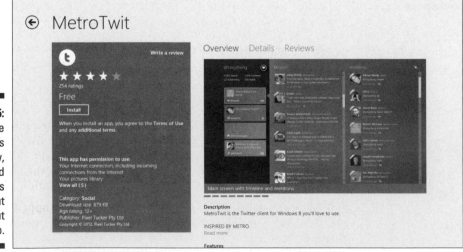

Figure 9-5:
Tap the words Overview, Details, and Reviews to find out more about the app.

- **Overview:** The app shows this page by default (refer to Figure 9-5). Here, you see a picture and description of the app, its features, and ways to see more information: the app's website, for example, as well as the app's support page, and legal terms.

  Slide your finger across the app's picture to see additional photos. Most apps offer two or more photos of how the app will look on your tablet.

- **Details:** This boring page may be the most important. It elaborates on the details shown in the app's far-right pane, lists what bugs were fixed in the latest release, what processors the app supports, and the permissions it requires.

  Windows RT tablets can install only apps written for ARM processors. Windows 8 tablets, by contrast, can run only apps written for x86, x64 processors. (As you browse, the Store only shows you the apps that will run on your particular tablet.)

- **Reviews:** The most enlightening part of choosing an app comes from reading the reviews. Here, owners leave comments based on their experience. Read the comments with a grain of salt, as different people have different expectations.

By looking at an app's pictures and reading an app's Overview, Details and Reviews pages, you can determine whether the app's right for you or whether you should continue browsing.

5. **Install or buy the app.**

   When you've found an app you want to place on your tablet, the app's page (shown earlier in Figure 9-5) displays any of three buttons:

   - **Install:** Found on free apps, this button lets you tap it to install the program onto your tablet. Within a minute or so after you tap the Install button, the app appears on the far right end of your Start screen, ready to launch with a tap of its tile.

   - **Try:** Found on paid apps, tap this button to try out the app for a week. After a week, the app expires unless you tap the Buy button, opening your wallet for the app's full price.

   - **Buy:** Paid apps cost anywhere from $1.49 to $999.99, but most cost less than five dollars. Tapping the Buy button lets you purchase the app immediately if you've already linked a credit card with your Microsoft account. No credit card link? Then the Buy button takes you to a secure website to enter that information.

   If you don't see a button, the words You Own This App appear, meaning you've already downloaded the app. If it's missing from your Start screen, tap the All Apps button on the Start screen's App bar (as I explain in Chapter 4), which presents an alphabetical list of *all* the apps installed on your tablet.

6. **Wait for the app to download.**

   Most apps download in less than a minute or two. Apps that take much
   longer usually warn you that you'll be pumping a lot of data into your
   tablet. If you're connecting via the Internet through a cellular service (as
   described in Chapter 6), wait until you're connected to a Wi-Fi connection,
   so you can avoid going over your data limit.

   When the app finishes downloading, a notice pops up in the screen's
   upper-right corner telling you the app was installed.

7. **Load the app.**

   The Start screen always hides your latest app downloads along its
   far-right edge. To find them, keep sliding your finger across the Start
   screen from right to left until you reach the end of the Start screen. (If
   you decide to keep the app, you can refer to Chapter 4 for information
   on how to organize the Start menu.)

Microsoft designed the Store to be as easy to use as possible. You can
browse for something that looks interesting, or you can search for exactly
what you want.

As the number of apps increases, you'll be able to add many extra powers
to your tablet quickly and easily — a welcome change from the days of old
when you needed to slide discs into your computer, hoping everything would
work.

> ✔ Apps you purchase from the Windows Store can be run on up to five
>   of the PCs or tablets linked to your Microsoft account. You can buy an
>   app for your tablet and then install the same app without charge on four
>   other Windows 8 PCs at home and work.
>
> ✔ When browsing for apps, be sure to tap the Reviews button on the app's
>   page in the Store. That lets you read what other people think of the app,
>   helping you weed out apps that don't perform well.
>
> ✔ The Store app is one of the few apps that don't *autorotate*: If you hold
>   your tablet in portrait mode, the Store app stays stuck in a sideways
>   position. Don't think something's wrong with your tablet. The Store app
>   insists on being held sideways.

Updating your apps

Apps constantly change. Companies release new versions to add features and
patch security holes. A few weeks later, they release yet another new version
to fix problems with the *last* update. It's a never-ending cycle.

When an update for one or more of your apps arrives, you'll know it by the Store app tile: A little number appears in the tile's bottom-right corner, letting you know how many of your apps have waiting updates.

Luckily, updating apps on a Windows 8 tablet works much more easily than it did on older desktop PCs. To update your apps, follow these steps:

1. **From the Start screen, tap the Store tile.**

   The Store app appears (shown earlier in Figure 9-2).

2. **Tap the word *Updates* in the Store app's upper-right corner.**

   The App Updates screen appears (see Figure 9-6), listing the waiting updates. They're all *selected* — ready to be updated — as seen by the little check mark in their upper-right corner. Want to download an update later? Then tap an unwanted app's tile, and the check mark disappears.

Figure 9-6: Tap the Install button from along the bottom of the App Updates screen to install the waiting updates for every selected app.

To download the app later when you have more time, repeat these steps; the app update will still be waiting.

3. **Tap the Install button at the bottom of the screen.**

   Windows immediately begins downloading and installing the updates.

Most programmers update their apps on a regular basis, adding new features and patching security problems. Some updates, however, add features you don't want. And some updates even cause unexpected problems.

How do you know whether to install an update or not? There's no one way of knowing, but try these tips when making your decision:

✔ When an update says it solves security problems, install it. You don't want to leave your tablet open to potential problems.

✔ Before updating, open the Store app, find the app that's receiving updates, and read the latest reviews. If an update causes problems, people who've updated usually complain about it, letting you know something's wrong.

✔ If you're not having problems with an app, and the update doesn't address any security issues, don't feel obliged to update it immediately. Wait a few days; then read the app's reviews in the Store app. If nobody complains of problems, the app's probably safe to install.

Uninstalling or changing an app

Before you can uninstall or change an app, you need to *select* its tile on the Start screen. Oddly enough, selecting an app's tile isn't something you'll stumble upon on your own.

So, here's the secret to selecting an app on the Start screen: Slide the app slightly upward or downward with your finger.

After you select an app, a check mark appears in the app's top-right corner, like the News app shown in Figure 9-7. The App menu also appears along the bottom, listing everything you can do with your newly selected app.

How much space does that app consume?

Running out of space on your tablet's skimpy hard drive? Some of your apps may be to blame. To see exactly how much space each of your apps consumes, follow these steps:

1. **Open the Charms bar, and tap the Settings icon.**

2. **When the Settings pane appears, tap the words *More PC settings*.**

3. **Tap the General category, and in the Available Storage section, tap View App Sizes.**

Windows quickly measures your app's sizes and then presents a list with the hoggiest ones at the top. It's only a list, though; it won't let you launch or uninstall apps.

I describe how to uninstall apps in the following section.

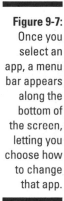

Figure 9-7:
Once you
select an
app, a menu
bar appears
along the
bottom of
the screen,
letting you
choose how
to change
that app.

✔ To uninstall an app, tap the Uninstall button from the App bar.

✔ App bar icons also let you change the size of an app's tile, start or stop the app's live updates, or unpin (remove) the app from the Start screen.

✔ In Windows 8, you select an item by sliding it in the *opposite* direction it normally moves. Because the Start screen scrolls from right to left, for example, you slide a tile up or down to select it. Use this trick whenever you want to select something in Windows 8 or within any of its apps.

✔ Selecting the Start screen tile of a traditional Windows desktop program brings a slightly different set of icons to the App bar. You can open the program in a new desktop window, pin it to the desktop's taskbar, or view its location in the desktop's File Explorer program.

✔ You can select more than one app at a time, which is handy when weeding out unwanted tiles to remove from the Start screen.

Installing Desktop Programs

Windows RT tablets include a traditional Windows desktop, but with one problem: Windows RT tablets won't let you install any programs onto the desktop. Instead, Windows RT tablets are limited to downloads from the Windows Store app, which usually isn't a problem because the Store adds more apps every day.

Windows 8 tablets, by contrast, include a fully functional desktop, just like the one found on desktop PCs. However, because tablets don't come with disk drives, how do you install a desktop program?

Windows 8 tablets give you several options:

✔ **Windows Store:** When you browse the Windows Store app with a Windows 8 tablet, many desktop programs appear on the Store's list of apps. When looking at a program you want, tap the Go to Publisher's Website link. The software publisher's website appears, where you can buy the program and download the program's installation file.

✔ **Website:** Desktop programs not listed in the Windows Store can still be downloaded directly from the Internet, just as in previous versions of Windows.

✔ **Flash drive:** All Windows tablets include a USB port. You can copy or download a program's installation file onto a flash drive with another computer and then insert the flash drive into your tablet and install it from there.

✔ **SkyDrive:** This online cubby hole (described in Chapter 6) works well for swapping files between your tablet and desktop PC. From your desktop PC, copy a program's installation file to any folder in SkyDrive. Then open the Start screen's SkyDrive app, visit the SkyDrive folder, and tap the program's installation file to install it.

There's another alternative, but it limits your tablet's portability. You can buy a DVD drive that plugs into your tablet, as I describe in Chapter 6, and then install the program directly from its CD or DVD. Be aware, though: plug-in DVD drives are battery hogs. Use them only when your tablet is plugged into the wall.

I explain how to download and automatically run files from a website in Chapter 7, but if you've downloaded a program and now need to find and run it, follow these steps:

1. **Open the Desktop app and tap the File Explorer icon.**

   The File Explorer icon appears, letting you peek into your tablet's folders.

2. **Navigate to the folder containing your program's installation file.**

   Downloaded files live in your Download folder, which you'll find listed in every desktop folder's left edge in the Favorites section.

   Tap the Download folder, and a window appears, listing every file you've downloaded from Internet Explorer.

3. **Double-tap the name of the program's installation file.**

   Two successive finger taps (which are the equivalent of a double-click) let the Windows desktop know that you're not just selecting the program for a name change — you want to *install* it.

4. **Tap through the warning screen.**

   A User Account Control window appears, warning you of potential damage. After all, you downloaded a program from the wilderness of the Internet, and now you want to install it on your computer.

   However, Windows 8's built-in malware detector already scanned the program as you downloaded it, so it's probably safe. So tap the Yes button, telling Windows to install your program.

5. **Follow the program's prompts, if necessary.**

   The program may ask you what language you prefer and in which folder it should set up camp, as well as recommend that you close all of your other programs. (Potential problems like this are what moved Microsoft to create Windows 8, with its simpler and more secure app system.)

When the program finally installs, it tosses a tile onto the Start screen's far-right edge. This annoyance can be fixed by shuffling the Start screen's tiles into more convenient positions (which I cover in Chapter 4).

Uninstalling a Desktop Program

You can remove desktop programs, as well as apps, directly from the Start screen. Unlike apps, though, desktop programs require you to jump through a few extra hoops.

To uninstall a desktop program from your tablet, follow these steps:

1. **From the Start screen, select your desktop program's app and choose Uninstall from the App bar.**

   Don't see your program's tile on the Start screen? Then move to Step 2.

   If you do see your desktop program on the Start screen, though, then select the program by sliding its tile slightly up or down. Then tap the Uninstall icon from the App bar along the screen's bottom edge. When the desktop's Control Panel opens to show its Uninstall or Change a Program window, skip ahead to Step 3.

2. **Not every desktop program appears on the Start screen. If yours doesn't, visit the Uninstall or Change a Program window manually:**

   1. From the Start screen, tap the Desktop tile. Then slide your finger in from the screen's right edge to fetch the Charms bar; then tap Settings icon. When the Settings pane appears, tap Control Panel from the pane's top.

   2. When the Control Panel appears, tap Uninstall a Program from the Programs section, and the Uninstall or Change a Program window appears.

3. **Tap the name of the program you want to uninstall; then tap the Uninstall button above it.**

4. **When asked if you want to remove the program, tap the Yes button.**

   Windows removes the program from your computer. If you've created files with that program, those files stay on your computer. However, unless your tablet has another app or program that knows how to open those files, you may not be able to access them.

Chapter 10

Working in Microsoft Office

In This Chapter

▶ Opening a document

▶ Starting a document from a template

▶ Saving and printing your work

▶ Taking notes with OneNote

*I*t's no coincidence that tablets with Windows RT include a free, installed copy of Microsoft's Office Home and Student 2013 RT. Those popular programs — Word, PowerPoint, Excel, and OneNote — are all many people need.

Tablets with Windows RT can read, save, and create Office files stored nearly anywhere: on your tablet, a flash drive, a networked PC, or on *SkyDrive*, the online storage place accessible by any PC.

These programs aren't pre-installed on tablets running Windows 8, but if you install them, this chapter helps bring you up to speed on the basics on opening, saving, and printing Office files.

Opening, Saving, and Printing in Office 2013 RT

Microsoft's Office Home and Student 2013 RT includes three popular programs designed specifically to run on tablets running Windows RT:

▸ **Word:** The industry-standard word processor, Word lets you create anything from letters to table-filled reports.

▸ **PowerPoint:** If you've sat through a corporate presentation shown on a projector or large TV, you've probably seen PowerPoint in action.

▸ **Excel:** A staple of accountants, Excel creates large tables for calculating complex formulas, handy for everything from household budgets to stock market projections.

Although the three programs do very different things, they all open, save, and print files in the same way.

This section walks you through each step of opening, saving, and printing files. I also explain how to save time by starting work with a free *template* — a pre-formatted document where you need only fill in the blanks.

OneNote, a note-organizing program, works a little differently, so I give it a separate section at the chapter's end.

Opening a document

Whether you want to create a new document, open an existing one, or start working from a template, follow these steps to open a document in Word, Excel, or PowerPoint:

1. **From the Start screen, tap the tile of the program you want to open: Word, Excel, or PowerPoint.**

   If you don't spot your desired program on the Start screen, tap the Desktop app's tile. When the desktop appears, tap your desired program's icon from the desktop's *taskbar*, that strip along the bottom, and your chosen program fills the screen.

2. **When your chosen program appears, tap what you'd like to open.**

   Microsoft Word, for example, shown in Figure 10-1, shows how each program offers four ways of starting work.

   • **Open a recently accessed document:** The Recent pane along the left edge lists your seven most-recently accessed documents. Tap a document name, and it returns to the screen, ready for more work.

   • **Start a new document:** Tap the Blank Document icon, and the program presents a blank page, ready for you to begin creating a new document from scratch.

Tap to open any of the last seven documents you worked on.

Search for free, downloadable templates.

Create a new document from scratch.

View a short tutorial.

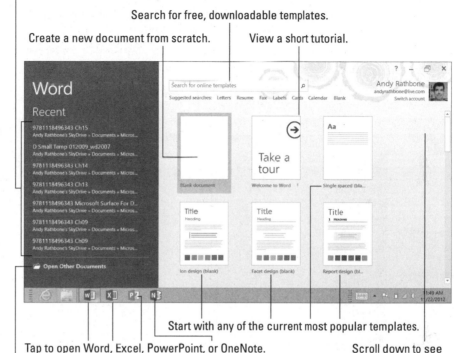

Figure 10-1:
Choose between an existing document, a template, or creating a new document from scratch.

Start with any of the current most popular templates.

Tap to open Word, Excel, PowerPoint, or OneNote.

Scroll down to see more popular templates.

Open documents not listed here.

- **Open a template:** Office's time-saving templates come pre-formatted, letting you concentrate on the content rather than the format or design. I give templates their own section later in this chapter.

- **Search for a new template:** Hundreds of templates await online. Type **resume** into the Search box, for example, tap the Enter key, and choose among dozens of pre-formatted resumés.

Taking the tour

Mixed in with other documents on the Open screen shown in Figure 10-1 is a tile called Take a Tour. By all means, tap the Take a Tour icon, even if you're familiar with the program. It offers a short guide and tips for how to put the program to work.

It's short, and it introduces some new features introduced in the version installed on your tablet with Windows RT: Office Home and Student 2013 RT, which Microsoft released in October, 2012. (It can still open your documents created in older versions of the program.)

If you want to open a document not listed here, move to Step 3.

3. **Tap Open Other Documents, navigate to your existing document, and load it with a tap of the Open button.**

Tap Open Other Documents from the bottom of the Recent pane, and the Open window appears, shown in Figure 10-2. The Open window lists your storage areas in the center column; to the right, it lists the currently selected storage area's most recently accessed folders and documents.

Tap to see documents stored in different areas.

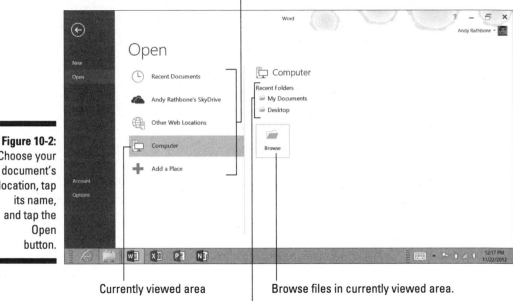

Figure 10-2:
Choose your
document's
location, tap
its name,
and tap the
Open
button.

Currently viewed area

Browse files in currently viewed area.

Recently opened folders in currently viewed area

To open a listed document, tap its name. Still don't see it? Then tap one of the Open window's five main storage areas:

• **Recent Documents:** The opening screen shown earlier in Figure 10-1 only shows your past seven recently accessed documents. This area, however, shows the past two dozen documents you've opened. If you've opened a document before, chances are, it's listed here, waiting to be opened with a tap.

• **SkyDrive:** This lets you open files stored on SkyDrive, your online storage space covered in Chapter 6. By storing your files on SkyDrive, you can work on them from any computer.

- **Other Web Locations:** Sometimes used by corporations, this lets you access folders stored on other websites.

- **Computer:** A popular choice, this shows recently accessed documents. It also offers a Browse button, where you can open files already stored on your tablet, or any stored on an attached flash drive or portable hard drive.

- **Add a Place:** Tap this shortcut to add other online storage places as Microsoft begins supporting them.

Tap the Browse button to navigate to documents inside a storage area, and then open your desired document with a tap on its name.

When you're having trouble finding a document, try any of these tips:

✔ When searching for a document you've worked on before, scan the Recent sections first. Tap likely suspects and take a peek. Guessed wrong? Close them with a tap in the program's upper- right corner and start again.

✔ Can't find a document *anywhere?* Then head back to the Start screen with a tap of your Windows key. Begin typing a keyword contained in your wayward document and tap the word *Files* in the Search pane that appears on the right. Your tablet lists every file containing the word you typed.

✔ To find and edit a file stored on a newly inserted flash drive or portable hard drive, tap Computer in Step 3 and then tap the Browse button. When a miniature File Explorer window appears, tap your flash drive's letter in the Computer section of the Navigation pane along the miniature window's right edge.

✔ You can also open documents directly from File Explorer. If you spot your desired document on your recently inserted flash drive, double-tap its name: The program that created the document appears, with your document in tow.

The fine print

The version of Office Home and Student 2013 bundled with Windows RT is the real thing: It's almost identical to the version of Office Home and Student 2013 sold in the stores for "normal" desktop computers. Microsoft explains the details of the differences at http://office.com/officeRT.

However, both versions of the program are licensed for *non-commercial* use only. To legally create documents for work, your business needs a volume licensing contract with Microsoft with commercial-use license coverage. Ask your business's IT person to see whether you qualify, and what additional options are available.

Starting from a template

In days of old, we often started from scratch with a sheet of paper. Yet that paper could probably be called a *template*: the preformatted lines across the page gave us something to follow as we wrote.

Today's templates offer much more than simple lines. Microsoft offers thousands of free templates for creating elaborate résumés, reports, invitations, schedules, calendars, and even stock reports that automatically create themselves when you type in a stock symbol.

To start working from a template, follow these steps:

1. **From the Start screen, tap the tile of the program you want to open: Word, Excel, or PowerPoint.**

2. **When the program appears, tap the template you'd like to open, and then tap Create to open the template.**

   Figure 10-1, shown earlier in this chapter, lists just a few of the many free templates available, sorted by current popularity. During the holidays, you see more party invitations in Word, for example; in September, you see more templates for school activities.

    To see other popular templates in Excel, for example, scroll down the screen by dragging the scroll bar down the screen. Tap any template's icon for a quick preview, shown in Figure 10-3.

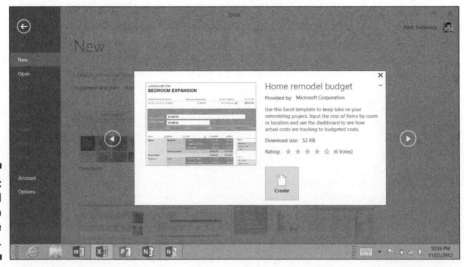

Figure 10-3: Tap a listed template to see more details.

If the current popular templates don't meet your needs, move to Step 3.

3. **Search for an unlisted template by typing a keyword in the Search for Online Templates bar along the top and tapping Enter. When you see a template you want, tap the Create button to download the template and begin working.**

Microsoft offers thousands of free templates online, searchable by key word. Type **Expense** into the Search bar (or tap the word *Expense* beneath the bar), for example, and Excel shows hundreds of expense-related templates shown in Figure 10-4.

Return to previous screen.   Tap to browse customized templates.

Type in a key word.   Tap categories to narrow your results.

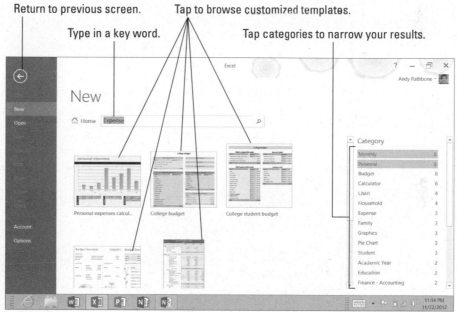

Figure 10-4: Tap a category to further narrow down your search.

Narrow your themes by choosing from the categories, shown along the right of Figure 10-4. Expense-related templates, for example, appear in the categories of Monthly and Personal.

Tap a template to see a preview, as shown earlier in Figure 10-3; tap the Create button to download and open the template.

Word, Excel, and PowerPoint offer thousands of templates from a wide variety of categories. It's much faster to adapt a template to meet your needs rather than starting from scratch.

✔ To save space, Microsoft didn't bundle Office templates with tablets running Windows RT. You must be connected to the Internet to download them.

✔ Before beginning a project, spend some time browsing and downloading potential templates. That way, you can still work from a template when offline.

✔ When installing Microsoft Office on your Windows 8 tablet, be sure to install the optional templates. Most tablets running Windows 8 offer more storage than tablets running Windows RT.

✔ To browse Microsoft's templates with Internet Explorer, visit `http://office.microsoft.com/en-us/templates`. Templates you download await you in your Downloads folder, available in the Navigation pane along the left edge of every folder.

Saving your work

As soon as you begin creating your document, *save it*. By saving it, you've done two things:

✔ You've created something to fall back on just in case you accidentally mess up your current work.

✔ You've created a starting point should you need to rush out the door and return later.

To save your work in Word, Excel, or PowerPoint, follow these steps:

1. **Tap the Save icon in the screen's top left corner.**

   The Save icon, which resembles a 25-year-old floppy disk, fetches the Save As window, shown in Figure 10-5.

2. **Choose a location for your document.**

   Two choices await you, depending on your plans for the document:

   • **SkyDrive:** Choose this, your storage space on the Internet, if you plan on accessing the document from other computers. I describe SkyDrive in Chapter 6.

   • **Computer:** If you plan on keeping the document on your tablet or e-mailing it to somebody, choose this option, and then select My Documents as your final destination. Every program and app can easily access files stored inside that folder.

3. **Choose a name for your document and tap the Save button.**

   Your program offers a generic name, like **Presentation1**, which certainly won't help you locate your work. Change the suggested name to something more descriptive that will help you remember the document next week.

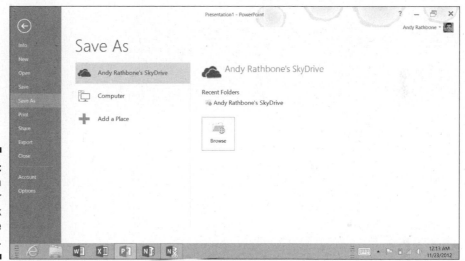

Figure 10-5:
Choose a
name for
your work
and a place
to save it.

Printing your document

After you've finished and saved your document, follow these steps to print your finished work in Word, Excel, or PowerPoint:

1. **Tap the word *File* from the Ribbon menu.**

   The Ribbon menu stretches across each program's top. Tapping different words on the Ribbon — *Format*, for example — shows different commands related to your document.

   Tapping File reveals *file*-related commands, shown in Figure 10-6, including Print.

Tap to print   Number of copies

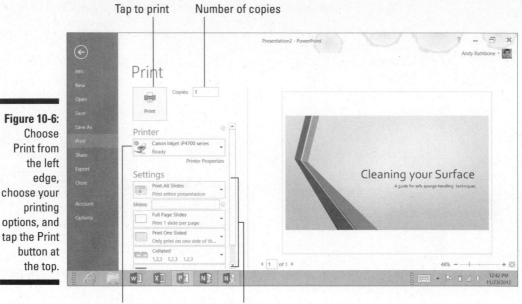

Figure 10-6:
Choose
Print from
the left
edge,
choose your
printing
options, and
tap the Print
button at
the top.

Select between printers   Printer options

2. **Choose your printer and adjust its settings, if necessary, and tap Print.**

   If you only want one copy of your document sent to the printer you normally use, just tap the Print button.

   If you need to do a little tweaking, adjust the settings shown in Figure 10-6 before tapping the print button.

   ✔ Desktop programs include built-in print commands that allow more customized print jobs. Start screen apps, by contrast, require you to open the Charms bar, choose Devices, and select your printer in order to print.

   ✔ Need to give a PowerPoint presentation? I explain how to connect your tablet to a projector or external display in Chapter 6.

Taking Notes with OneNote

A computerized three-ring tabbed binder, Microsoft's OneNote organizes your notes. It's not picky, letting you add notes in *any* form: typed by hand, copied from websites, recorded as audio, captured as a photograph or video, or even handwritten with a stylus on the tablet's screen.

Students have embraced OneNote because it lets them open a Chemistry section, create a new tab for each new lecture or subject, and fill it with freeform notes, including photos of the blackboard or hand-written equations.

OneNote organizes your notes in three main ways:

✔ **Notebooks:** Everything starts with a notebook, which holds all of your notes. You can create as many notebooks as you wish, each designed around its own theme. OneNote starts with two notebooks: The Personal notebook contains notes dealing with you and your home; the Work notebook helps you track your work-related projects.

✔ **Categories:** Each notebook can have several categories to separate your projects. The Home notebook can have a Remodeling category, for example, as well as a Shopping List category.

✔ **Pages:** Here's where you break down your categories even further. The Home notebook's Recipe category can have a page for each recipe.

Follow these steps to create a new Notebook in OneNote, add new categories, and add pages to the categories:

1. **Open OneNote, tap File from the top menu and tap New.**

   To create a new notebook, begin by choosing a storage location, usually SkyDrive, so it can be accessed from any of your computers. Then type a name for your Notebook, in this case, Shopping List.

2. **Choose whether to share your notebook with others.**

   When the Microsoft OneNote window appears, you can tap the Invite People button to give others access to your OneNote file. That's handy when creating projects at work, for example, or creating a shopping list that can be on every family member's phone.

   To keep it private, tap the Not Now button; you can always share it later.

3. **Type notes into your project, adding Categories and Pages as needed.**

   OneNote appears, shown in Figure 10-7, letting you add Categories and pages to organize your notes. If you want, save time by starting from a template: Tap Insert from the top menu, choose Page Templates from the drop-down menu, and choose from the templates offered on the screen's right edge.

4. **To add a category tab, tap the plus sign to the right of the last tab and then type the category's name.**

   Figure 10-7 offers two categories, for example: one for 99 Ranch Supermarket, the other for a local health food store. Each category contains a shopping list for a different store.

Choose other notebooks

Current category

Other category

Current notebook   Add new category   Other pages   Add page

Current page

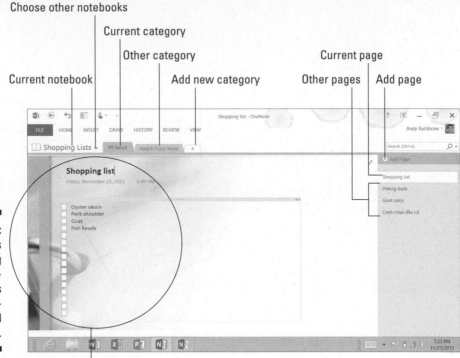

Figure 10-7:
This
Shopping
List note-
book shows
two cat-
egories and
three pages.

To-Do list template

To change or delete a tabbed category, rest your finger on its tab until the pop-up menu appears, and then choose your option.

5. **To add a page to the currently viewed category, tap the words** *Add Page* **atop the right column and type in a page name.**

   For example, the 99 Ranch category lists some recipes for favorite dishes, making it easy to look over the ingredient list while at the store.

When you're through taking notes, simply stop and close the program with a tap on the X in its upper-right corner. The program automatically saves your work with the name and location you chose in Step 1.

Microsoft offers OneNote for PCs, Apple computers, and every smartphone, letting access your notes from nearly any location.

Part III
Media

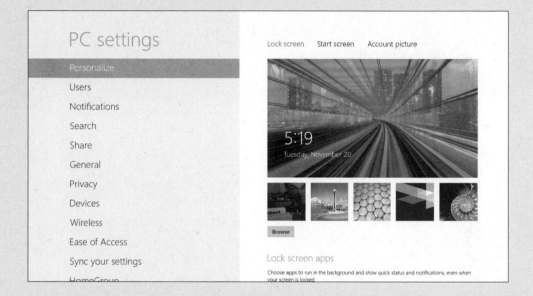

To find out how to play your own media on your Windows 8 tablet, go to `www.dummies.com/extras/windows8fortablets`.

In this part . . .

✔ Know how to open, create, save, and print documents in Microsoft Word, Excel, PowerPoint, and OneNote.

✔ Copy photos from your digital camera to your tablet, as well as download and watch movies.

✔ Listen to music through Xbox Live, as well as music copied onto your tablet.

Chapter 11

Photos and Video

Most Windows 8 tablets include two cameras, one on the front and the other on the back. Taking photos with a tablet rarely satisfies, though. There's no viewfinder, and reflections tend to obscure the subject on the screen. Forget about flash or zooming in.

As for quality, your ever-present smartphone probably takes better pictures. Shooting pictures with a tablet just feels awkward compared with shooting through a phone or camera. No, your tablet shines when *displaying* photos and videos, and this chapter walks you through doing both.

Note: Need to import photos from your digital camera or cell- phone? I explain how in Chapter 6.

Snapping Photos or Videos

Your tablet displays photos much better than it can capture them. But if you're struck with a Kodak moment and your tablet is the only camera you have handy, follow these steps to snap a photo or movie:

1. **From the Start menu, tap the Camera app's tile.**

   The Camera app appears, shown in Figure 11-1, immediately filling the screen with what it sees before its tiny front or rear lens. (Note how the Camera app's light begins glowing next to the lens, letting you know you're on camera.)

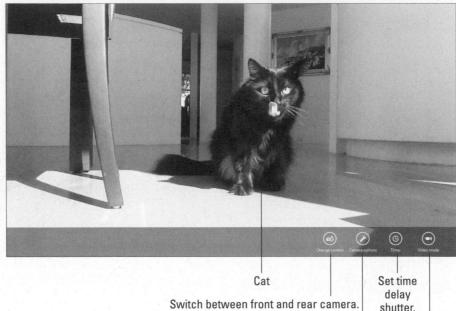

Figure 11-1: Change your desired controls from the App bar, and then touch any other part of the screen to snap the photo.

Cat

Switch between front and rear camera.

Set time delay shutter.

Change camera options.

Switch between camera and video mode.

2. **Change controls, if desired.**

Contrary to most apps, the Camera app *always* displays its App bar, which offers these options:

- **Change camera:** Tap this to toggle between the front and back cameras. (A light glows next to the camera lens in use.)

- **Camera options:** Rarely used, this button switches the settings from automatic to manual. The limited manual controls rarely work better than the automatic settings.

- **Timer:** Tap this to set a three-second shutter delay, which is *almost* enough time to spring in front of the camera for a group shot.

- **Video/Camera mode:** This toggles between shooting snapshots or videos.

3. **To snap a photo or shoot a movie, touch the screen.**

    When shooting a photo, the Camera app emits a mechanical shutter click sound, and then quickly saves the snapshot. Your new picture quickly scoots out of sight to the screen's left edge, letting you snap another photo.

    When shooting videos, a timer appears in the screen's lower- right corner, letting you track your movie's length. To stop shooting the movie, tap the screen.

To view your newly shot photo or movie, slide your finger from the screen's center toward the right edge. That drags your photo (or the first frame of your movie) back into view. To return to shooting, slide your finger in the other direction, and the live view reappears.

Whether you're looking at a recently shot photo or movie, the Camera app offers a few ways to edit your work, all found on the App bar. (Slide your finger up from the screen's bottom to reveal the App bar):

 ✔ **Crop:** Tap this when viewing a photo, and a rectangle appears. Drag the entire rectangle or just its corners to frame a different portion of the photo. Tap OK to crop, and the app saves your crop as a new picture, preserving the original photo.

 ✔ **Trim:** Tap this when viewing a movie, and a circle appears at each end of the video's timeline, shown along the screen's bottom. Drag the circles along the timeline to mark the video's new start and stop points. Then tap OK to save your video.

Your photos and videos both live in your Picture library's Camera Roll folder, where they can be viewed with the Photos app, described in the next two sections.

Viewing Photos

The Photos app, just like the People app, makes the rounds of your social networks, picking up any photos it can find. Open the Photos app with a tap of its Start screen tile, and the results appear, shown in Figure 11-2.

Figure 11-2: The Photos app shows photos currently on your tablet, as well as online locations like SkyDrive, Facebook, Flickr, and networks.

The Photos app shows a different tile for each place your photos reside. In Figure 11-2, for example, the first tile contains photos in your tablet's own Pictures library. (The other tiles require an Internet connection for access.)

Follow these steps to view your photos:

1. **Tap the storage area you want to open.**

   To view photos stored directly on your tablet, including ones shot with your tablet's camera, tap Pictures Library. If you have Internet access, tap the other tiles to view photos stored online.

2. **Browse the folders.**

   Tap the Pictures library tile, for example, and the screen shows tiles representing each folder inside that library. Tap a folder to open it.

   To back out of a folder, tap the backward-pointing arrow in the top-left corner. Keep tapping the arrow, and you'll eventually return to the Photos app opening menu, shown earlier in Figure 11-2.

3. **Tap a photo to view it full screen.**

   When the photo fills the screen, zoom in or out by pinching or stretching the photo between your fingers. To see its menus, shown in Figure 11-3, slide your finger up from the screen's bottom.

Return to previous view.

Figure 11-3: The Photos app lets you zoom in and out of photos with your fingertips and watch slide shows.

View original photo on web.

Start slide show of photos.

Set photo as background for Lock screen or Photos apps.

Depending on whether you're viewing a single photo, a folder's worth of photos, or several folders, the App bar sprouts different buttons:

 ✔ **Back Arrow:** A tap of the back arrow in the upper-right corner returns you to the folder containing the currently viewed app.

 ✔ **Set As:** This opens a pop-up menu, letting you turn your currently viewed photo into the background for your tablet's Lock Screen, the background for the Pictures app, or the Picture app's tile.

 ✔ **View on Web:** Seen only when viewing photos stored online, this takes you to the photo's location on Facebook, Flickr, SkyDrive, or elsewhere.

 ✔ **Slide Show:** A tap of this button launches a slide show of every photo in the currently viewed folder. To stop the show, tap a photo.

 ✔ **Select All:** This selects all the currently shown photos for later action, including Delete, Share, or Print. (If tapped by mistake, tap Clear Selection to return the selected items to normal.)

 ✔ **Browse by Date:** Seen when viewing folders, this lets you view your photos in chronological order, handy when showing a timeline of your vacation photos.

Tap the Import button to import photos from an attached camera or your memory card, as I describe in Chapter 6.

When displaying a single photo full-screen, the app bar offers buttons for letting you rotate and crop the image, handy for making profile photos out of group shots.

Sharing or Printing Photos

The Photos app lets you share or print photos by following these steps:

1. **Open the folder containing your photos, and then select the photos you want to share or print.**

   With your finger, swipe down on your desired photos. As you select them with a downward swipe, the selected photos sprout check marks in their upper-right corner.

2. **Visit the Charms bar and choose Share or Devices.**

   Swipe your finger inward from the screen's right edge to fetch the Charms bar, and tap either Share (for sharing with friends) or Devices (for printing your images).

   - **Share:** The Share pane opens, listing every app able to share your photo or video. A tap of the Mail app, for example, opens the Mail pane, where you enter the recipient's e-mail address and tap the Send button. (I cover mailing attached files in Chapter 8.)

   - **Devices:** The Devices pane appears, listing your installed printers. Tap your printer's name, and the Printer window appears, offering you a preview of the printed page. (I cover connecting printers and printing in Chapter 6.)

As more apps appear in the Windows Store, the Share pane offers more ways to share your photos and videos with different social networks. If your social network doesn't yet have an app, visit the site through Internet Explorer to share the photo.

Watching Movies

More a shopping mall than an app, Microsoft designed the Video app to pull you into its two storefronts: The Movies Store entices you buy or rent movies, and the Television Store sets the hook for TV shows. To make sure your wallet's available, you can only use the Video app when logged in with a Microsoft account.

Watching your *own* movies

Movies shot with your tablet's Camera app aren't listed in the Video app. To play them, slide your finger up from the screen's bottom to reveal the Video app's App bar. Tap the Open File icon, and then use the File Picker, covered in Chapter 4, to find your videos in your Pictures library's Camera Roll folder.

Your tablet works best with videos encoded in WMV or H.264/MP4 movie formats. If you already own movies in those formats, head for the Desktop app, covered in Chapter 5. There, you can copy your movies to a flash drive, insert the drive into your tablet, and copy the movies to your tablet's Videos library.

The app doesn't support other video formats, like shows recorded by Windows Media Center or TiVo. If your movies are encoded in another format, you need a conversion program to copy them into MP4 format.

To open the Video app and browse its wares, follow these steps:

1. **From the Start screen, tap the Videos tile.**

   The Video app appears, shown in Figure 11-4. The app immediately confuses things by changing its name to *Xbox Videos*. That's because the Video app lets you play videos to your Xbox game console, if you have one, so you can watch your movies on the big screen.

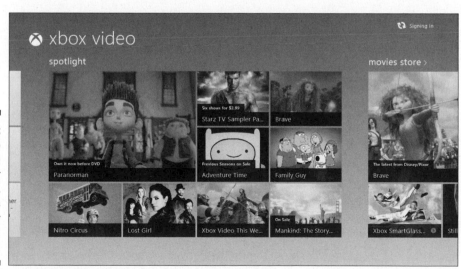

Figure 11-4: The Video app lets you watch your own videos, as well as rent or buy movies and TV shows.

2. **Browse to the type of video you want to watch.**

   The Video app offers four main sections:

   - **My Videos:** Scroll to the hidden area beyond the screen's left edge to see videos living in your tablet's Videos library.

   - **Spotlight:** Time-dated offers often appear here, letting you buy movies before they're released to DVD, for example.

   - **Movies Store:** Tap any tile to browse trailers, buy, or rent movies.

   - **Television Store:** Television shows appear here. (Some shows offer a free episode, usually a season opener.)

3. **Tap a video's tile to see more about it.**

   A window appears, with buttons that let you buy the video, see more about it, watch its trailer or, in the case of TV shows, buy a season package or individual episodes.

4. **Watch a video.**

   Tap a movie or TV show tile from the storefronts to rent, buy, or download the video to your My Videos section. The app charges the credit card associated with your Microsoft account, or prompts you to set one up.

   Tap any video in your My Videos section to begin watching. Swipe up from the screen's bottom to expose buttons for pausing, playing, and skipping forward/backward. The Play To button lets you play the video through your Xbox 360 game console, if you have one.

Before diving into the Video app with your credit card, keep these tips in mind:

- View free things at first to familiarize yourself with the process. Look for free TV pilots, movie trailers, or "behind the scenes" promo videos.

- Rental items and some specials are time-dated, meaning they'll disappear from your Videos library after a certain date.

- Before traveling, look for items with a Download option. After these items are downloaded, they can be viewed when you're out of range of a Wi-Fi connection.

- Before buying anything, you must type in your Microsoft account password, a safeguard against accidentally brushing against a Buy button.

- Don't think you're restricted to your tablet's Video app for movies. Netflix has its own app, letting you watch streaming movies. Amazon's videos are available too, if not in app form, then through your web browser.

Chapter 12

Listening to Music

Some people spend more time organizing their music than listening to it. They store each album in its own folder, meticulously renaming each song's title to include the album name and recording year.

Your tablet, however, isn't built for micromanaging your music collection. No, your tablet works best for *playing* music, and the Music app tries to simplify that task.

In fact, you don't even need your own music: Your tablet lets you stream music for free through something called an *Xbox Music Pass*. Or, you can stick to tunes you've copied onto the tablet.

This chapter covers both ways to listen to music: Listening to your own files, or streaming millions of songs from the Internet with Microsoft's new Xbox Music Pass.

Listening to Music through the Xbox Music Pass

When you first open the Music app on a new tablet, you won't find much but an empty shelf. After all, you haven't had time to copy any music onto it yet, a task I describe in Chapter 5.

Even an empty tablet, though, can dish out just about any song you want to hear. Those songs come from an *Xbox Music Pass,* a service Microsoft entices you with when you open the Music app.

If you have no interest in Microsoft's Xbox Music pass, jump to the next section, where you can simply start playing your own tunes.

But if you're curious as to Microsoft's way of letting you listen to more than 30 million songs for free, follow these steps to sample the Xbox Music Pass. (I explain the fine print at this section's end.)

1. **Load the Music app with a tap of its tile on the Start screen.**

   You must sign in with a Microsoft account to hear music through the Xbox Music Pass. The Music app, shown in Figure 12-1, contains four parts:

Figure 12-1:
The Music app's four sections cater to different interests.

• **My Music:** Hidden off to the left, the Music app shows songs or albums you've copied to your tablet's Music library.

• **Now Playing:** Shown when you first open the program, this area lists your currently playing song. Tap any of the surrounding buttons to begin hearing free music.

• **All Music:** Shown to the right of the Now Playing section, this area lists popular artists and albums, all ready to play with a tap.

• **Top Music:** Scroll to the far right to hear something quickly: a list of the latest chart- toppers, ready to play with a tap of a finger.

2. **In the Now Playing section, tap the Play an Artist tile, type in your favorite artist's name, and tap the Play button.**

   Before the music begins to play, however, you're interrupted by Step 3.

3. **Tap the Sign in Now button to sign up with Xbox, and then tap the I Accept button.**

   Microsoft's Windows division and its Xbox division work out of separate offices. So, even though you've signed up with a Microsoft account, you *also* need to sign up for an Xbox profile. (It's free.)

4. **Tap OK to approve the process and listen to music by your chosen artist.**

   Your new Xbox profile gives you a nonsensical "gamer tag," which is simply an Xbox nickname. You can safely forget it, as Xbox Music begins greeting you by that name whenever you log on.

After you've dispensed with the red tape, the Music app slips into its Xbox Music clothes and begins playing songs by the artist you chose in Step 2.

You're now free to listen to millions of songs by thousands of artists, simply by tapping the Play an Artist button and typing in the artist's name. Or, tap an artist or album listed in the All Music or Top Music sections listed in Step 1. It's just waiting to be played.

Now, a moment for the fine print:

✔ You need an Internet connection to hear the music because that's how Microsoft sends the tunes to your tablet. When you're out of range of a Wi-Fi connection, the music stops streaming.

✔ Microsoft occasionally slips ads in between songs. Sometimes you just hear a voice-over; at other times, the Music app plays a full-screen video ad. And after six months, Microsoft limits your ad-supported-but-free streaming to ten hours a month, which is about 20 minutes a day.

✔ To bypass the ads and the ten-hour monthly limit, sign up for a free 30-day trial. After 30 days, Microsoft begins automatically charging $10 a month to your credit card.

✔ During that 30-day trial (and if you subscribe to the service), you can play, stream, or download any of the music on your tablet, a Windows Phone, a Windows 8 PC, or an Xbox 360 console (provided you're an Xbox Live Gold member). Those platforms all run Xbox Live, and you can only play the songs through Xbox Live by signing into the service.

✔ If your subscription lapses, you can no longer play your music, including music you've downloaded – *unless* you've bought the music, that is, which costs extra. After they're purchased, however, those individual songs are yours to copy to CD or play on other PCs and music players.

✔ Xbox Music Pass isn't cheap, and it's filled with fine print. But if you pony up $10 a month for the service, it's very convenient – until you stop paying, that is. Then your music disappears, and you're back to ten hours a month of ad-supported music.

Listening to Your Own Music

Whereas the Xbox Music Pass thrives on stipulations, the Music app's other side sets very few rules. You can play music stored on your tablet, its memory card, or on other networked computers. You can even play tunes you've stashed on SkyDrive.

To play your own music on your tablet, follow these steps:

1. **From the Start screen, tap the Music tile.**

   The Music tile opens, shown earlier in Figure 12-1. Eager to push its Xbox Live service, the app places your music out of sight, barely peeking from around the screen's left edge.

2. **Scroll to the screen's farthest left side to see the My Music section.**

   The My Music section lists music stored in your tablet's Music library. If you haven't added any music to your tablet's Music library, the screen looks as empty as the screen in Figure 12-2.

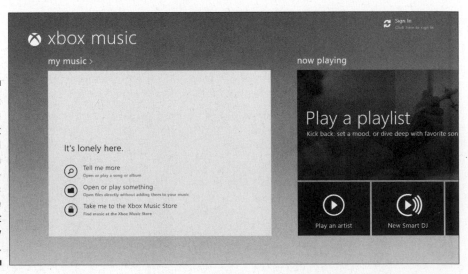

Figure 12-2: If you haven't stored music in your tablet's Music library, the app doesn't show any music.

After you copy music into your tablet's Music library, the screen updates to show up to eight of your albums, as shown in Figure 12-3.

Figure 12-3:
After you copy music to your tablet, the Music app shows up to eight of your albums.

3. **If you spot the album you want to hear, tap it, and then jump to Step 5.**

If you *don't* see your album, however, tap the words *My Music*, shown in the top left corner of Figure 12-3. Your My Music screen appears, shown in Figure 12-4, listing all of your music.

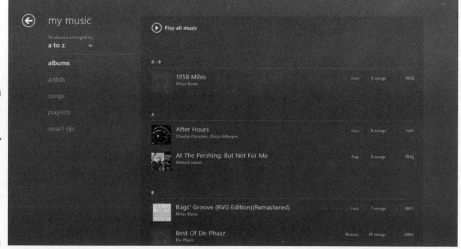

Figure 12-4:
Tap the words *My Music*, and the Music app shows all of your available music.

4. **Browse through your music by album, song, or artist.**

   Tap the drop-down menu beneath the words *My Music* in Figure 12-4 to view your music sorted by alphabet, release year, genre, artist, or date added.

   To begin listening to an album or artist, tap its name. A box appears, listing your choice, as shown in Figure 12-5.

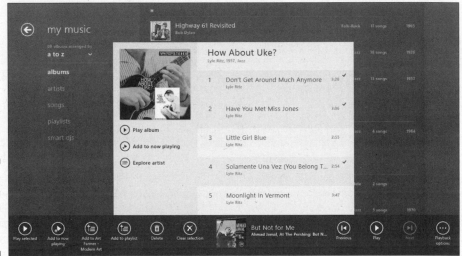

Figure 12-5: Choose how to listen to your chosen music.

5. **Choose whether to play the chosen item, or add it to your Now Playing list.**

   Depending on whether you tapped an album, a song, or an artist, you may see several options in the box shown in Figure 12-5.

   • **Play Album:** This simply begins playing all songs on the album, beginning with the first track.

   • **Add to Now Playing:** This tacks the selected item onto the end of your Now Playing list, so it plays after the currently listed music.

   • **Explore artist:** Tap this to bring a new window listing more information about the artist, his biography, and his availability on Xbox Music Pass.

- **Play Smart DJ:** Tap this, and the Xbox Music appears, playing a customized radio station built around that artist's style. (And, unless you've paid, you'll hear advertisements, too.)

- **Play all:** This plays all of the songs by the artist you've chosen.

To see more options, slide your finger inward from the screen's bottom or top edge. The App bar appears, shown along the bottom of Figure 12-5, offering different ways to play your music, as well as controls for pausing, fast forwarding, or skipping to the next track on your list of currently playing songs.

 ✔ To create a playlist from the My Music view, select items by sliding your finger horizontally across them; a check mark appears next to selected items. After selecting what you'd like to hear, tap the Add to Playlist button from the App bar along the screen's bottom edge.

✔ You won't hear ads when playing your own music, or music stored on your SkyDrive account. You only hear ads when streaming something from the app's free Xbox Music Pass side.

 ✔ If you hear ads when playing your own music, some Xbox Music streaming files (marked by the icon in the margin) have slipped into your collection. Delete them from your My Music section to stop triggering the ads. Then fetch the Charms bar, tap Settings, tap Preferences, and turn off Xbox Music Cloud.

 ✔ Tablets with Windows RT don't include the desktop's Media Player, found in earlier Windows versions. Media Player lives on in tablets that run Windows 8, however, offering more ways to manage and play your music.

✔ The Music app plays only MP3 and WMA files, including WMA lossless. It won't play formats like .flac, .ogg, or .ape.

 ✔ To hear music stored in places besides your Music library, slide your finger up from the screen's bottom edge to fetch the App bar. When the App bar appears, tap the Open File icon to fetch the File Picker, covered in Chapter 4. That lets you navigate to the music's location, be it on your memory card, a flash drive, SkyDrive, or another networked computer.

 ✔ Keyboards designed for Windows 8 include dedicated music playback keys along the top row. The first key mutes the sound, the second lowers the volume, the third raises it, and the fourth toggles between play and pause.

Making the Music app concentrate on *your* music

If you prefer listening to your own music, tell the Music app to stop tempting you with the Xbox Music Pass: Follow these steps to make the Music app open with a view of your *own* music library:

1. **From the Music app, open the Charms bar with an inward swipe from the screen's right edge.**

2. **Tap Settings, and then tap Preferences from the Settings pane.**

3. **When the Preferences pane appears, turn on the toggle called When the App Opens, Show My Music.**

That tells the Music app to open with a view of your own music, rather than music from Xbox Music Pass's artists of the day.

Part IV
Tweaks

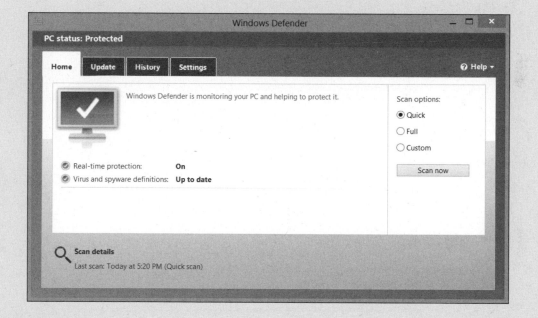

For instructions on how to manage the Family Safety feature of Windows 8, go to www.dummies.com/extras/windows8fortablets.

In this part . . .

- ✔ Change the settings of your apps, programs, your tablet, and Windows 8 itself.

- ✔ Troubleshoot your tablet when it's not working correctly.

- ✔ Turn on File History to automatically back up all of your files every hour.

- ✔ Refresh and reset your tablet to return it to working condition.

Chapter 13

Changing Settings

· ·

In This Chapter

▶ Customizing your tablet's settings

▶ Personalizing your tablet in the PC Settings area

▶ Changing settings on the desktop's Control Panel

▶ Preventing your tablet from adjusting the screen brightness

▶ Turning on the Guest account

· ·

*O*ccasionally, your tablet will misbehave. Sometimes it's just a minor irritation; other times, your tablet simply refuses to obey orders.

To keep your tablet running smoothly, this section explains how to tweak your tablet through its bundle of switches in the PC Settings area. Another section explains how to find switches hidden on the desktop's Control Panel.

If adjusting the settings doesn't fix your tablet, head for Chapter 14. There, I offer troubleshooting advice, as well as maintenance tasks to keep your tablet running smoothly.

Customizing Your Tablet through PC Settings

The Start screen's control panel, called the PC Settings screen, lets you shave off your tablet's rough edges. Each section in the PC Settings screen lets you customize a different area of your tablet's behavior.

To open the PC Settings screen, and begin tweaking your tablet to meet your needs, follow these steps:

1. **From any screen, slide your finger inward from the right edge to fetch the Charms bar, and then tap the Settings icon.**

2. **When the Settings pane appears, tap the words *Change PC Settings* from the bottom edge.**

The PC Settings screen appears, shown in Figure 13-1. The pane on the left lists the categories of settings; tap a category, and that category's options spill out to the right.

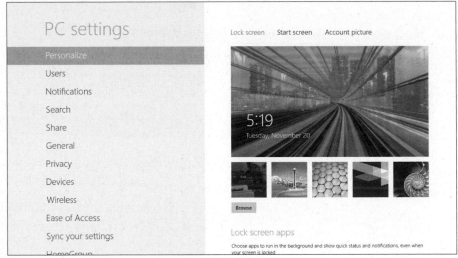

Figure 13-1:
The PC
Settings
screen
lets you
customize
your tablet's
behavior.

The rest of this section explains each category in PC Settings, and the settings most likely needing a bit of tweaking. The changes you make, usually by tapping a toggle switch, take place immediately.

TIP

Settings not found in this section, like Family Safety, and changing your tablet's name, can be found in the Desktop app's Control Panel. To find that, open the Desktop app, tap the Charms bar's Settings icon, and tap Control Panel from atop the Settings pane.

Personalize

Your doorway to changing Windows' appearance, the Personalize screen lets you change three areas: the lock screen that appears when you turn on or wake up your tablet, the Start screen's background colors and patterns, and your account photo.

✔ **Lock Screen:** Tap the words *Lock Screen* to see and change your current lock screen photo. Tap one of the existing images, or tap Browse to select your own photo from your Photo library. At the screen's bottom, choose which icons should display bits of information on the Lock screen.

✔ **Start Screen:** This lets you merge 20 background patterns with 25 colors to create 500 different Start screen combinations.

✔ **Account Picture:** To change your account photo, tap Camera and take a quick snapshot. Or, tap Browse to create an account photo from pictures in your Pictures library.

Users

This section lets you upgrade your user account from a Local to a Microsoft account, if desired. Head here to change your password, as well. Chances are, however, you'll visit here most often to add a new user account to your tablet by tapping the section's Add a User button.

Newly added users need to download waiting updates, as described in Chapter 14, both from Windows Update and the Windows Store.

If you're adding a child, choose to Turn On Family Safety, if desired, so you may monitor their computer use.

Notifications

When one of your apps does something exciting, it sends you a *notification:* a little box in your screen's top right corner that displays the reason for the excitement: a new instant message, for example, or an upcoming appointment.

Head to the Notifications section to choose which, if any, apps may send announcements, as well as whether they can make noises when doing so. It's an easy way to silence noisy apps without having to remove them completely from your tablet.

The notification settings are all On/Off toggle switches. To turn a switch off or on, just tap it.

The Charm bar's Search option lets you search for missing apps, lost files, or hard-to-find Settings. Beneath the Apps, Files, and Settings icons, you also see a list of searchable apps.

Changing your Sign In account

You may want to change the account you use to sign in on your tablet. For example, you may want to sign on with the same account you use for your Xbox, or you may want to switch to a newly remembered Microsoft account.

The simplest solution is to create a new User Account for your new Microsoft account by following these steps:

1. **From the Charms bar, open the Settings icon, and then tap Change PC settings.**

2. **From the Users category in the left column, tap Add a user.**

   Type in the e-mail address associated with your newly remembered Windows Live ID (or the e-mail address associated with your Xbox gamertag).

3. **Log back onto your old account, and then move all of your data to your tablet's Public folders.**

From the desktop, double-click a library — Music, for example, and you'll see both the My Music folder and the Public library, where you should now copy all of your music.

Finally, log onto your new account, and copy your files from the Public folders back into your own folders. When you're through, you can log off your old account and log onto your new account. After a few days, feel free to delete your old account, when you're sure you no longer need it. (Make sure you've elevated your new account to Administrator, so you're able to delete the old account.)

Deleting your old account also deletes anything you've purchased with it, including apps, movies, songs, and other items.

Search

Tap the Search pane's Maps app, for example, type **Alaska**, and the Maps app pops up, ready to offer driving directions.

If you *don't* want an app listed as searchable within the Search pane, this area of PC Settings lets you toggle its removal. If nothing else, it's an easy way to combat clutter.

Share

This rarely used section lets you choose which apps appear on the Share pane's list of destinations. (To see the Share pane, open the Charms bar and tap Share.) For example, when Facebook graces Windows 8 with an app, this section lets you choose whether to share items with Facebook.

General

Although this section sounds the most boring, you just might spend most of your time here. Here are a few gems, as well as a few misleading items:

✔ **Touch Keyboard:** The settings offered here apply only to the *onscreen* keyboard. Unfortunately, the settings don't apply to external keyboards, including Bluetooth, USB, or the Touch or Type keyboards bundled with the Microsoft Surface tablets.

✔ **Screen:** Most tablets normally adjust their screen's brightness automatically, dimming the screen indoors and brightening it when you step outside. But if the constant dimming/brightening drives you batty, tap the Adjust My Screen Brightness Automatically toggle to turn it off. (You can still adjust the screen brightness manually by tapping the Screen icon in the Settings pane.)

✔ **Language:** Bilingual tablet owners can tap this to head straight to the Language area of the Desktop app's Control Panel. There, you can choose from keyboard layouts popular in other countries.

✔ **Available storage:** If you're running out of storage space, tap this to see a list of apps, sorted with the largest ones at the top. Delete the biggest hogs to regain some space. (Apps can't be stored on your memory card, unfortunately.)

I cover this section's last three options, Refresh, Remove Everything, and Advanced Startup, in Chapter 14.

Privacy

This bone tossed in for privacy advocates lets you choose whether apps can use your general location (handy with maps and weather) and your name and account picture (used by many social networks).

A third option lets Microsoft receive lists of websites used by apps, hopefully so Microsoft can weed out apps doing unscrupulous things.

Devices

This handy list shows all the devices now-or-once attached to your tablet. Unfortunately, it doesn't let you do anything but remove them by tapping the minus sign to the right of their name.

The gem here is Add a Device, listed at the top. Tap that to add Bluetooth gadgets like mice, keyboards, and headsets, as described in Chapter 6.

Wireless

Only three toggle switches live here, but they're all handy. Tap the Airplane Mode toggle to turn off your Wi-Fi before heading onto a plane. The other two toggles control Wi-Fi and Bluetooth. Feel free to turn off Bluetooth to extend your battery life if you never connect with Bluetooth gadgets like wireless mice and keyboards.

 For a quick way to turn Airplane Mode on or off, fetch the Charms bar, tap the Settings icon, and tap the Settings pane's Wireless network icon (shown in the margin). When the Networks settings pane appears, tap Airplane Mode to toggle the setting On or Off.

Ease of Access

These switches help adapt the tablet to people with physical challenges. The High Contrast switch, for example, helps the vision-impaired by reducing all distraction. And Windows' Narrator, a Windows chestnut for years, reads menus and text with its same robotic tone.

Sync Your Settings

Microsoft kindly remembers the settings of Microsoft account owners. Log onto another PC with your Microsoft account, and your settings, passwords, app purchases, favorite websites and more ride along, making that other PC behave much like your own.

This section lets you choose which settings, if any, you *don't* want to travel with you. (For example, if you prefer your tablet's desktop wallpaper to be different than that on your Windows 8 desktop PC, tap the Desktop Personalization toggle to switch it to Off.)

Homegroup

Tablets running Windows RT can't *start* a Homegroup, but they can join an existing one. Tablets running Windows 8, by contrast, can both start and join an existing Homegroup. This section lists the password of the Homegroup you've joined, if any.

Windows Update

Windows 8 tablets are very new, and updates arrive frequently to fix problems and smooth out rough spots. You can tap Check Updates here to find and install the latest. For more information about Windows Updates, flip ahead to Chapter 14.

Changing Settings on the Desktop's Control Panel

Although the Start screen's PC Settings area contains most of the settings needed by tablet owners, the Windows 8 desktop includes its own Control Panel. That Control Panel includes switches that affect not only your Windows desktop, but your entire tablet.

This section covers the portions of the desktop's Control Panel most frequently sought after by tablet owners.

Opening the desktop's Control Panel

Sequestered deep inside the Desktop app, the desktop's Control Panel opens fairly easily when you follow these steps:

1. **From the Start screen, tap the Desktop tile to enter the Desktop app.**

   Easily identified, the Desktop app's tile always wears the same background image that's splashed across your desktop.

2. **From the desktop, slide your finger in from the right to fetch the Charms bar, and then tap the Settings icon.**

   The Settings pane appears along the screen's right edge.

3. **Tap the words *Control Panel* at the top of the Settings pane.**

   The Control Panel window appears, shown in Figure 13-2.

The Control Panel breaks down its settings into eight categories that loosely describe their contents. Adding to the confusion, sometimes choosing a Control Panel item shuttles you off to the PC Settings screen, where you flip the required switch.

Figure 13-2:
The desktop's Control Panel contains switches that affect your entire tablet, not just the desktop.

Because every Control Panel category contains several *more* categories, these tips will help you navigate the Control Panel's meandering corridors:

- To find a setting quickly, open the Charms bar from the Start screen, and then tap the Search icon. Tap in the Search pane's Search box, and type in the name of your sought-after setting — **security**, for example. Then tap the Search pane's Settings icon to direct the search to Settings. The screen immediately lists every security-related setting; tap a setting to head there quickly.

- Make the desktop Control Panel show icons instead of categories by tapping the View By drop-down menu in the window's top right corner, and then choosing either Large Icons or Small Icons. The Control Panel then lists alphabetized icons for every setting, sparing you from hunting through categories.

Finding a particular switch

The desktop's Control Panel breaks down its settings into eight categories, but finding the right switch from among the hundreds quickly turns into a game of cat and mouse.

When you're having trouble finding a particular switch, head for the Search box in the Control Panel's upper, right corner. Tap inside the Search box and summon the onscreen keyboard with a tap on its taskbar icon.

When the onscreen keyboard appears, begin typing your setting's name or function. As you type, the Control Panel quickly lists settings that match your search. When you spot your desired setting, tap its name to bring it to the screen.

Keep trying various keywords, and you eventually stumble upon a matching setting.

Turning off adaptive brightness

Windows 8 adds *adaptive brightness* to its tablets. A little sensor in your tablet constantly measures the room's brightness level, and then adjusts the screen's brightness to reach a comfortable level. The adjustments make the screen easier to read as well as prolong your battery life.

However, overly sensitive adapters on some tablets lead to constant, distracting brightness changes.

You can turn off adaptive brightness from the General category of the Start screen's PC Settings screen, as described earlier in this chapter. But if that's not enough, fire up the desktop's Control Panel and follow these steps:

1. **From the desktop Control Panel, tap the System and Security category, and tap the Power Options subcategory.**

   The Power Options section opens to show two power plans, Balanced (recommended) or Power Saver.

2. **In the Balanced (recommended) section, tap Change Plan Settings.**

   When the balance settings section appears, tap Change Advanced Power Settings near the window's bottom. The Power Options window appears, letting you fine-tune your tablet's power-saving controls.

3. **In the Power Options window, tap the plus sign next to the Enable Adaptive Brightness setting.**

   Two options drop down, shown in Figure 13-3: one for when the tablet runs on its battery, and the other for when it's plugged in.

4. **Tap the word *On* next to both the On Battery and Plugged In settings; when the drop-down menu appears, tap Off to turn off the adaptive brightness.**

5. **Tap the OK button to save your changes.**

That stops your tablet from constantly changing the screen's brightness. However, the job of adjusting your screen's brightness now falls in your lap.

To manually adjust the screen's brightness, fetch the Charms bar, tap Settings, and tap the Screen icon. When the bar appears onscreen, adjust the brightness by sliding the bar up or down.

To return to your tablet's default power plan, follow these steps again, but choose Restore Default Settings for this plan in Step 2.

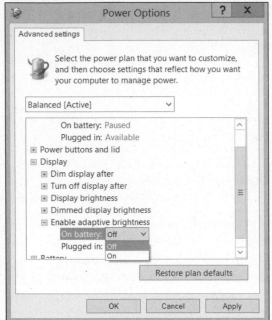

Figure 13-3:
Choose Off
to stop the
tablet from
changing
the screen's
brightness.

Turning on the Guest account

The Start screen's PC Settings screen lets you add several user accounts, handy for letting several people share one tablet. But the PC Settings area won't let you remove or change accounts. Nor will it let you turn on the Guest account, which is a handy way to let friends or visitors check their e-mail through Internet Explorer.

To change existing accounts or turn on the Guest account, open the desktop's Control Panel and follow these steps:

1. **Tap the User Accounts and Family Safety category.**

   This category opens to show a section for User Accounts, as well as for Family Safety, which lets you set up limited-access accounts for children.

2. **Tap User Accounts, and then tap Manage Another Account.**

   The Manage Accounts window lists every account on your tablet.

3. **Tap Guest.**

   The settings for the Guest account appear.

4. **Turn on the Guest account by tapping the Turn On button.**

   The Guest account is turned on, and subsequently appears as an option on your tablet's sign-in screen.

To let a friend borrow your tablet, tap Guest from the sign- in screen. (Or tap your user account in the Start screen's top right corner and choose Guest from the drop-down menu.) Your tablet opens to the Guest account, which offers access to four Start screen apps: Desktop, Internet Explorer, File Explorer, and the Store app.

Guest accounts come with some welcome restrictions that keep your files and your tablet as safe as possible:

✔ Guests can't download apps — paid or free — from the Store, unless they enter a Microsoft account. If you want, you can also type in your own Microsoft account to complete the transaction.

✔ Guests can't install desktop programs or software onto your tablet, nor can they change any of its settings. (The wireless setting will be listed as unavailable, for example, to prevent them from connecting to other wireless networks. If your tablet is already connected to a wireless network, though, your guest can browse using that connection.)

✔ The Guest account's desktop doesn't include Microsoft Office. If your guest needs Office access, create a Limited account for them, instead, from the PC Settings screen's Users section described earlier in this chapter. (I describe the process in Chapter 2.)

✔ Guests can't view or copy any of your files. However, they can access anything stored in your library's Public folders, making those folders a handy way to give everybody access to favorite photos, songs, or movies.

✔ Guests can access any of the desktop's bundled programs, but they can't access Windows Media Center, if you've installed it on your tablet.

✔ To keep your tablet as secure as possible, turn off the Guest account when it's not being used. To turn it off, follow the previous steps, but choose Turn Off Guest Account in Step 4.

Chapter 14

Maintenance, Safety, and Troubleshooting

. . . .

In This Chapter

▶ Keeping your tablet healthy

▶ Prolonging battery life

▶ Backing up your tablet

▶ Avoiding viruses

▶ Fixing problem apps

▶ Troubleshooting and fixing problems

▶ Refreshing and resetting your tablet

. . . .

*H*opefully, you can ignore this chapter, because Windows 8 tablets automatically perform all their maintenance chores.

For example, your tablet's built-in malware detector, Windows Defender, automatically scans incoming files for embedded viruses. And every evening, it scans your computer for any bad guys that may have slipped in unnoticed. When you turn on File History, Windows 8 automatically backs up your files.

When the maintenance tasks work well, you rarely need to perform any troubleshooting. But if something should go wrong with your tablet, this chapter explains how to find and correct problems.

It also explains how to use Windows 8's new troubleshooting tools Refresh and Reset, which return even the most troubled tablet back to working order.

Performing Maintenance Chores

Windows 8 tablets generally perform all their maintenance tasks automatically in the background. Occasionally, though, some tasks require a few tweaks, or a click of an OK button. This chapter describes how to make sure your tablet's maintenance tasks run automatically, as well as how to preserve battery life when on the road.

Running Windows Update

Perhaps the most important maintenance task of all, Windows Update automatically sends security patches to your tablet every Tuesday. If possible, your tablet installs the patches immediately. If the patches require you to restart your tablet, however, Windows Update waits for you to restart your tablet, and then installs the patches as your tablet starts up again.

If you want to make sure your tablet is up-to-date with Microsoft's security patches, or if you want to check for any waiting updates, follow these steps:

1. **From any screen, slide your finger inward from the right edge to fetch the Charms bar, then tap the Settings icon.**

2. **When the Settings pane appears, tap the words Change PC Settings from the bottom edge.**

3. **When the PC Settings window appears, tap Windows Update from the bottom of the left column.**

The PC Settings screen shows the Windows Update section, shown in Figure 14-1.

Your tablet normally checks daily for updates and installs them automatically, but if you're impatient or expecting an update, tap the Check for Updates Now button to check immediately for any waiting updates:

✔ After the updates have downloaded, you can install them immediately by fetching the Charms bar, tapping the Power icon, and choosing Update and Restart from the pop-up menu. (If you don't see that option, the updates have politely installed themselves, without your having to restart your tablet.)

✔ Windows Update requires a working Internet connection to download new updates or check for new ones.

✔ Windows Update only updates your tablet's *operating system* — Windows 8 or Windows RT. It doesn't update your *apps,* — the mini-programs available through the Windows Store. I describe how to update your apps in Chapter 9.

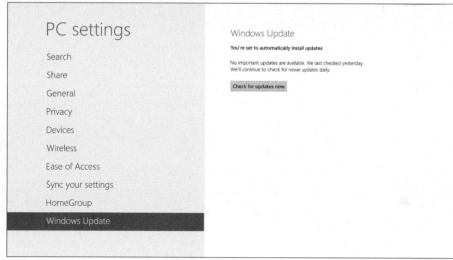

Figure 14-1: Tap Check for Updates Now to look for any waiting updates.

Checking maintenance tasks

Windows 8 runs common maintenance tasks automatically at 3 a.m. each evening. At the appointed hour, Windows 8 connects to the Internet to download any waiting software updates, update its virus definitions, check your computer for viruses, and perform other bits of computerized housekeeping.

Depending on how you use your tablet and the strength of your Internet connection, however, your tablet might not have a chance to perform some maintenance tasks, and they pile up in the background.

To view and complete any missed maintenance tasks, or to change the 3 a.m. maintenance schedule, follow these steps:

1. **From the Start screen, open the Desktop app.**

2. **Fetch the Charms Bar, tap the Settings icon, and tap Control Panel at the top of the Settings pane.**

   The desktop's Control Panel appears.

3. **Tap the System and Security icon, tap the Action Center icon, and tap the Maintenance category.**

   The Action Center window appears, showing the Maintenance section in Figure 14-2.

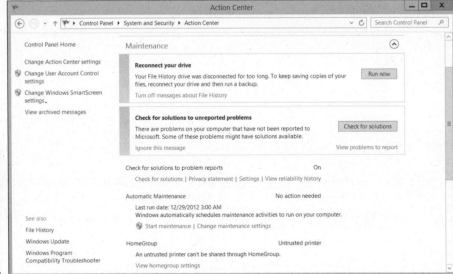

Figure 14-2:
The Action
Center lets
you perform
needed
mainte-
nance tasks.

The window shown in Figure 14-2, for example, shows two missed maintenance items: Reconnect Your Drive, and Check for Solutions to Unreported problems. Each task offers a button; tap the button to begin running the adjacent task.

If your tablet is sleeping at 3 a.m., Windows runs its maintenance tasks the next time you turn on your tablet. But if you prefer a different maintenance time, tap the Change Maintenance Settings link; when the drop-down menu appears, choose a new time instead of the default 3 a.m. time.

Prolonging your tablet's battery life

A tablet running Windows RT easily boasts a full day of battery life, and sometimes two. Tablets running Windows 8, by contrast, last only about five hours between charges.

But whether you own a power slurper or a power gulper, your tablet's battery life always remains a concern.

The tips in this section help you keep your tablet working for as long as possible between sips at the power outlet.

Dimming the screen

Roughly half of your tablet's battery strength goes directly to your tablet's screen. That's why most tablets come set to turn off the screen when they haven't been touched for a minute or two.

It's easy to control your screen brightness whenever it looks brighter than necessary. By dimming the tablet's screen to the lowest point that still meets your needs, you can extend your battery life even further.

To dim your screen, follow these steps:

1. **Slide your finger in from the screen's right edge to open the Charms bar, and then tap the Settings icon.**

2. **When the Settings pane appears, tap and hold the Screen icon.**

   As you touch the Screen icon, it turns into a sliding bar for changing the brightness level.

3. **With your finger, slide the bar up to increase the screen's brightness; slide it down to decrease the brightness.**

As you work on your tablet, keep an eye on the light around you. As the light fades, lower your tablet's brightness accordingly.

Dimming your screen manually is especially important if you've turned off your tablet's adaptive brightness, as I describe in Chapter 13.

Turning off unused gadgets and services

Anything plugged into your tablet's USB port — mice, portable drives, portable music players, and flash drives — treats that port as a power outlet, draining power to light up, spin, or transmit information.

Portable hard drives and CD/DVD drives are some of the worst offenders. To preserve battery life, try to copy necessary files onto your tablet *before* hitting the road. Then keep the portable drive stashed in your bag to be used only during emergencies or when you're plugged into an outlet.

Turning off unused services — Wi-Fi, Bluetooth, GPS and cellular — can also save power. To turn off unneeded services, follow these steps:

1. **Slide your finger in from the screen's right edge to open the Charms bar, and then tap the Settings icon.**

2. **When the Settings pane appears, tap Change PC Settings.**

3. **When the PC Settings screen appears, tap the Wireless section, and tap the toggle switches for the wireless services you want to turn on or off.**

   Depending on your tablet, that section includes toggles for Wi-Fi, Bluetooth, GPS, or other services.

   Tapping a toggle switch reverses its setting, so repeat these steps to reverse your actions.

Adjusting your power saving options

Microsoft designed Windows 8 tablets to conserve as much power as possible. For example, your tablet goes to sleep when you haven't used it for a while; it doesn't turn off completely. Normally, that's exactly how it should be, as it lets your tablet turn back on more quickly when needed.

Tablets running Windows RT can sleep for days, even weeks. You don't ever need to turn them off. They drift off to sleep by themselves when neglected, and wake within seconds at the press of the power switch.

Tablets running Windows 8, however, consume more power. If you're trying to preserve battery life, run your Windows 8 tablet on Power Saver mode by following the steps below:

To switch to Power Saver mode, follow these steps:

1. **From the Start screen, open the Desktop app.**

2. **Fetch the Charms bar by sliding your finger in from the screen's right edge, and then tap the Settings icon. When the Settings pane appears, tap Control Panel from the top.**

   The desktop's Control Panel appears.

3. **From the desktop Control Panel, tap the System and Security category, and tap the Power Options subcategory.**

   The Power Options section opens to show two power plans, shown in Figure 14-3, Balanced (recommended) or Power Saver.

4. **Tap Power Saver.**

   This power setting wrings the most life out of your battery by dimming the screen after one minute, and turning it off if you haven't touched it within two minutes.

   After being ignored for ten minutes, your tablet automatically goes to sleep. If your tablet's battery runs *really* low, abandon Sleep mode and simply turn it off:

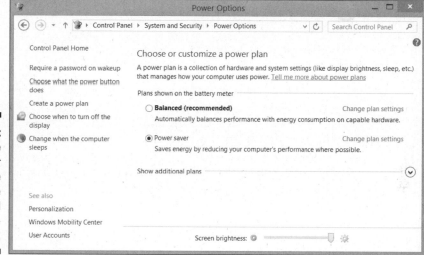

Figure 14-3:
Choose
the Power
Saver mode
when you're
worried
about bat-
tery life.

 To turn off your Windows 8 tablet, fetch the Charms bar by sliding your finger inward from the right edge, then tap the Settings icon. When the Settings pane appears, tap the Power icon and choose Shut Down.

Hibernate and Sleep: What's the difference?

While poking around in your tablet's power set-tings, you may find an option to choose between *Sleep* and *Hibernate*. Each option saves power in a slightly different way.

Sleep: Normally, your tablet sleeps when not being used. The Sleep mode keeps all of your programs loaded in its memory, but your tablet stops using them. It turns off the screen, and waits. When woken up, your computer snaps back into action with everything just as you left it.

Sleep mode still consumes some battery life, though. If your tablet's battery reaches a critical low point, your tablet switches quickly into Hibernate mode, described next, and then turns itself off.

Hibernate: As opposed to Sleep mode, which keeps everything stored in memory, Hibernate mode writes all that memory to your tablet's hard drive, and then turns off your tablet. When turned back on, your tablet reads the memory from the hard drive and leaves you where you were when you turned on Hibernate. All your open programs will be waiting for you.

Because Hibernate mode involves the hard drive, it makes your tablet take a little longer to start up and shut down. However, it saves your battery life over the long term because your tablet's completely turned off.

The moral? Sleep mode works best for most day-to-day conditions. But if you won't be using your tablet for a few days, it's best to turn it off.

Safety

Windows 8 does its best to keep your tablet safe and secure. It requires a password before anybody can enter your user account, for example.

But two other chores will also keep your tablet and your files safe: backing up regularly, and making sure Windows Defender — Microsoft's built-in antivirus program — is up- to- date and running automatically. I describe both in this section.

Backing up your tablet

Backups are essential with tablets, where the fumble of a finger or leap of a cat can accidentally delete your files. Even worse, tablets rank highly among thieves, as they're easy to wipe clean and sell to a pawn shop.

Windows tablets offer two types of backups:

- **File History:** File History automatically backs up your Documents, Music, Photos, and Video libraries *every hour.* That not only keeps your work safe, but gives you a long string of backups to choose from: You can easily grab yesterday's document if you've irreparably messed up the current version.

- **System Image:** Found only on tablets running Windows 8, System Image contains your entire tablet's C: drive: Windows 8, your programs, settings, and files. It's the whole enchilada. If your tablet's stolen, you can restore the System Image onto your replacement, and be right back where you started.

The next two sections explain how to create both types of backups.

Turning on File History

Turning on File History is as simple as tapping a toggle switch. Your only decision boils down to where to store the backups. File History offers four storage options, each with its own pros and cons:

- **Your tablet's memory card:** The simplest but weakest solution, this creates backup copies on a memory card. (Almost all Windows tablets include a slot that accepts an inexpensive memory card.) Unfortunately, if somebody steals your tablet, they've also stolen your backup. Also, most people fill their tablet's memory card with favorite movies, music, and photos — not boring backups.

✔ **Flash drive:** Flash drives rarely hold enough files to make File History worthwhile. And until you remember to manually to insert the drive into your tablet's USB port, File History won't be working automatically. But if your flash drive holds at least 32GB, it's better than nothing.

✔ **Portable hard drive:** A better solution is to plug a portable hard drive into your tablet, and wait while File History creates its backup. However, not everybody owns a portable hard drive. Plus, only the most disciplined tablet owners always remember to plug in their drive to create a backup before leaving on a trip.

✔ **A network location:** The best solution, this automatically backs up your tablet's files onto a PC on your home network. It's automatic, and it happens whenever your tablet comes within range of your home network. (I explain how to set up a wireless home network in my other book, *Windows 8 For Dummies*, published by John Wiley and Sons, Inc.)

To turn on Windows' File History, follow these steps:

1. **From the Start screen, open the Desktop tile.**

2. **Slide your finger in from the right edge to fetch the Charms bar, and then tap the Settings icon. Then tap Control Panel from the top of the Settings Pane.**

3. **When the desktop Control Panel window opens, find the System and Security section, then tap the words, *Save Backup Copies of Your Files with File History.***

   The File History window opens, shown in Figure 14-4.

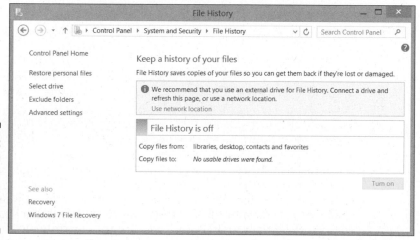

Figure 14-4: Choose where to store the File History backups.

4. **Choose where to save your backup copies and tap the Turn On button.**

The File History window, shown in Figure 14-4, lists any attached drives or memory cards for you to choose with a tap of your finger.

Don't see your drive listed? Tap the Select Drive link from the window's left edge, and navigate to your drive before tapping the Turn On button.

After you choose your drive and tap the Turn On button, File History begins saving copies of your drive every hour. At least, that's the way Microsoft wants it to work. But if your drive keeps filling up too quickly, you can adjust this setting in several ways:

✔ Tap the Advanced Settings link shown in the preceding Figure 14-4, and the Advanced Settings page appears, where you can change the backup time from one hour to 3, 6, 12 hours, or even daily.

✔ The Advanced Settings page also lets you change how long Windows should keep your backups. It normally saves them forever, which is unrealistic. Instead, change it to Until Space Is Needed, or 3 Months.

✔ If you don't want a folder backed up, exclude it from File History. In Figure 14-4, tap the Exclude Folders link on the left, tap Add, and then choose the folders you want excluded from the backups.

✔ If you have a wireless network at home, save backups on one of your network's PCs. File History then automatically backs itself up wirelessly whenever you're within range of your home network. To choose a network location for File History, tap the Select Drive link shown earlier in Figure 14-4, tap the Add Network Location button, and navigate to a folder on your desktop PC.

Creating a system image

File History saves the things *you've* created. It copies all the documents, photos, movies, and music you've stored in your libraries.

A System Image, by contrast, saves *everything:* your files, programs, settings, and even Windows itself. It's a complete copy of your tablet's hard drive.

Should your tablet be stolen, you can buy another tablet of the same make and model, restore your System Image onto the new tablet, and be back to where you were before you left the house.

You can only create a System Image on a tablet running Windows 8. Tablets running Windows RT should store their most important files on SkyDrive, or use File History to save backups to a flash drive, portable hard drive, or home network.

To create a System Image, follow these steps:

1. **From the Start screen, open the Desktop tile.**

2. **Slide your finger in from the right edge to fetch the Charms bar, and then tap the Settings icon. Then tap Control Panel from the top of the Settings Pane.**

3. **When the desktop Control Panel window opens, find the System and Security section, then tap the words, Save Backup Copies of your files with File History.**

4. **When the File History window opens, look in the far bottom left corner and tap the words Windows 7 File Recovery.**

5. **When the Backup or Restore your Files window appears, tap Create a System Image from the window's top left corner.**

   Follow the instructions to save the System Image on a portable hard drive or a place on your home network.

I explain how to restore a System Image onto your tablet in this chapter's "Resetting your tablet" section.

System images are quite large, so you want to save them on a portable hard drive or network location that's at least as large as your tablet's hard drive. (The hard drives in most Windows 8 tablets range from 128GB to 256GB.)

Staying safe with Windows Defender

Windows 8's built-in antivirus program, Windows Defender, constantly runs in the background, automatically scanning everything that enters your computer. If Windows Defender detects something dangerous trying to enter, it quarantines the bad guy before it can do any damage.

If you're feeling suspicious, however, you can tell Windows Defender to scan your computer anytime you like by following these steps:

1. **From the Start screen, slide your finger up from the screen's bottom edge to reveal the App bar. Then tap the All Apps icon.**

2. **Tap the Windows Defender icon, listed in the Windows System section of apps.**

   Windows Defender appears, shown in Figure 14-5.

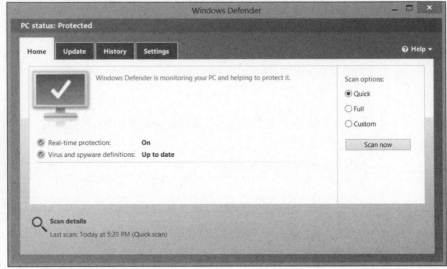

Figure 14-5:
Tap Scan
Now to
scan for
viruses and
spyware on
your tablet.

3. **Tap the Scan Now button.**

   Windows Defender performs a quick scan of your computer, concentrating on the locations where the evil beings usually try to enter your computer.

You can customize Windows Defender several ways with these tips:

✔ Windows Defender normally updates itself daily as part of your computer's automatic maintenance tasks described earlier in this chapter. But to make sure it has up-to-the-minute updates, tap the program's Update tab, and tap the Update button.

✔ When you're feeling extraordinarily suspicious, scan your *entire* computer. Tap the Full option, and then tap the Scan Now button below. That scan takes longer than the default Quick Scan but it's much more thorough.

✔ To scan a portable drive or flash drive, tap the Custom button, and then tap the Scan Now button. A window appears, letting you tap your portable drive from a list. Tap the OK button.

Troubleshooting

Occasionally, your tablet either misbehaves, or falls ill. This section covers possible treatment plans, as well as a few tweaks to solve specific problems.

I can't connect to the Internet!

I describe how to connect with the Internet in Chapter 6. But if you're having trouble, try these troubleshooting tips:

- ✔ Restart your tablet. Sometimes that's all it takes for the tablet to wake up feeling renewed and ready to tackle an Internet connection.

- ✔ If you're connecting to a wireless network for the first time, reenter the password to make sure you've entered it correctly.

- ✔ If you're within range of your wireless router, unplug the router, wait 30 seconds, and then plug it in again. Wait 30 more seconds, and then try to reconnect.

Returning Internet Explorer to default status

Lots of nasties try to latch onto Internet Explorer, adding unwanted toolbars, changing your Home page, or sending barrages of pop-up ads.

If Internet Explorer seems to be running out of control, follow these steps to return your browser to out-of-the-box condition:

1. **From the Start screen, tap the Desktop app tile. When the desktop appears, tap the Internet Explorer icon in the screen's bottom left edge.**

2. **When Internet Explorer opens, tap the Settings icon in its upper-right corner. (It looks like a gear.)**

3. **Choose Internet Options from the Settings menu.**

4. **When the Internet Options window appears, tap the Advanced tab, and then tap the Reset button at the window's bottom.**

   A window appears, reminding you that you're about to disable all toolbars, add-ons, and Internet Explorer Settings. To delete everything, tap the Delete Personal Settings check box. That erases your history, web form information, and saved passwords.

5. **Tap the Reset button at the confirmation window.**

When Internet Explorer finishes restoring itself to like-new condition, restart your tablet to complete the changes.

Turning off a frozen app, program or tablet

When the screen freezes on a desktop PC, you can usually hold down the Ctrl+Alt+Del keys simultaneously to get out of a jam. That strategic key sequence catches Windows' attention, making it ignore its current errant behavior and pay attention to you, the owner, once again.

Lacking physical keyboards, tablets lack that escape hatch. The alternative? Hold down the Windows key beneath your tablet's screen and simultaneously press the tablet's Power button.

That brings up Windows 8's Task Manager, which offers these options:

- **Lock:** A handy option to choose if you leave your tablet for a few moments, this locks the tablet. To begin working again, you must enter your password.

- **Switch User:** Choose this to let another account holder sign in to use the tablet. When they sign back out, your programs and apps remain open, just as you left them.

- **Sign Out:** This closes down your apps and programs, signs you out, and leaves you at the sign- on screen for other account holders to use the tablet.

- **Change a Password:** Seen only by local account owners, this lets them change (or remove) their existing password.

- **Task Manager:** Choose this to see a list of currently running apps and programs. To close a frozen program, hold your finger on its name; when the pop-up menu appears, choose End Task.

If none of these options works, tap the Power icon in the screen's bottom-right corner. A pop-up menu appears, letting you choose Sleep, Shut Down, or Restart. (If any updates are waiting, you'll see options to Update and Shutdown/Restart, as well.)

Fixing problem apps

When an app doesn't seem to be working correctly anymore, follow these steps to uninstall it, and then reinstall it from the Windows Store. (This works for both free and paid apps; the store remembers your purchase, and lets you download the app again without paying twice.)

1. **From the Start screen, select your problem app's tile or icon.**

   To select an app, drag it down slightly with your finger. A check mark appears by the app, and the App bar appears along the screen's bottom edge.

2. **Tap the Uninstall icon on the App bar.**

    Your tablet uninstalls the app.

3. **Visit the Windows Store and reinstall the app.**

    From the Windows Store, slide your down finger down slightly from the screen's top, and then tap the words *Your Apps* that appear along the screen's top edge. Tap the name of your formerly misbehaving app, and then tap the Install button from the App bar along screen's bottom edge.

Your app reinstalls itself onto your Start screen's farthest right edge. Hopefully, your app will have enjoyed its vacation and returned in a better mood.

Refreshing your tablet

When a tablet that runs Windows RT isn't working correctly, you can tell it to reinstall its operating system, but save your files. Called *Refresh*, it's a quick fix, as you can easily reinstall your apps from the Windows Store. But refreshing poses a problem for tablets running Windows 8:

 On tablets running Windows 8, the Refresh feature also removes all of the *programs* you've installed on your Desktop app. Before using the Refresh feature, make sure you have your program's original installation discs handy, as you will need to reinstall them all.

To Refresh your tablet, follow these steps:

1. **Swipe in from the right edge of the screen, tap Settings, and then tap Change PC settings.**

2. **Tap the General section.**

3. **In the Refresh Your PC Without Affecting Your Files section, tap the Get Started button.**

4. **When your tablet wakes up, you're left with a few tasks:**

   • Visit the PC Settings screen's Windows Update section and download any waiting updates.

   • Open the Windows Store app and reinstall your apps.

   • On tablets running Windows 8, open the Windows desktop. There, you find a waiting list of your uninstalled desktop programs, along with links to where you can download and reinstall many of them.

Refreshing a tablet that runs Windows RT takes much less time, as you needn't worry about reinstalling desktop programs. (The Office programs will still be there.)

But when you use Refresh on tablets running Windows 8, the process takes much longer: Tracking down and reinstalling all those desktop programs can be a nightmare.

Resetting your tablet

This last-resort option wipes your tablet completely clean, removing *everything.* When it wakes back up, your tablet behaves like it was just removed from its shiny new box. It's a drastic measure, but it's one that always works when your tablet seems beyond repair.

Resetting your tablet is also a good way to restore your tablet to factory conditions before giving it away, either to friends or charity.

Resetting your tablet deletes all of your personal files, apps, desktop programs, and settings. Before resetting, back up any files you don't want to lose.

Restoring from a System Image

To restore your Windows 8 tablet from a System Image you created with the instructions earlier in this chapter, open the Charms bar, tap Settings, tap PC Settings, tap the General section, and tap the Restart Now button in the Advanced Startup section.

When your computer restarts, it offers the option to restore your computer from the System Image you so prudently created earlier.

To reset your tablet to factory conditions, follow these steps:

1. **Swipe in from the right edge of the screen, tap Settings, and then tap Change PC settings.**

2. **Tap the General category.**

3. **In the section called Remove Everything and Reinstall Windows, tap Get Started, tap Next, and follow the instructions.**

When your tablet returns to life, page back to Chapter 2. Your Surface behaves just as it did when you first turned it on, and you need to choose a language, and begin installing updates.

Part V

the part of tens

In this part . . .

- ✔ Ten things to do now to your tablet to save you time and trouble down the road.

- ✔ Ten essential free apps to download.

- ✔ Ten essential tips and tricks to make your tablet work better and faster.

- ✔ Ten handy accessories to pack with your tablet.

- ✔ Ten essential Windows shortcut keys for when you attach a keyboard.

Chapter 15

Ten Things to Do Now to Your Windows Tablet

*W*hen you first turn on your tablet, it's a faceless, nameless device. After you've completed these ten tasks, though, your tablet becomes truly *yours*, stocked with the latest updates, backed up in case of calamity, organized to make things easy to find, and ready to work in tandem with your desktop PC.

Even if you've owned your tablet for a few weeks, run through this checklist to make sure everything's working the way it should.

Run Windows Update

Microsoft constantly releases a huge stream of updates and patches through its Windows Update service, and the flow only increases with tablets. With Microsoft Surface, for example, running Windows Update from the desktop is the quickest way to update its trial version of Office to the final version.

Your brand new tablet is most certainly not up-to-date with the latest software, and it won't be until you run Windows Update.

To run Windows Update, fetch the Charms bar, tap Settings, and tap Change PC Settings. When the PC Settings screen appears, tap Windows Update, and tap Check for Updates Now.

I give more complete instructions on how to use Windows Update in Chapter 14.

Update Your Apps

Windows Update keeps Windows running safely and smoothly. But Windows Update won't update apps you download from the Windows Store. For that, you need to visit the Windows Store.

To update your apps, open the Start screen's Store app and tap Updates in the screen's top- right corner.

I give more details on updating your apps in Chapter 9.

Make Your Desktop Fit Your Fingers

The following steps enlarge everything on the desktop by about 25 percent, making your desktop's buttons and bars much easier to control with a finger.

1. **Launch the Desktop app from the Start menu.**

   The traditional Windows desktop fills the screen.

2. **Summon the Charms bar by sliding your finger inward from the screen's right edge. Tap the Charms bar's Settings icon to fetch the Settings pane. Then tap Control Panel from the top of the Settings pane.**

   The desktop's Control Panel appears.

3. **On the Control Panel window, tap the Hardware and Sound category, and then tap the Display.**

   The Display window appears.

4. **In the Change the Size of All Items area, tap the setting called Medium — 125% and then tap the Apply button.**

5. **When Windows asks you to sign out of your computer and apply your changes, tap the Sign Out Now button.**

I explain more about enlarging everything on your desktop in Chapter 5.

Organize and Label Your Start Screen

Earlier versions of Windows included a neatly organized Start menu that sprouted from the Start button in the screen's corner. The menu showed several different categories, letting you jump quickly between programs, documents, music, pictures, and other popular destinations.

Windows 8 not only dropped the Start button, but dropped the organization, as well. Instead, your tablet's Start screen becomes a sprawling mess of unorganized tiles that spreads as far to the right as you can scroll.

To combat the sprawl, spend a few minutes organizing your Start screen, as I describe in Chapter 4. Organizing your Start screen places your Start screen apps into manageable categories. Plus, it helps you figure out some of the Start screen's most unintuitive tasks: select tiles, delete unwanted apps, and add icons for places you'd like to revisit with a single tap.

Pin Your Favorite Programs to the Desktop's Taskbar

Windows 8's desktop lacks a Start menu for launching programs. Whenever you want to open a program, you must visit the Start screen and hunt for your favorite program's tile. That's a distracting trip to a different world.

But launching a program needn't be so awkward. If you prefer spending your time on the desktop, make the most of your *taskbar* — that strip along the desktop's bottom edge — and your favorite programs will be one click away.

I explain how to add your favorite programs to the taskbar in Chapter 5.

Turn On File History and Back Up Your Tablet

Windows 8's File History backup program automatically copies your files every hour. Backing them up so frequently turns backups into a convenience to be enjoyed: If afternoon rolls in and you've messed up your report, grab the version from this morning's backup and start over.

To begin backing up your files, all you need to do is turn on File History and pick a storage location for your backup, tasks I cover in Chapter 14.

For the most automatic and trouble-free backups, tell your tablet to back itself up to a folder on your wireless network. That way, your tablet backs itself up automatically whenever you're within range of your network, both before you take your trip and as soon as you return home.

Install SkyDrive for Windows on the Desktop

Windows RT tablets come with a SkyDrive app that lets you store and access files stored on *SkyDrive*, Microsoft's online storage space. The minimal app works best when copying a few files to or from your tablet.

Tablets running Windows 8, by contrast, can install the full-fledged SkyDrive for Windows program. That places a SkyDrive folder in File Explorer. Anything you copy or move into that folder is automatically copied to SkyDrive.

Because your tablet's SkyDrive folder automatically stays synchronized with SkyDrive on the Internet, you can access your files even when not connected to the Internet. As soon as you find an Internet connection, SkyDrive kicks in, automatically updating your SkyDrive files in the cloud to match your tablet's SkyDrive folder.

There's more: When you install SkyDrive for Windows on your desktop PC, your tablet can then browse *all* of your desktop PC's files.

I describe how to use the SkyDrive app and SkyDrive for Windows in Chapter 6.

Set Up Your Tablet as "Trusted"

Whenever you create a Microsoft account on a new Windows 8 PC — and your tablet counts as a PC — Microsoft asks you to trust this PC. The words *Trust This PC* may appear on a menu on your tablet, or in an e-mail.

Trust it with what, you may ask? Actually, Microsoft wants to know if you trust this PC with your information. This security precaution ensures that *you're* the one accessing the PC. Here's how it works:

To verify your identity, Microsoft sends a secret code and a web address to the cellphone or e-mail address that you entered when first setting up your Microsoft account. When you receive the code, visit the listed web address and enter the code into the online confirmation box.

That way, Microsoft can confirm that *you* are the person creating the Microsoft account on the tablet. After that's out of the way, Microsoft begins syncing the tablet with your passwords and sign-in information for your apps, websites, networks, and your network's Homegroup, if you have one.

If you haven't trusted your tablet yet, follow these steps to begin:

1. **Fetch the Charms bar by sliding your finger in from the screen's right edge, and then tap the Settings icon.**

2. **When the Settings page appears, tap Change PC Settings.**

3. **In the PC Settings screen's left side, tap the Sync Your Settings category.**

4. **In the Sync Your Settings category's right side, tap Trust This PC.**

Microsoft walks you through the process of trusting your tablet.

After you've trusted all of your Windows 8 PCs, the settings stay synced between them.

Install Desktop PC Apps onto Your Tablet

Your Windows 8 PC can run the same apps as your tablet. And if you own a Windows 8 PC, you've probably downloaded an app or two to see what the fuss is all about.

When you log onto your tablet with the same Microsoft account you use for your desktop PC, apps you've installed on your desktop PC will be waiting for you.

To see and download apps you've downloaded on other Windows 8 PCs, follow these steps:

1. **From your tablet's Start screen, tap the Store app.**

2. **When the Store app appears, slide your finger down from the screen's top edge to reveal the App bar.**

3. **Tap Your Apps from the App bar.**

   The Store lists all the apps associated with your Microsoft account, but not installed on your tablet.

4. **Tap the tiles for the apps you want to install (or tap the Select All icon to select them all.) Then tap the Install button to install the apps onto your tablet.**

Apps you purchase for your desktop PC can be installed onto your tablet and vice versa. Each purchased app can run on five PCs associated with your Microsoft account.

Note: Apps written for Windows phones aren't related to apps written for tablets.

Buy a USB Hub and a Flash Drive

Chances are, your tablet came with one USB port. That's enough to plug in a mouse— but nothing else. A USB hub adds extra USB ports to your tablet, letting you plug in a mouse, keyboard, and even let you charge your phone.

Hubs are inexpensive, lightweight, and flat, so they don't hog much space in your tablet's bag.

Flash drives work like tiny, inexpensive hard drives, making it easy to copy files to and from your tablet. After you use one, you wonder how you got along without it.

I describe USB hubs, flash drives, and other accessories, in Chapter 18.

Chapter 16

Ten Essential Apps

Windows 8 comes with several core apps pre-installed; I cover the Mail, People, Calendar, and Messaging apps in Chapter 8.

But the Windows Store offers thousands of other apps, with hundreds more pouring in each week. Too many, in fact, to know which ones are worth installing. This short guide should get you started because every app on this list is free.

I explain how to install apps in Chapter 9; that chapter also explains how to uninstall apps that don't meet your needs.

Clock

Windows 8 is the first version of Windows to leave something important off every screen: a simple clock.

The original clock lives on in the bottom-right corner of the Desktop app. But the Start screen doesn't show the current time and date until you fetch the Charms bar with a finger swipe inward from the screen's right edge.

If you miss seeing the current date and time on the Start screen, many apps aim to fill that void. For example, Clock, by Jujubar Software, shows the time, date, and day in both a full-size tile, as well as a half-size tile.

Netflix

Although Microsoft wants you to buy, rent, or watch movies through its own Video app, you're not limited to Microsoft's offerings.

Netflix subscribers can download the Netflix app and stream thousands of TV shows and movies whenever they're within range of an Internet signal.

The app doesn't let you manage your Netflix queue, but Netflix will hopefully add that capacity soon.

Remote Desktop

Like its desktop cousin, Microsoft's Remote Desktop lets you log onto other PCs on your home or work network. After you've logged on, your tablet shows what's running on the other PC, just as if you were sitting in front of it.

Remote Desktop comes in handy on Windows RT tablets that can't run Windows programs. With Remote Desktop, they can run those on their other networked PCs, just as if they were running them on their own Windows RT tablet.

Microsoft Solitaire Collection

Many people shed a tear when Windows 8 dropped FreeCell, the timewaster of many a bored office worker. Microsoft has made amends with its Microsoft Solitaire Collection.

The package of games brings FreeCell back to Windows, as well as chestnuts like Klondike and Spider. (It also brings some new card games to the mix: Pyramid, TriPeaks, and the Daily Challenges.)

If you thought you were addicted to FreeCell before, just wait until you start moving cards around with your fingers. . .

File Browser

When your hand rests on a mouse, it's fairly easy to shuffle files around on the desktop. But file management becomes downright laborious with your fingers, especially because the Start screen doesn't include a built-in file manager.

That forces you to visit the desktop whenever you want to move files to or from a flash drive or folder.

Recognizing an opportunity, several programmers have released file-management apps, and the best free one could be the aptly named File Browser by Dozrekt.

File Browser presents files and folders as large, finger-sized icons. You can browse your tablet's libraries, as well as the libraries shared by computers on your home network.

You can add specific locations as Favorites: Fetch the Charms bar, tap Settings, tap Favorites, and the File Picker appears. There, you can navigate to other folders or network locations you'd like to see listed.

It sure beats a trip to the desktop.

MetroTwit

Twitter fans will find plenty of third-party Twitter clients to tide them over until Twitter releases its official app. Until then, I've been using MetroTwit by Pixel Tucker Pty Ltd.

MetroTwit lets you group incoming Twitter information into columns. Your friends' tweets can fill one column, for example, while a search string, or tweets from a particular person, can fill the other.

The program includes a relatively unobtrusive ad that can be removed by upgrading to the Pro version.

TuneIn Radio

I've always loved Internet Radio stations: They fill nearly every musical niche from every culture. The TuneIn Radio app by TuneIn offers stations from nearly every genre worldwide, and it includes your local stations, as well. (It also carries police and fire scanners from major cities.)

It's an easy way to hear any type of music whenever you have an Internet connection, as well as a way to keep posted about that fire over yonder hill.

Draw a Stickman Epic

Sometimes a silly game is just what you need when you're killing time at the repair shop during a brake job. That's a niche filled by Draw a Stickman Epic from Hitcents.

In a world where video games try to outdo each other with realism, Draw a Stickman Epic opens by having you doodle a stickman on your tablet's screen. Your hastily scribbled stickman thus becomes the game's central character, as you walk it through an uncharted land, searching for treasures.

It's a refreshing change to see a game concentrate on playability rather than eye candy.

Kindle

Amazon holds the lead on e-books, and its Kindle software lets you read those books on nearly any device, including your Windows 8 tablet.

Amazon's Kindle app lets you read any e-book you've purchased from Amazon, as well as browse and purchase new books.

As all Kindles do, the Kindle app remembers which page you've last read, whether it was on your smartphone, your Kindle tablet, or the Kindle app on your Windows 8 tablet.

Amazon's trying to grab the entire digital book market, of course, but the quality of its app shows that it's taking its goal seriously.

Word Blast

For people who like picking words out of letters, Word Blast by Cobra Tap fills that need quite well. It presents a honeycomb grid of letters; your job is to slide your finger over them to create words.

It adds a few twists, like letting you rotate grids to bring that "u" closer to the "q". And it lets you compete against other players' scores, if you choose to sign in.

It's free, and you can spend way too many hours on it.

Chapter 17

Ten Essential Tips 'n' Tricks

A *For Dummies* book isn't the same without a Part of Tens chapter. With a Windows tablet, the hard part is limiting it to just ten. So, without further ado, here are ten essential tips 'n' tricks to wring the most out of your tablet.

When Lost, Swipe in from the Screen's Left Edge

Whenever you tap a link or another app on your tablet, the new item fills the screen, pulling you in deeply. When you finally close the app, the Start screen jumps in to fill the void.

But what were you working on *before* you went off track by tapping the link?

To find out, swipe in from the screen's left side. Your original app fills the screen, bringing you full circle to where you were before the distraction.

Shrink Information into Groups

When faced with an overwhelming amount of information, pinch it into smaller groups. The pinch shrinks the information down into manageable groups, as shown in Figure 17-1, letting you tap the group you want to read.

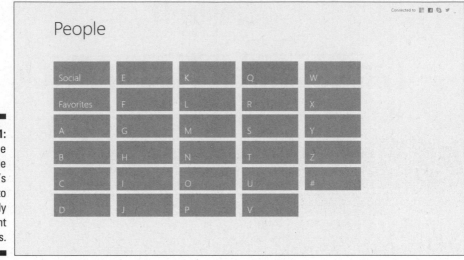

Figure 17-1:
Pinch the
People
app's
screen to
jump quickly
to different
contacts.

This works on the Start screen, as well as many bundled apps: News, Finance, Weather, Travel, People, Store, and others.

After the information is shrunken into categories, you can jump between categories much more quickly.

Search for Items by Typing Directly on the Start Screen

When you're searching for something, start typing its name directly onto the Start screen. Windows clears the screen and begins listing matches.

For example, type **camera** directly into the Start screen.

As you type the first letter, the Start screen switches to Search mode, listing every app containing the letter "c." As you keep typing, the list narrows, eventually showing only camera-related apps.

The Search pane clings to the screen's right edge, letting you direct your search away from apps and into other areas:

- ✔ **Settings:** Tap Settings from the Search pane, and your tablet lists camera-related settings.

- ✔ **Files:** To see any *files* containing the term *camera*, tap Files; the screen shows any of your files mentioning the word *camera*.

- ✔ **Specific apps:** Beneath the list of Apps, Files, and Settings, the Search pane lists specific apps. Tap one of those — Netflix, for example — to search for movies relating to the word *camera*.

Don't have a keyboard attached to your tablet? Then fetch the onscreen keyboard: Summon the Charms bar, tap the bar's Settings icon, and tap the Settings Pane's keyboard icon. When the pop-up menu appears, tap Touch Keyboard and Handwriting Panel.

Select Start Screen Tiles

Some items seem difficult to select, a precursor to deleting, moving, renaming, copying, or any other host of tasks. For example, a tap on a Start screen tile opens it rather than selects it. Holding down a finger on the tile doesn't fetch a menu. Perplexed finger jabs just scroll the item back and forth.

The trick to selecting difficult items like Start screen tiles is to slide your finger across them in the *opposite* direction that they scroll.

Start screen tiles normally slide from right to left. So, select them by sliding your finger *up or down* across the tile. This works when selecting photos, e-mails in the Mail app, and many other seemingly difficult-to-select items.

Move Your Favorite to the Start Screen's Top- Left Corner

The tile resting in your Start screen's top- left corner holds a special power: It launches when you press Enter. Put the Desktop tile there, for example; then, when you plug in a keyboard and press Enter, the desktop will be waiting for you.

I describe how to select a tile in the preceding tip. After selecting a tile, keep your finger held down, and then slide your finger to the screen's top- left corner. When the tile reaches the Start screen's top- left corner, lift your finger, and the tile stays in its new location.

Stop the Screen from Rotating

Most of the time, you want the screen to rotate as you hold your tablet. That way, the screen's always "right side up." Occasionally, though, you don't want it to rotate – perhaps you're reading a book or browsing websites.

 To keep the screen from rotating, open the Charms menu and tap Settings. When the Settings pane appears, tap the screen icon near the bottom right (shown in the margin).

When the brightness bar appears, look at the Rotation Lock icon atop the bar; tap that icon to toggle autorotation on and off.

Some tablets also come with a dedicated Rotation Lock button on one side. (Next to the Rotation Lock button, look for a symbol of a rectangle and two arrows.)

Tweak Your App's Settings

Every app offers a way to fine-tune its behavior through the Charms bar's Settings area. When something about an app irks you, see if you can change it: Fetch the Charms bar by sliding your finger in from the screen's right edge and tapping Settings. If an app can be changed, the Settings pane offers a way.

Keep Your Apps Up-to-Date

Windows 8's app ecosystem is new, and many publishers release updated versions of their apps on a regular basis. To find and install updates for your apps, keep an eye on the Start screen's Store app.

When apps are available, a small number appears in the Store's lower-right corner. Spot a number? Tap the Store app to find and install waiting updates.

Use the Charms Bar for Apps

It's easy to open an app, and then begin searching its menus for basic things like search, print, or even a way to adjust settings.

Yet, they're all there, and you've used them before: The Charms bar works not only on the Start screen, but on every app you download from the Windows Store.

Looking for a movie in the Netflix app, for example? Fetch the Charms bar, and tap Search, and enter your sought-after film in the Search pane.

And if you need to print, open the Charms bar, tap Devices, and choose your printer from the Devices pane. (Not all apps can print, unfortunately.)

Zoom in on Awkward Websites to Touch Tiny Buttons

When faced with a tiny button on a website, straddle the button between your thumb and index finger. Then move your fingers apart as if you're stretching the screen. As you move your fingers, the screen enlarges. The screen looks a little hazy as it enlarges.

But when you lift your fingers, the screen pops back into focus, with everything much larger. And, of course, that tiny button is now finger-sized and easy to tap.

Pinch the screen between your fingers to return it to a comfortable size.

I explain pinching, stretching, and other finger gymnastics in Chapter 3.

Chapter 18

Ten (or So) Essential Accessories

*F*or many people, their Windows 8 tablet comes with everything they need. Who needs a bulky gadget bag?

Other people may prefer adding a few accessories to their tablet, which isn't difficult. Tablets running Windows 8 work with just about any accessory you can plug into your desktop computer.

This chapter covers the most important accessories to add to your tablet. Your needs may differ, of course, so I've listed them in general order of importance and portability.

A Memory Card

Nearly every Windows 8 tablet includes a microSDXC (Secure Digital Extended Capacity) memory card slot for sliding in a memory card. Pictured in Chapter 6, these tiny cards are smaller than a dime.

A microSDXC slot accepts three types of cards: microSDXC, microSDHC, and microSD. It won't accept the larger Secure Digital cards found in many digital cameras.

Will it work with Windows 8?

When you're not sure if a particular gadget works with Windows 8 or Windows RT, it's easy enough to find out: Plug it in. Windows 8 tells you whether it works within seconds.

For a hint before you buy, however, visit Microsoft's Windows 8 Compatibility website (www.microsoft.com/en-us/ windows/compatibility/). There, you can type in the name of a gadget, and the site says whether it's compatible.

Many of the compatibility verdicts are cast by the general public, however, so take the reviews with a grain of salt. Save the receipt after buying your new gadget, just in case it doesn't work.

Buy the largest capacity card you can afford and slide it into your tablet's memory card slot to expand your tablet's storage for adding extra music or movies.

Or, use a memory card as your tablet's File History storage space, described in Chapter 14. That ensures your tablet stays backed up, wherever you take it.

Recommendation: I like SanDisk's 64GB microSDXC cards, but card manufacturers don't differ much in quality. Also, a card's speed rating doesn't matter much when used in a tablet, unless you watch a lot of high-definition video or you are constantly copying huge files to and from the card.

A Padded Case

Few tablets include a case, but without one, you'll have second thoughts when tossing your tablet into a suitcase or standard laptop bag. That exposed glass may be tough, but it still looks fragile.

Cases designed for iPads usually won't work with Windows 8 tablets; iPads are shaped slightly differently. Instead, look for a case designed specifically for a Windows 8 tablet. Or, check out cases designed for ultrathin laptops, as you might have more luck.

Also, a Cocoon gadget holder, like the one shown in Figure 18-1, lets you pack flash drives, cables, adapters, USB hubs, and other doodads in a flat package.

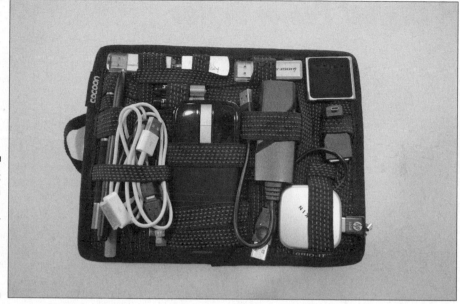

Figure 18-1:
The Cocoon
Grid-It!
organizer
lets acces-
sories lie
flat for easy
storage.

An AC Adapter

Your tablet's AC adapter always belongs in your bag, unfortunately. Under heavy use, your tablet's batteries might not last all day. The best adapters include prongs that fold inward when not in use, keeping them from scratching your tablet's screen.

Recommendation: The best adapter comes with your tablet. If you need another one, buy the same type from your tablet's manufacturer.

A Soft Cleaning Cloth

Spread this across your tablet's glass front before placing it in the case; it offers a little protection from scratches.

A cloth also lets you wipe your fingerprints off the glass. You can't see the fingerprints much when the tablet's turned on. But when it's turned off, the glass will look full of smudges.

Recommendation: Microfiber or lint-free cloths won't scratch the screen or leave lint behind.

A Digital Pen or Stylus

Some tablets include a digital pen or stylus for note-taking. (I give more information about digital pens in Chapter 3.) But even if you never plan to write on your tablet, a stylus works quite well as a mouse substitute when working on the desktop.

Because a stylus is easier to slip in a bag than a mouse, I rank it fairly high on the list of must-have gadgets.

Recommendation for capacitive stylus: Although it's pricey and looks odd, the Adonit Jot Pro Stylus works quite accurately. Budget buyers can pick up the inexpensive AmazonBasics Stylus for Touchscreen Devices.

A Keyboard

Many people learn to type quite speedily on their tablet's glass keyboard. But no matter how comfortably you can type, the tablet's glass keyboard consumes *half* of your screen, making it difficult to see your work.

If you type a lot of information into your tablet, pick up a portable Bluetooth or USB keyboard.

I cover keyboards in Chapter 3.

Recommendation: Keyboards are very much a personal preference, so try several before buying one to make sure you like the key spacing and format. I like Microsoft's Wedge Mobile Keyboard; it comes with a cover that doubles as a tablet stand, and it includes dedicated Windows 8 keys for fetching the Charms bar and controlling music playback.

If you own a Microsoft Surface, buy either the Touch or Type cover. You won't be sorry.

A Mouse

Essential for the desktop, a mouse and keyboard turn your tablet into a makeshift laptop. You'll find many portable mice for sale on Amazon and at other stores. Because most tablets only include one USB port, you need either a wireless mouse or a wireless keyboard. (Or, you can buy a small USB hub, which I cover next, which lets you plug in several USB gadgets.)

Recommendation: Microsoft's Arc Touch Mouse folds flat when not being used, making for easy storage. It requires a USB port for its Bluetooth receiver, however, so you need a USB hub if you want to plug in other USB peripherals.

A USB Hub

This gadget expands your tablet's lone USB port into two or more, hopefully enough to accommodate all of your gadgets. Buy one with at least three USB ports, letting you plug in a keyboard and mouse, but still leaving another port open for a flash drive or other gadget.

Recommendation: I love the Belkin USB 2.0 4-Port Ultra-Mini Hub from Amazon for five dollars.

A USB Flash Drive

These tiny little drives cost very little. Yet they not only expand your tablet's storage, but they provide a quick way to transfer files to and from your tablet.

A 32GB flash drive costs very little and provides enough storage space for thousands of songs, photos, or a handful of movies.

Recommendation: Don't pay extra for a *USB 3.0* flash drive unless you're sure your tablet includes a *USB 3.0* port. (Most tablets include a USB 2.0 port, which isn't nearly as fast as the newer USB 3.0 ports.)

A Video Cable

Although many retailers charge extravagant fees for these, don't fall for the scam. You can buy them online for less than ten dollars. Be sure to buy one with a standard HDMI port on one end, and a micro-HDMI or MiniDisplay port on the other end. (Choose the type that matches the video port on your tablet.)

Plug the cable's small end into your tablet; the larger end plugs into the HDTV or monitor. It's a handy thing to have when you want more real estate for your desktop than your tablet's screen can offer.

Recommendation: Don't spend more than ten dollars; digital cables either work, or they don't. Expensive ones won't "work better."

Travel router

If you've set up a wireless network in your home, you've already set up a router. If that experience didn't turn you off — and you travel a lot — consider picking up a *travel router*. This tiny gadget, the size of a deck of cards, turns a hotel room's network jack into a Wi-Fi hotspot for the entire room. (And even adjacent rooms, if you give them the password.)

Travel routers can be tricky to set up. But when you're staying in a hotel that only offers wired Internet access, a travel router lets all your wireless devices simultaneously share that same connection.

A Portable Hard Drive

Most people won't need this, because they can find enough storage from their tablet, its memory card, flash drives, and SkyDrive. But if you need to carry around a *lot* of files, pick up a portable hard drive.

Recommendation: I've had good luck with Western Digital's My Passport series of drives. I use a 500GB drive and a 2TB drive.

A Microphone/Speaker

Your tablet's built-in microphone and speakers meet most sound needs. But if you want to move a step up, perhaps for conference calls, or when recording your local ukulele group, pick up a portable microphone and speaker.

Recommendation: I like the MXL AC-406 USB speakerphone. It's a microphone *and* a speaker in one fairly compact package, and it works with tablets that run both Windows RT and Windows 8.

Chapter 19

Ten (or So) Essential Keyboard Shortcuts

*T*ablets work best with your fingers — until you find yourself on the Windows desktop. Then, most people plug in a mouse and keyboard to help them grab the desktop's tiny window borders and information-packed menus.

That's when these keyboard shortcuts come in handy. Don't try to memorize them all; just pick out the ones that look helpful to how *you* work. You can always peek back here if you need the others.

The shortcut keys in Table 19-1 all use the Windows key on your keyboard, not the Windows key built into the front of your tablet's case.

Table 19-1	Windows Keyboard Shortcuts
Press this . . .	*To do this . . .*
Win	Toggles between the Start screen and your last-used app.
Win+1	While on the desktop, pressing this launches the first program listed on the taskbar. (That's Internet Explorer, unless you've changed it.) Similarly, pressing Win+2 launches the second program on the taskbar, which is File Manager.
Win+C	Toggles the Charms bar (and shows the time and date, as well) on and off.
Win+D	Loads the Desktop app.
Win+E	Opens File Explorer to the Computer section.
Win+F	Opens the Charms bar and search for Files.

(continued)

Table 19-1 *(continued)*

Press this . . .	To do this . . .
Win+I	Opens the Charms bar's Settings icon, for changing the open app's settings, as well as access to settings for networks, volume, screen brightness, notifications, power, and keyboard (language).
Win+L	Returns to the Lock screen.
Win+M	On the desktop, minimizes all open windows.
Win+O	Toggles screen rotation lock. (The Surface RT's clip-on keyboard prevents the screen from rotating when the keyboard is attached.)
Win+P	Configures second monitor or projector.
Win+Q	Opens the Charms bar to search for apps.
Win+U	Switches to the Desktop's Ease of Access Center.
Win+W	Opens the Charms bar to search for settings.
Win+X	Displays a shortcut menu in the screen's bottom, left corner.
Win+Z	Displays an app's menus.
Win+Tab	Cycles through all the open apps.

Index